Controlling the Chaos

A FUNCTIONAL FRAMEWORK FOR ENTERPRISE ARCHITECTURE AND GOVERNANCE

Robert Fox

Technics Publications
BASKING RIDGE, NEW JERSEY

Published by:

TECHNICS PUBLICATIONS

TECHNOLOGY / LEADERSHIP

2 Lindsley Road
Basking Ridge, NJ 07920 USA

https://www.TechnicsPub.com

Cover design by Lorena Molinari

Edited by Lauren McCafferty

First Edition

First Printing 2018

Copyright © 2018 Robert Fox

ISBN, print ed.	9781634623414
ISBN, Kindle ed.	9781634623421
ISBN, ePub ed.	9781634623438
ISBN, PDF ed.	9781634623445

Library of Congress Control Number: 2018937528

Contents

Introduction

Most large businesses today have very complex information systems – or, more accurately, systems of systems. It's difficult to manage all of this IT Infrastructure complexity under a single unified vision that supports the business model.

Since at least the 1970's, analysts have been trying to convince businesses to invest in an **Enterprise Architecture and Governance (EAG)** program. Over the years, these efforts have resulted in a confusing array of overlapping standards, frameworks, and implementations. Despite thirty years of evolving best practices, IT is more fragmented than ever before. The industry is in desperate need of a "big picture" that ties all of these efforts into a unified whole.

Unfortunately, that big picture doesn't exist. With remarkably few exceptions, I have found that almost no one has a clear idea of just what architecture and governance really are. Some can give long-winded definitions full of big words, but those definitions are often vague or limited in scope and usability

At a conference in Detroit recently, I spoke to enterprise architects from 14 different companies. They all said that setting up governance was one of their top five priorities, yet every single one of them admitted they had no clear idea what they were doing or what their end goal was.

I've seen vendors claim to have architecture or governance "in a box" for the low, low price of only $99.95. Due to the ambiguity of terms, this "box" can contain just about anything. Vendors get to define the problem in terms of the solution they sell, be it a workflow management product or a glossary tool. These are some great products, many of which you're going to need as part of your overall enterprise architecture and governance program. However, EAG as a whole isn't something you can simply buy and install.

So what is it? What's the big picture we're all trying to implement?

I'm convinced that conceptual clarity demands visualization. As an architect, most of my discussions quickly turn into whiteboard or paper sketches. In meetings, people will often hand me a dry-erase marker as they ask me a question. These conceptual sketches are vital to reducing complex subjects into a few easy-to-understand, high-level symbols – a "napkin drawing."

This book will sketch a "napkin drawing" of enterprise architecture and governance. What are they, really, and how do they work at the enterprise level? How do you get them up and running and how do they work on an ongoing basis? How do you break them down into manageable chunks? How do those functions interact with each other and with the rest of your infrastructure? Where and how do all the various existing frameworks, models, and best practices out there fit in this picture?

This sketch is based on my own experience with governance and architecture. Your experience will differ from mine. That's fine! Anyone who has ever sat in a room full of architects will attest that no two architects will ever fully agree on anything. I welcome the discussion, and I believe the result of that dialog will benefit all of us.

Flipping through this book, you might expect to find a short course on IT disciplines like data modeling, software development, and hardware acquisition. If that's the case, you're going to be *sorely* disappointed. Instead, this book will address the *coordination* of those functions at the enterprise level. The goal is to integrate all those functions into a cohesive whole that spans *all* IT functions across *all* the information systems in your company. The result should create a single framework for architecture and governance.

If that sounds like something you could use, read on!

CHAPTER 1

EAG History

This book isn't the first attempt to try to organize IT complexity and manage it at an enterprise level. The industry terms for these efforts are "Enterprise Architecture" and "Governance."

Very few big ideas appear out of a vacuum. My own understanding of enterprise architecture and governance owes a great deal to the dialog that has been going on in this field for the last thirty years. Before adding my own thoughts, I want to sketch some of the foundational work of **Enterprise Architecture (EA)** and **Enterprise Governance**. These two disciplines have always been closely related, and are now considered the single topic **Enterprise Architecture and Governance**, or **EAG**.

1987 - The Zachman Framework (John Zachman)

John Zachman was an early pioneer in breaking down IT complexity into manageable "chunks." In 1987, he wrote an article describing *A Framework for Information Systems Architecture* in the IBM Systems Journal. His conceptual framework organized discussions and work products into six silos: "what" (information), "how" (applications), "where" (technology), "who" (people), "when" (scheduling and priorities), and "why" (motivation and goals). He then divided each of these silos into five levels of abstraction. His framework is shown in Figure 1.1.

For each cell in this grid, Zachman described the decisions required before continuing down to a lower level of detail, and he recommended the artifacts that should be used to document these decisions and share them with other silos at that same level. For example, in the *Data* column of the grid, a logical model is at a higher level of abstraction than the physical model, and must be completed first. Further, an information architect might document the physical model using an Entity Relationship Diagram (ERD), but pass certain structures to the application architect using an XML document artifact, so that the application architect working at that same level of abstraction can easily incorporate the data structures into the enterprise services they are developing.

	DATA *What*	FUNCTION *How*	NETWORK *Where*	PEOPLE *Who*	TIME *When*	MOTIVATION *Why*
Objective/Scope (contextual) *Role: Planner*	List of things important in the business	List of Business Processes	List of Business Locations	List of important Organizations	List of Events	List of Business Goal & Strategies
Enterprise Model (conceptual) *Role: Owner*	Conceptual Data/ Object Model	Business Process Model	Business Logistics System	Work Flow Model	Master Schedule	Business Plan
System Model (logical) *Role:Designer*	Logical Data Model	System Architecture Model	Distributed Systems Architecture	Human Interface Architecture	Processing Structure	Business Rule Model
Technology Model (physical) *Role:Builder*	Physical Data/Class Model	Technology Design Model	Technology Architecture	Presentation Architecture	Control Structure	Rule Design
Detailed Reprentation (out of context) *Role: Programmer*	Data Definition	Program	Network Architecture	Security Architecture	Timing Definition	Rule Speculation
Functioning Enterprise *Role: User*	Usable Data	Working Function	Usable Network	Functioning Organization	Implemented Schedule	Working Strategy

Figure 1.1 The Zachman Framework

The most important concepts Zachman brought to the discussion of Architecture and Governance were:

- Dividing complexity into "domains" of architecture, each with its own subject area experts

- Working through concepts at higher levels of abstraction first before drilling down into detail

- Agreeing on a common standard for documenting and exchanging work products across levels of complexity, and across the domains of architecture

The **Zachman Framework** is particularly helpful in organizing software development lifecycle (SDLC) functions. In that context, it is just as relevant today as it was thirty years ago, and should be required reading for every architect. It's less useful for managing other IT infrastructure areas such as the hardware lifecycle functions and security provisioning and de-provisioning functions.

Several software development tool sets support the Zachman Framework. For example, The IBM Rational suite has a data modeling tool and an application development tool that support the UML documentation artifacts proposed by Zachman, and interchange data between domains in the ways Zachman proposed in order to facilitate cross-domain enterprise architecture. It isn't necessary to purchase a suite of architecture tools like this, but it is necessary to define and manage how the different architectural domains communicate with each other to achieve cohesive software development process results.

Recommended reading:
Enterprise Architecture Using the Zachman Framework (MIS), by Carol O'Rourke and Neil Fishman

1989 - National Institute of Technology (NIST) Model

A couple of years later in 1989, the **National Institute of Standards and Technology (NIST)** developed a model for enterprise architecture. This model didn't initially incorporate Zachman's concept of architectural segments, but did introduce the idea that architecture is *hierarchical*. According to the NIST model, the flow is:

- Industry - Regulatory or certification requirements

- Corporate - Executive leadership goals, which are typically adjusted annually

- Departmental – Specific projects that support the goals of the executive leadership

- IT - priorities in support of departmental business goals. Within IT, NIST prioritized information first, followed by applications and technology.

According to the NIST model, at the highest level there are governmental and industry requirements and standards which are non-negotiable. You can't design a complete business solution first, and then pause to consider compliance requirements afterward.

Within those compliance restrictions, the executive leadership of the company will make decisions about how the company will comply and compete. Executive goals typically support one of the big three cross-industry business drivers:

- Increase revenue

- Decrease expenses (both cost and risk)

- Grow the company

Based on the executive leadership decisions, each business unit will then decide how they will contribute to and support the corporate vision with products and services. Then the IT architecture team will design the information systems to support the business unit vision. It's a bit more complicated than that, the point being that there's a decision hierarchy in which each layer has the freedom and responsibility to exercise their best judgment and experience, but only in a way that supports decisions made at the next higher level. NIST was the first organization to consistently use the term Enterprise Architecture (or EA) to describe this attempt to organize the chaos of individual departmental or project architectural decisions into a cohesive enterprise vision.

In the NIST model, business architecture drives information architecture, which in turn drives the infrastructure architecture. This is represented in Figure 1.2.

The NIST model continues to evolve and remains very relevant today. In particular, **the NIST Cyber Security Framework (NIST CSF)** is one of the most widely used security compliance programs.

Recommended Reading:
NIST Enterprise Architecture Model, by Lambert M. Surhone,

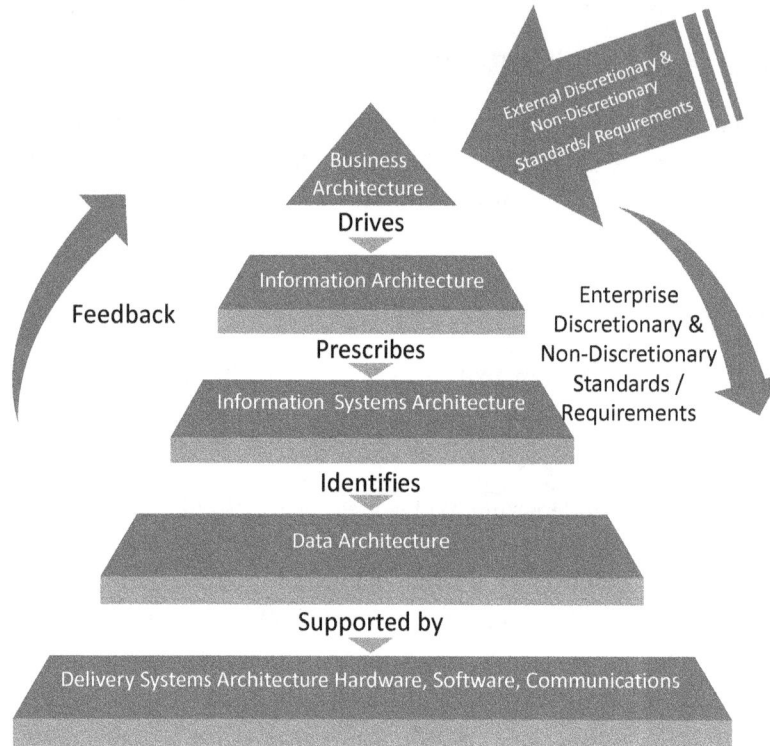

Figure 1.2 NIST Enterprise Architecture Model[1]

1992 – Stephen Spewak – Enterprise Architecture Planning (EAP)

In 1992, Stephen Spewak published his seminal book entitled *Enterprise Architecture Planning (EAP)* which merged Zachman's concept of architectural segments with the NIST concept of a hierarchical tree or pyramid of decision-making responsibility. Spewak defined Enterprise Architecture Planning as "*the process of defining architectures for the use of information in support of the business and the plan for implementing those architectures.*"

Following the precedent set by NIST, Spewak insisted that a business-oriented (rather than IT-oriented) approach to architecture planning is critical to providing an architecture that supports the business and contains costs. To Spewak, enterprise architecture exists to better use information in support of the business.

Unlike Zachman, Spewak used only four architectural areas, saying that the business architects owned the *who*, *when,* and *why* columns of Zachman's framework. Spewak arranged the architectural segments as follows.

1.   Business Architecture (Zachman's People, Time, and Motivation domains)
2.   Information Architecture (Zachman's Data domain) in support of the business
3.   Application Architecture (Zachman's Function domain) in support of the information
4.   Technology Architecture (Zachman's Network domain) in support of the applications

[1] https://en.wikipedia.org/wiki/File:NIST_Enterprise_Architecture_Model.jpg.

We now know these four architectural areas as the **domains** of enterprise architecture and governance, or EAG. In the Zachman Framework, the domains were equal peers.[2] In Spewak's model, the business architect is in the driver's seat. The architect determines which feature is most pressing, how that function should work, and when it must be available. Note that this function falls to a "business architect," rather than to the more generic "business." This architect is a business professional especially selected to give strategic direction to the IT organization.

Based on the direction provided by the business architects, the information architects will determine what data needs to be collected to support the business and how the different data elements relate to each other. Then the application architects will decide how to implement the business processes that the business architects have defined, using the information that the information architects have defined. Finally, the technology architects will define components such as servers, disks, and networks necessary to support the information and application required by the business process.

Spewak's work left a significant contribution to the discussion of enterprise architecture and governance: he defined four architectural domains and their precedents. He seemed to view the IT organization as an orchestra of different IT instruments, all under the control of the business *conductor*.

This is an accurate metaphor for IT management. You've probably heard those moments before a conductor takes the stand when all the various musicians are warming up, each practicing the section they consider most important. It's a cacophony of noise and an accurate picture of many IT organizations. Then the conductor takes the stand, focuses all the players on the same page, and the chaos is transformed into a beautiful symphony.

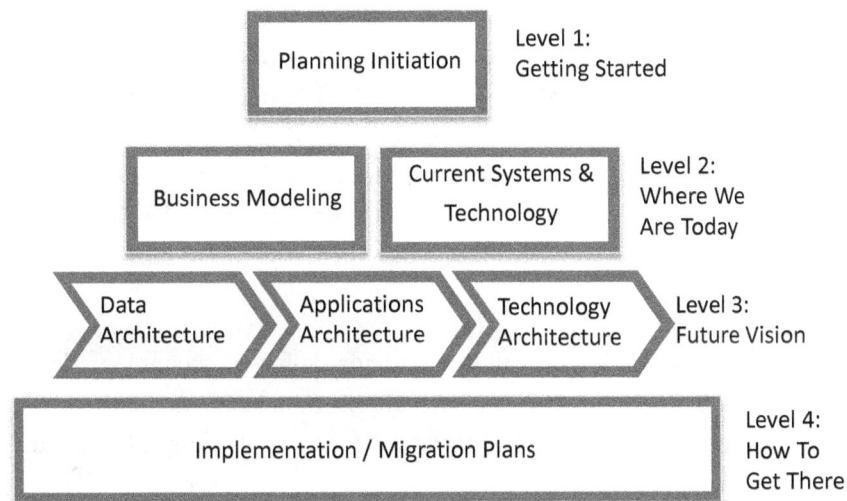

Figure 1.3 Stephen Spewak's Levels of Enterprise Architecture Planning

Spewak's organization of IT into three domains under the control of the business is still a best practice today.

Recommended Reading:
Enterprise Architecture Planning: Developing a Blueprint for Data, Applications, and Technology, by Steven H. Spewak and John A Zachman, 1993, Wiley.

---

[2] Some claim that Zachman's decision to order the first three columns in his framework into data, application, and technology, implies a priority, but Zachman never made this explicit.

1994 - The Open Group Architectural Framework (TOGAF)

In the early 1990's, businesses in every industry were feeling the pain of internal systems that did not play well with each other or adequately support real business needs. Everyone was ready to invest in enterprise architecture and governance in order to solve this problem. At the time, the problem was that EA was defined in theory, but not in practice. EA frameworks offered no real guidance on how to get from point A (inefficient IT chaos) to point B (well-managed, flexible IT that supports the business efficiently). Everyone wanted to see an example of a successful EA/EAG program, complete with strategies, policies, processes, standards, and roles all documented, so that they could copy it and modify as necessary. If you want to build a custom house that meets your needs, it's far easier to modify plans of an existing house than to start with a blank sheet of paper. This is where TOGAF came in.

In 1994, The Open Group attempted to address the need for a practical EAG implementation by taking some Department of Defense standards as a starting point to build **The Open Group Architectural Framework (TOGAF)**. In the minds of many, this was less a *framework* than it was a *sample implementation*.

TOGAF consisted of a technical reference model and a list of recommended standards. TOGAF also provides much more guidance on governance policies that the previous frameworks lacked. As we will discuss later, these robust policies and standards made TOGAF the transition point between Enterprise Architecture (EA) and Enterprise Architecture and Governance (EAG).

Version 9.1, introduced in 2011, adds some level of guidance that was previously missing, but in reality, TOGAF is still a reasonably generic published implementation of EAG that a company can look at to get an idea of how they might solve similar problems in a way that works for them. As of 2016, The Open Group claimed that 80% of the global 50 and 60% of the Fortune 500 companies employ TOGAF.[3] That's no doubt true, but in most cases, what that really means is that these companies have all looked at the detailed blueprint for the TOGAF house and stolen ideas they thought would work well with minimal modification in the house they were building. They didn't actually build the TOGAF blueprint. No one really *adopts* TOGAF as an enterprise framework – they just copy large parts of it to use in their own architecture and governance framework.

That said, TOGAF is extremely helpful, especially its standards for the technology domain. I suspect this is because technology architecture concepts transfer easily from industry to industry. A bank and a utility company have very different business models, information, and applications, but the technology in their computer rooms will look very similar.

Nevertheless, while TOGAF is a very interesting architectural blueprint, it isn't as helpful in guiding you through the thought process of changing your current architecture to more efficiently and effectively serve the needs of the business.

Finding a blueprint with design ideas you like is great, but you'll still need a lot of additional knowledge and experience before you can tear down the walls of the house you currently live in. TOGAF provided the design ideas, but not the systematic implementation guidance.

---

[3] http://bit.ly/2mY5Gg8.

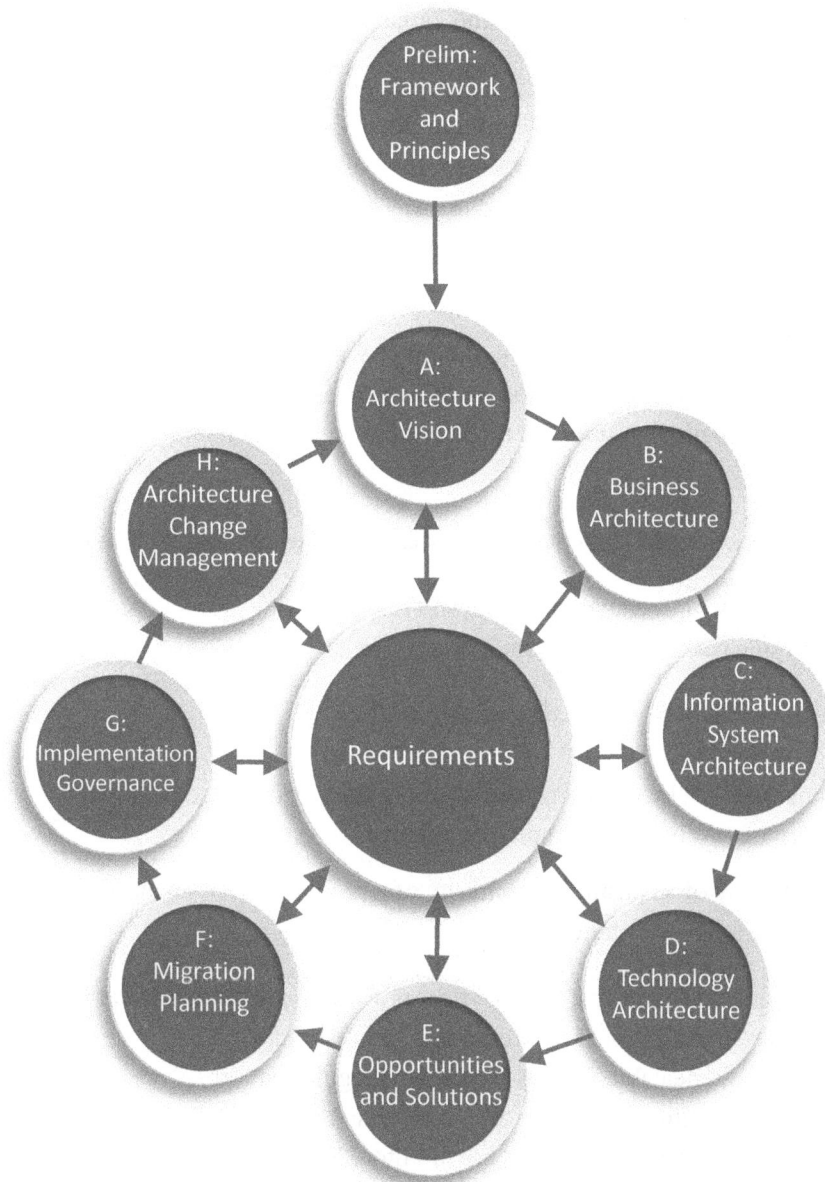

Figure 1.4 TOGAF Architecture Development Methodology[4]

Recommended reading:
TOGAF Version 9.1, by Van Haren Publishing.

1996 – Control Objectives for Information Technology (COBIT)

The **International Systems Audit and Control Association (ISACA)** released its "Control Objectives for Information and Related Technologies" in 1996. The "and Related" was soon dropped from common usage, and the standard became known as **COBIT**. This standard supposedly provided an implementable

---

[4] https://commons.wikimedia.org/wiki/File:TOGAF_ADM.jpg.

"set of controls over information technology and organized them around a logical framework of IT-related processes."[5]

IT architects didn't develop COBIT. It was initially developed by auditors who would go into various companies to document and assess those companies' processes. These auditors needed a standard list of questions to ask about IT functions, and a standard way to document policies, standards, processes and roles so that the documentation produced by all the different auditors could be compiled into a cohesive and unified whole.

One of the new ideas that COBIT brought to the table was their focus on *processes*, rather than the information, applications, and technology used by those processes. The real focus is on the *risks* inherent in the process and the *controls* that mitigate those risks – hence the name "Control Objectives for IT." The original intent of COBIT was controlling the risks in IT processes.

COBIT is a set of best practices for documenting processes and evaluating their maturity, including:

- A standardized way of documenting roles and responsibilities for a process using the "RACI" model, specifying personnel details including:

  - Responsible – Who does the actual work?
  - Accountable – Who must sign off/approve work?
  - Consulted – Which experts have the necessary knowledge and skills?
  - Informed – Who should know the results?

- A standardized way of assessing the maturity of a process during an audit, which can be described by the following stages:

  - Level 0 – Non-Existent. Management processes are not applied at all.
  - Level 1 – Initial. Processes are ad-hoc and disorganized.
  - Level 2 – Repeatable. Processes follow a regular pattern.
  - Level 3 – Defined. Processes are documented and communicated.
  - Level 4 – Managed. Processes are monitored and measured.
  - Level 5 – Optimized. Best practices are followed and automated.

COBIT isn't a list of processes that you can pick up and drop into your company so much as it is a way to develop, document and asses the processes you already have. Think of it as a best practice for documenting and evaluating processes. COBIT isn't an enterprise architecture framework; it's a way of documenting the processes and roles in an enterprise architecture framework. COBIT can't tell you what roles to use; it tells you how to document those roles.

Regardless, COBIT has a lot of outstanding information when it comes to thinking about the processes in your architecture. They are thought leaders for documenting IT governance and measuring risk and maturity. COBIT belongs in the toolkit and on the bookshelf of every architect and technical writer.

Recommended reading:
- COBIT 5 Framework, by ISACA.
- Enterprise Governance of Information Technology – Achieving Alignment and Value Featuring COBIT 5, by Steven De Haas and Wim Van Grembergen.

---

[5] http://bit.ly/2qBtdUA.

1989-1996 – Information Technology Infrastructure Library (ITIL)

Between 1989 and 1996, the UK government's **Central Computer and Telecommunications Agency (CCTA)** published a series of recommendations to standardize IT services management, controlling and managing the services IT used to support the business. In their **Information Technology Infrastructure Library (ITIL)**, a "service" is something performed by IT, but it is defined in a way that describes a service provided to the business.

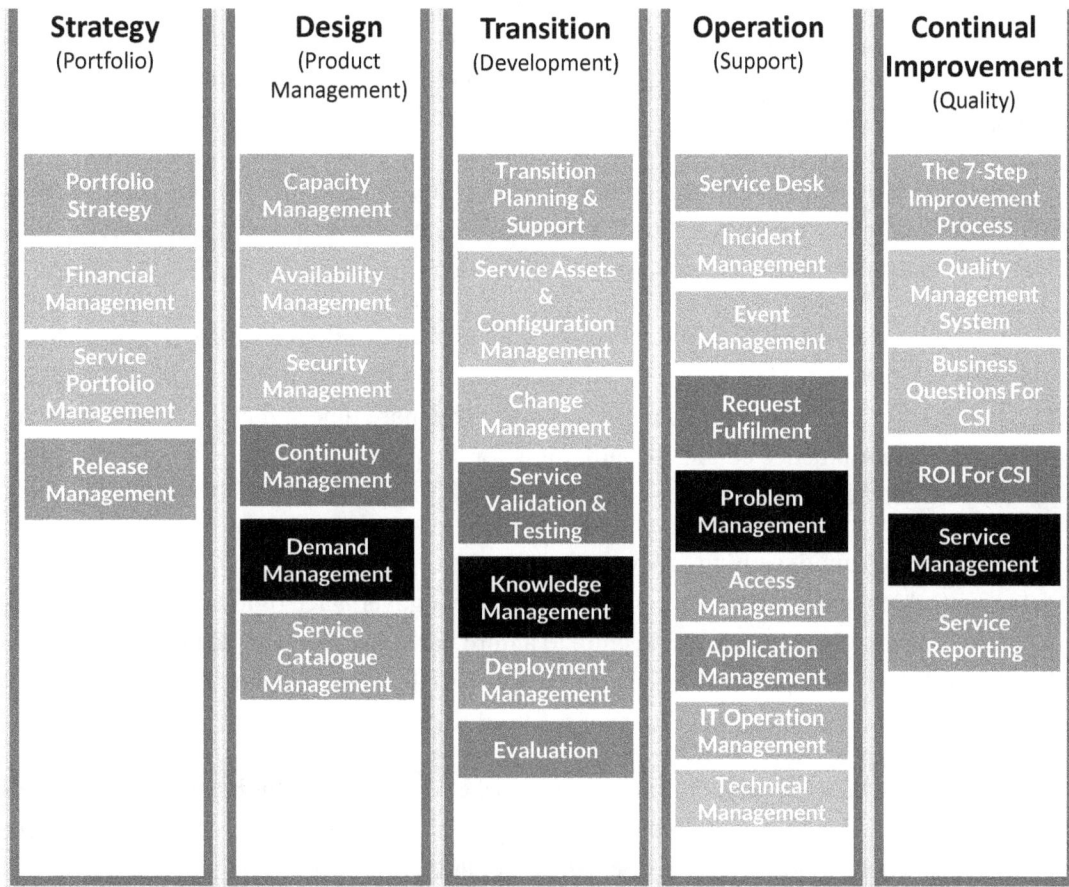

Strategy (Portfolio)	Design (Product Management)	Transition (Development)	Operation (Support)	Continual Improvement (Quality)
Portfolio Strategy	Capacity Management	Transition Planning & Support	Service Desk	The 7-Step Improvement Process
Financial Management	Availability Management	Service Assets & Configuration Management	Incident Management	Quality Management System
Service Portfolio Management	Security Management	Change Management	Event Management	Business Questions For CSI
Release Management	Continuity Management	Service Validation & Testing	Request Fulfilment	ROI For CSI
	Demand Management	Knowledge Management	Problem Management	Service Management
	Service Catalogue Management	Deployment Management	Access Management	Service Reporting
		Evaluation	Application Management	
			IT Operation Management	
			Technical Management	

Figure 1.5 The ITIL library[6]

ITIL isn't an enterprise architecture framework in the sense that it can be used to document and manage all of your company-specific IT processes, but it does include definitions, best practices, and standards for many processes that need to be included in any IT architectural framework. It maintains a very good focus on the fact that these services exist to support the business, and it contains a strong emphasis on continuing process improvement.

ITIL is one of the most useful frameworks for ensuring completion of processes (both in breadth and depth of detail) for most IT functions. For relatively common, cross industry processes such as change management and disaster recovery, the ITIL library is a fantastic template to use to make sure you are considering everything you need to include in your architecture and governance programs.

---

[6] https://en.wikipedia.org/wiki/File:ItilstructWiki.png.

Unfortunately, ITIL isn't nearly as helpful for less common processes that are specific to your particular industry. A 2004 survey of companies that had adopted ITIL revealed that 77% agreed, "ITIL does not have all the answers."[7]

While ITIL is extremely valuable, it is also extremely proprietary. CCTA and a professional services company now jointly own the ITIL framework and the books and training have become quite expensive.

Many other frameworks for managing IT services have emerged since the inception of ITIL, including Business Service Management (BSM) and IT Service Management (ITSM), FitSIM (lightweight service management), ISO/EIC 20000 and the Microsoft Operations Framework (MOF). Each of these has strengths and weaknesses. The main obstacles with leaning on these frameworks for your enterprise architecture are:

- **The services are very generic.** In order to be widely useful to companies across all industries, the framework must be rather generic. Generic guidelines trap adopters in a mindset of applying guidelines *exactly* as documented, regardless of industry or company-specific constraints.

- **They may become quickly outdated.** At the time of their development, they reflected the best practices in technology. Technology is advancing all the time, and a very detailed, complex set of guidelines just can't keep up with the advances. The more time and effort a framework invests in describing best practice detail, the harder it is for the framework to keep these details updated with rapidly changing technology.

- **They stop you from dreaming.** They tend to focus on what you should do today, not how to determine what you should do tomorrow. They address governance of today, but not strategy for tomorrow. If you give up your architecture to a third party, you become dependent on them to build your future. You stop making plans to respond to disruptive innovations like big data, blockchain, and cloud and simply wait for the third party to tell you how to respond.

- **They don't provide a roadmap.** They describe what you should be doing, but don't provide any recommendation on how to implement change. They describe how much greener the grass is on the other side, but don't describe the path to get there from where you are today.

In the next chapter, we'll try to assimilate all of these various standards and best practices into a single, comprehensive framework, in what I believe is a logical next-step in the evolution of the attempt to manage IT complexity on behalf of the business.

---

[7] Survey: "The ITIL Experience – Has It Been Worth It", author Bruton Consultancy 2004, published by Helpdesk Institute Europe, The Helpdesk and IT Support Show, and Hornbill Software.

CHAPTER 2

EAG Functional Framework

Unfortunately, there's no such thing as architecture or governance in a box. It isn't a simple matter of saying that you've chosen TOGAF or ITIL as your EA framework. Nothing out-of-the-box is going to be a complete drop-in solution. You're going to have to build your own IT management solution, and you're going to need a plan.

You need to be able to hang all the complicated pieces of your own program on a simple EAG framework, with as little re-inventing of the wheel as possible. You no doubt already have quite a few documented policies, standards, and processes in place, and you can fill in many of the remaining gaps by borrowing ideas from TOGAF, COBIT, and ITIL. However, you still need some sort of framework that will organize all the parts so you can see where those gaps are and prioritize them. You need a way of visualizing the complexity. You need a napkin drawing of the "big picture."

The big problem with getting from where you are today to a fully functioning enterprise architecture and governance program is that it's a *big problem*. There are an overwhelming number of different parts to keep track of without the use of some sort of system. Companies in every industry have been trying to come up with "some sort of system" for the past 40 years. Some of these systems have been successful, but many have not. You want to leverage what has worked, while avoiding the mistakes of the past.

Why architecture and governance programs fail

Many companies have tried to move forward with an enterprise-level architecture and governance program, and many of those programs have failed to show any business value. In my experience, these programs fail for one or more of the reasons listed on the following page.

In order to avoid these common routes to failure, you need committed leaders who understand the need to bring IT complexity under control. You need a simple, clear vision that spans all of IT, and focuses on supporting the business. You can't simply ignore the last thirty years of best practices. Your program must be able to incorporate existing policies, standards, and processes with little or no change, and you need involvement from the IT departments you're trying to manage.

Top Reasons why Architecture and Governance Programs Fail
Leadership Issues
• No executive sponsor with both the will and the power to bring about change.
• No program manager with the vision and people skills to keep the team focused.
Vision Issues
• The program is IT-centric, rather than business-centric, and does not involve the business or focus on supporting business goals.
• Driven by personal agendas, too much focus is directed on one or two functional areas at the expense of other, equally important IT functions.
• The various pieces don't integrate together into a cohesive, manageable whole.
• The solution is too complicated to be clearly understood by the people who have to use it.
Approach Issues
• The program ignores existing governance and attempts to rebuild everything from scratch.
• The program uses dedicated architecture and governance resources unattached to business units, and hands down decisions from an ivory tower.
• The program attempts to force all functional areas to conform to a single implementation rather than allowing some degree of departmental flexibility.
• The program is billed as a project. Projects have completion dates. Programs do not.
• The best practice priority of EAG IT domains isn't followed.

Using TOGAF, ITIL, and more

Where we don't have existing architecture and governance in place, we want to be able to easily adopt material from recognized best practices such as TOGAF, ITIL, and COBIT. The reason we don't just adopt one of these industry standards is that none of them are going to completely suit your business. Indeed, each of these approaches has a particular focus – particular strengths and weaknesses. No matter what conceptual framework we come up with for our architecture and governance, we should easily map these industry-standard approaches to it. If your framework is so different that it can't be related to industry standards, it's time to rethink your framework.

Unfortunately, there is no one-size-fits-all EAG drop-in framework. Every industry has a different business model. Often business models can vary dramatically even within an industry. Different organizations will have different goals and will need different kind of support from their IT organization. Different organizations are at different levels of maturity and have different pre-existing infrastructure to accommodate. If this weren't so, every IT department in every company would look exactly the same.

All the different EAG standards and frameworks claim to be describing the same thing. They all claim to organize and manage IT architectural complexity, yet each approach is quite different. Consider the story of five blind men encountering an elephant for the first time. Each describes the part of the elephant he encounters: a tusk, a leg, the ear, the trunk, the body. Each man experiences the elephant from his own perspective, even though they're all attempting to describe the same elephant. ITIL, TOGAF, Zachman, COBIT, and others all claim to be describing architecture and governance, but they seem, on the surface, to be as different as the descriptions given by the five blind men. It's our task to take all those different descriptions and figure out the common truth behind them. *What does the architecture and governance elephant really look like?*

Figure 2.1 "Blind men and elephant," from Martha Adelaide Holton & Charles Madison Curry[8]

It seems all of those industry-standard approaches describe different combinations of IT functions and the things we do to manage those functions. So I would start my picture of the EAG elephant by creating a grid, where I list all of the functions IT performs for the business as columns, and all the things we do to manage those functions as rows. This grid is the beginning of our EAG framework.

	FUNCTIONS All the *things we do* to support the business…								
ARCHITECTURE AND GOVERNANCE — All the things we do to *manage* the functions…									

When I start to place the different historical approaches on this framework, I find that

- NIST and Spewak mainly describe how IT functions fall into various domains of responsibility, so it's probably going to be easier to follow that best practice if our function columns are grouped together by IT domain.

- TOGAF focuses more on policies and standards; with the most re-usable being those for the technology and security functions. Policies and standards aren't functions; they're how you

_____

[8] Holton-Curry readers, 1914.

manage functions, so we're going to need rows in the framework for these important governance documents.

- ITIL focuses on listing the most common cross-industry functions, organizing them into high-level functional areas. Functions are our columns, but since there are so many IT functions, we need to follow ITIL's example of grouping functions together into functional areas to keep the concept manageable. A large part of ITIL is process and role documentation. We want these important governance artifacts as rows in our framework.

- COBIT defines templates for documenting the policies, standards, processes, and roles that are complete and consistent across the enterprise. We don't need extra columns or extra rows for COBIT, but when we begin to create the document artifacts in the cells of this grid, we need to be ready to steal freely from all the thought that COBIT has put into their templates.

- Zachman focuses on policies, standards, processes, and roles, but mainly for the software development lifecycle. We are going to be able to apply many of Zachman's concepts when we begin creating the governance documents for those functions. Zachman also standardized which UML diagramming techniques, such as ERD diagrams, swim lane, and use case diagrams to consistently and effectively communicate complex ideas. We aren't going to want to re-invent any of that.

Some of these approaches focus more on standards, some more on strategy, some more on processes. Some reference a few specific functions, like SDLC or security. However, when you step back and listen to all of these different descriptions of our elephant, a picture starts to emerge.

These various approaches generally share two major commonalities:

- Firstly, they all define lists of the functions IT provides for the business. They also organize these functions into meaningful, higher-level "functional areas," which are owned by domain experts. To be clear, a domain can be comprised of multiple functional areas, and each functional area can be comprised of multiple individual functions.

- The second way these approaches are similar is that they each include a list of all the different tasks that must be completed to manage those functions. Some of these tasks fall under the category of architecture, or managing the future of the functions. Other tasks relate more to governance, or managing the day-to-day execution of functions.

That picture, in my opinion, comes together in the drawing below. I call this a **Functional Framework**, because the basic organization, similar to COBIT and ITIL, is a hierarchical arrangement of all the "things we do." For each of these functions, we can document the relevant architecture and governance structures needed to manage that function, resulting in one cohesive vision of the IT infrastructure that supports the business. This is the napkin-drawing that we've been looking for to tie all of the IT complexity into a unified concept that is easy to understand and manage.

Like ITIL, this approach is focused on the functions (ITIL "services") your organization does in support of the business. Suppose for a minute that you have a friend who works in the IT department at another company, perhaps even in a different industry. You meet this friend for lunch, and they ask you about your organization. "What all is your IT organization responsible for?"

A Functional Framework for Architecture and Governance																			
FUNCTIONAL FRAMEWORK	ORGANIZATION	BUSINESS				IT													
	EA DOMAIN	BUSINESS				INFORMATION				APPLICATION						TECHNOLOGY			
	FUNCTIONAL AREA	AREA 1		Area 2		AREA3		AREA 4		AREA 5		AREA 6		AREA 7		AREA 8		AREA 9	
	FUNCTION	Function 1	Function 2	Function 3	Function 4	Function 5	Function 6	Function 7	Function 8	Function 9	Function 10	Function 11	Function 12	Function 13	Function 14	Function 15	Function 16	Function 17	Function 18
ARCHITECTURE	LONG TERM STRATEGY																		
	ROADMAP																		
GOVERNANCE	POLICIES																		
	STANDARDS																		
	PROCESSES/ROLES																		

Figure 2.2 A Generic Functional Framework

Can you answer? In theory, everyone should certainly know what they're responsible for, but in reality that's a far grayer subject than it should be. Even if you can answer the main parts, can you immediately list off all the little peripheral responsibilities? If you can't immediately bring them to mind,

- How do you plan a strategy for them?
- How do you create standards and policies for them?
- How do you analyze the broad impacts of new or changing business requirements?
- How do you clarify who is responsible for each?
- How do you remember them all when it comes time to plan next year's budget?

We should all have a list somewhere of the things for which we are responsible. The first step in organizing your architecture isn't changing org charts or creating an inventory of assets. The first step is creating a list of all the functions performed by your area of influence. These are the columns in the functional framework from which you plan your IT management. You can't start planning until you know what it is you're managing.

With that in mind, we'll begin not with a discussion of how to manage IT functions, but with a discussion of how to create a list of the functions you'll be managing. In our functional framework, that means starting with the columns (functions) before we get to the rows (management tasks).

Everyone's functional framework will be different. Odds are that if five different people in your organization try to list the functions you manage, you'll get five different lists. That's to be expected. You must work together to compile an agreed-upon list.

What is a "function"?

Let's clarify some of the concepts. Just what is a "function"?

Functions are things that happen, whether or not they are currently managed. From an IT standpoint, they are the things you do to support your business. Ideally, those "things you do" have a strategic plan, policies, standards, processes and roles defined, but they are still IT functions even if you're just winging it today.

There seems to be a great deal of confusion regarding the differences between the things that are truly functions, and the things that are projects or job titles. Let's address that right up front.

Functions are organization independent

You'll be tempted to build your list of the existing IT functions by simply dropping in your org chart of departments, managers, and supervisors as the high-level functional areas, then having each list the detail functions they are responsible for within that department.

Whatever you do, avoid that temptation! This is critical. You're not trying to document the way you're organized today. The whole point of this exercise is that you are struggling today, and are trying to find a different, more streamlined means of managing IT complexity. Simply document the hierarchy of functions, not the hierarchy of your organization chart. Certainly you should consider all your job roles in order to discover and document the detail functions, but don't impose a hierarchy of those functions based purely on the job titles.

In a later phase, you'll want to make sure your organization reflects your functions, but that doesn't mean you want to base your functional model on your old organization structure.

This can be a frightening thing to all the people you're interviewing when compiling that list of functions. The impression is that, "Jobs are on the line" and "Empires will be overthrown." In reality, this isn't what happens. Implementing EAG may involve some job shifts, but that shift ends up *creating positions* rather than eliminating them. In my experience, you'll find more *management gaps* than you'll find management redundancy. What you'll find is that there are some functions that one manager was technically responsible for, but never really focused on. By moving functions into related groups, you'll more than likely actually be creating groups of functions that need new, dedicated teams. Maybe data dictionary responsibility falls to the developers today, but always suffers from lack of priority. After creating a functional framework independent of your current org chart, you may well decide that you need a new team to focus on metadata, including data dictionary, process documentation, references tables, and other descriptive information.

A functional framework shouldn't split one function into two just because more than one manager works on it. You shouldn't see functions such as "Sam's application support" and "Sarah's application support." Those are organization breakdowns. Likewise, you shouldn't see duplication of functions merely to separate full time employees from contractors. If the function is the same, then don't split it up because of an artificial distinction imposed by your current organization structure.

At the high level of the functional framework, you shouldn't see duplication of function for different departments or lines of business. Those breakdowns may be necessary to run the business, but at the highest level, the architecture and governance for those areas will be defined only once per function. Don't worry! You'll see as we progress that there's plenty of room for departmental flexibility deeper down within this framework.

Don't change your functions to match your organization – change your organization to match your functions.

Functions are independent of projects and time

Your functional framework shouldn't contain a list of projects. While you're responsible for projects, the purpose of IT isn't to create projects; it's to perform the functions that are required to support the business. Projects end after a short period. Functions don't end without a significant change in the business model. If you decide as a company to move *all* your software to a third-party hosted cloud solution, your software upgrade/maintenance function may end, but this would be very rare. Projects end all the time.

Your functional framework shouldn't contain any temporary tasks. With rare exceptions, temporary tasks are really projects, and should be treated as such. Don't ignore the work – but do assign the task to a high-level "function."

Organizing your functions

The reason architecture and governance are so difficult is that they are complicated. There are a *lot* of functions - so many that an exhaustive list would be unmanageable. The sole purpose of this book is to give you a practical way to organize and manage that complexity. One key component of our EAG approach is to cluster functions together into manageable groups, called **functional areas**.

This organization of the complexity has to happen before you can start to manage it. That's the whole point of the functional framework – organizing how you think about all those thousands of details into something more conceptually understandable, then putting the management structures in place on those abstractions.

How then do you go about building this functional framework with its hierarchy of functions?

The organization layer of the functional framework

At the top level, this organization structure is divided into business and IT.

A Functional Framework for Architecture and Governance

FUNCTIONAL FRAMEWORK	ORGANIZATION	BUSINESS		IT													
	EA DOMAIN	BUSINESS		INFORMATION		APPLICATION			TECHNOLOGY								
	FUNCTIONAL AREA	AREA 1	Area 2	AREA3	AREA 4	AREA 5	AREA 6	AREA 7	AREA 8	AREA 9							
	FUNCTION	Function 1	Function 2	Function 3	Function 4	Function 5	Function 6	Function 7	Function 8	Function 9	Function 10	Function 11	Function 12	Function 13	Function 14	Function 15	Function 16	Function 17	Function 18
ARCHITECTURE	LONG TERM STRATEGY																
	ROADMAP																
GOVERNANCE	POLICIES																
	STANDARDS																
	PROCESSES/ROLES																

Figure 2.3 The Organization Level of the Functional Framework

Perhaps this is a bad thing. It promotes "us versus them" mentality, and is often an obstruction to true teamwork. As we've said before, one of the main reasons for architectural and governance program failure is that IT tries to go it alone, building out complex programs without any business input. Putting the business in the framework ensures that they are a part of the discussion.

Once you leave the ivory towers of academia, you'll find a huge difference between the answers given by a computer science professor and the answers that work in the real world. I love to say, "We are a business, not a science project!" I have it written at the top of the white board in my office, and I'll keep coming back to it throughout this book.

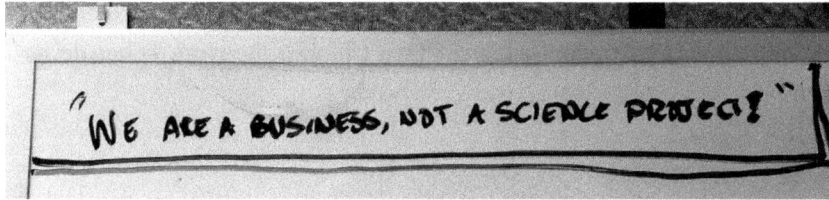

Figure 2.4 The Top of my White Board

When left to their own devices, IT people sometimes come to believe that the world revolves around them. I know - I am IT people! We could have dispensed with the organization level of abstraction and begun with the four EA domains, which do call out business architects as a separate domain. But I suggest that we *want* to call attention to that IT/business divide, to the fact that *we* work for *them*.

The reason the organization tier is so important is the way most company's org charts are built, where the business and IT roll up to different C-level executives. The point of the organization level of this framework is that you are going to have to get executive sponsorship from both sides of the house, or from a level that is over both. *You can't build a successful architecture or governance program using IT-only resources and IT-only sponsorship.*

In some cases, your business *is* IT. I worked for many years for a company that developed software for the finance industry. We weren't a financial institution, but we did develop and sell software to financial institutions. We were a software development company. In one sense, the entire company was IT. However, even in that context, there are people whose roles involve decisions about the business of the company: what products and features do we need to focus on to remain competitive? What are the bottlenecks in the infrastructure that supports our sales, marketing, and customer service organizations? Should we be investigating new lines of business or expanding our existing business through new channels?? The people whose job it was to answer these questions were our "business" people, even in an IT-centric software development company.

You always have business people, and they always need to be part of in your enterprise architecture planning. Not just *involved*, but actually *leading* the discussion. Therefore, they need to be included in your functional framework.

I've seen some sources recently[9] that separate the organization layer differently. You still have the business organization, but the IT organization is split out into a **semantic/content organization** (the information domain) and an **infrastructure organization** (the application and technology domains).

---

9 For example, The Journal of the American Health Information Management Association, October 2017, p.60.

In that model, the thought process is that there are three levels at which you manage IT complexity:

- Functional Interoperability – consistent, integrated business processes
- Semantic Interoperability – consistent, integrated business information and exchange structures
- Technical Interoperability – consistent, integrated software and hardware infrastructure

This is a relatively new trend. I'll mention it here, but this approach doesn't reflect the way IT functions are typically managed or the way IT departments are typically organized today. For the remainder of this book, I'll consider the information domain to be part of the IT organization. In the context of our goal of a functional framework that can be used to make the management of IT functions simpler, I don't want to introduce anything that wouldn't be intuitively understood by all the players. That said, if your company *is* organized this way, it's a small change at the organization level of the framework, and the rest of the discussion still applies.

The domain layer of the functional framework

At this level of the framework, we bring in the architectural domains defined by Zachman, Spewak, and the NIST model.

A Functional Framework for Architecture and Governance

FUNCTIONAL FRAMEWORK		ORGANIZATION	BUSINESS				IT										
		EA DOMAIN	BUSINESS				INFORMATION			APPLICATION					TECHNOLOGY		
		FUNCTIONAL AREA	AREA 1		Area 2		AREA3		AREA 4		AREA 5	AREA 6		AREA 7		AREA 8		AREA 9	
		FUNCTION	Function 1	Function 2	Function 3	Function 4	Function 5	Function 6	Function 7	Function 8	Function 9	Function 10	Function 11	Function 12	Function 13	Function 14	Function 15	Function 16	Function 17	Function 18
ARCHITECTURE	LONG TERM STRATEGY																		
	ROADMAP																		
GOVERNANCE	POLICIES																		
	STANDARDS																		
	PROCESSES/ROLES																		

Figure 2.5 The Domain Level of the Functional Framework

Each of these architectural domains represents different expertise and different priorities. These will be discussed in detail later. Unless you're a very small organization, don't be tempted to assign the architecture and governance for two different domains to the same resources. Even if you can find someone who truly understands the needs of each, no one can wear both hats at the same time. It's something like the need for separating development and operations (see page 45).

You can't let your application architects take care of the information architecture, and so forth. You need individual architects to focus on each domain and champion its architectural needs. This will create a lot more conflict and drama, but the organization will be better off because of it.

According to Spewak and NIST, these domains are not peers of equal priority and precedence. The business architect is the real driver, defining what functionality the business needs. The information architect designs the information needed to support those business functions. The application architect designs the applications needed to build, maintain, and deliver the data, and the technology architect designs the infrastructure necessary to host the applications.

Think of Enterprise Architecture as a rope. Business is out front, setting the architectural direction and pulling everything else behind it. Information architecture is next in line, being pulled by the business, and in turn pulling application architecture, which in turn pulls the rope that guides technology architecture. *Starting your EA program with technology architecture is rather like trying to push a rope.*

Many EA programs start with their priorities reversed. Technology is in the driver's seat, with application close behind. Information was invited as an afterthought, and business was not invited at all. I think there are several reasons why this happens so often:

- Technology is more portable across industries, so a larger body of useable implementation and best practices has been available to draw upon for much longer than other domains. This is why TOGAF is much more relevant to the technology domain than to the information and application domains. Technology is the most mature domain in terms of the availability of domain-specific architecture and governance best practices.

- Technology, by its very nature, is more centralized. We're in an age where most application developers still focus on one or two applications, but technology resources host solutions that are shared as a service across the enterprise. Security concerns, leveraging virtual servers and disks, consolidated backups and disaster recovery – these are just a few of the compelling business cases for pooling technology into a centrally managed data center. Because of this, the technology domain has probably been working at the enterprise level in your organization longer than the other IT domains, with more mature organization structures to support enterprise-wide decision-making. This makes the technology domain a natural choice for leadership in enterprise architecture discussions. The technology domain has the most mature org chart roles.

- Many of the most pressing EAG issues today appear to be technology-domain issues. Compliance with security mandates, for example, is at the top of everyone's list of objectives. Security must be addressed at an enterprise level, and is often the project that's driving companies to focus on enterprise architecture and governance in the first place. Because of this focus, the technology domain seems a natural choice for leadership.

However, before you set up your programs with the technology domain at the helm, please review the best practices that have held true for the last thirty years. Beginning with technology is a case of the tail wagging the dog. You don't build technology first, and then consider application, data, and business needs. Technology issues are definitely in the spotlight today, but they are there because of business needs, not the other way around. While many consider the business requirement for security to be a technology domain issue, I suggest it belongs to the information domain instead. You aren't securing cabling and disk drives; you're securing the data on the cabling and disks. You can't implement a PHI, PII, or PCI security solution until you understand what the data requirements are. Yes, in the end, a good part of the solution will be in the technology layer, but the requirements don't *ever* begin there. Don't skip past the domain precedents recommended by Spewak and NIST thirty years ago, or your programs will not be business focused. This is a business, not a science project.

Full-time versus matrixed domain EAG architects

I've seen two different approaches to setting up an Enterprise Architecture and Governance organization, but only one of them should be considered a best practice.

One approach is to put someone in charge of Enterprise Architecture and Governance and have the all the domain architectural roles report directly to that EAG director as dedicated resources. The other approach is to leverage architects that work in different areas of the company, but come together regularly in a *dotted-line*, or *matrixed* reporting structure:

- **Full-time, dedicated architects** reporting directly to an EAG director, working full time on strategic architecture.
- **Matrixed architects**, reporting to different parts of the organization, working on real projects, with dotted-line relationships to a full time EAG director.

It might seem counterintuitive, but I've found that the direct-reporting architect approach doesn't work well. In fact, I've never once seen it be successful. In every case, it becomes a silo of people who make decisions amongst themselves, then pass those decisions as mandates to the rest of the company. There are several problems with this approach. The isolated architects are:

1. **Disconnected from reality**. These architects are not in tune with the daily challenges of the company and are operating in the dark, despite best intentions. This results in elegant solutions that ignore practical integration messiness, timelines, and budgets. What tends to come out of these organizations look like the ivory-tower, perfect world solutions you would give your college professor in response to an exam question, and not what's actually useful in the real world. A three to five year strategic vision isn't intended to paint a picture of architectural nirvana. Rather, it is a best-case, real-world scenario where there are still a lot of legacy infrastructure limitations in the mix. It probably doesn't make business sense in that period to invest limited resources in replacing those older infrastructure components rather than building out more important new functionality around them. A perfect-world infrastructure vision is more likely an IT architect goal than a business goal. Once again, this is a business, not a science project.

2. **Generating ill-will**. This becomes *us versus them*, where *they* are trying to tell *us* how to do our jobs, when they don't have a clue what's really going on. This is taxation without representation. Architects working on actual projects can't be thrilled about having design constraints imposed upon them by a group of people with fancy titles who work in isolation, with no effective input from the average person.

3. **Not growing**. The architects who work in isolation are not growing their skills through real world implementations. Their titles give them a false sense of their own abilities, but in this world of rapidly changing technology, you need to be constantly learning and applying new skills in real world contexts.

4. **Out of touch with budget**. These architects working in isolation tend to have a great deal of difficulty tying their goals to business value. Their strategic roadmaps are self-centered and

unrealistic. They aren't just isolated from their IT peers; they are isolated from the fiscal reality of the business operations.

5. **Not in a position to influence**. Because they are not part of the normal business project pipeline, they don't have the opportunity to influence the architecture of real business initiatives.

6. **Become a dumping ground**. Senior resources are rare and valuable. If you want access to the most talented resources in your organization, you're going to have to be willing to share. You can't hire from outside, because for these positions, you need people who know your infrastructure intimately. If departments believe they'll be losing their best people, they'll send you instead the people they would prefer gone. To them, it's an easy way to take out the trash without going through the confrontation and emotion of firing someone.

I've found that the *far* better approach is to take real-world architects facing real-world problems and allow them to carve off a portion of their schedule to meet together under the shelter of the EAG umbrella and hash out solutions together. The one person in charge of the EAG program is fully dedicated, but all of the architects underneath that position are matrixed in from other areas. This works far better than the ivory tower approach, giving individual architects a voice to air real-world concerns and a chance to "own" the resulting decisions.

The full-time, dedicated architects in the ivory tower tends to result in a group of out-of-touch elitists coming up with rules that no one else is committed to, architects that are out of touch with the real world problems and the project pipeline, and an architectural roadmap unable to find business value in each step.

The second approach tends to result in real world issues being addressed by the best resources within your company. The people actually doing the work throughout the organization then champion the decisions.

Enterprise Architecture and Governance (EAG) program roles

This discussion of the organization and domains of the functional framework provides a good opportunity to discuss the roles involved.

- The Executive Sponsor

  o The C-level executive sponsor *must be on the business side*, preferably a COO or CEO. IT architecture and governance cannot be an IT internal project or it will lose focus. The sponsor will need to "get" the concept of investing in the architecture and governance necessary to effectively and efficiently manage the IT functions that support the business. CIO, CTO, CDO, CAO positions should also be supportive of the mission since their most valuable resources will be investing large amounts of time to support it, but the business should ultimately be in charge. You must constantly remind IT that they work for the business, not the other way around. IT does everything to support the business. The executive sponsor won't actually be spending a great deal of their own time, but they will need to actively *champion the commitment of the necessary resources* (human and financial) to the mission. The director may also occasionally ask the sponsor to *resolve conflicts* that affect the program. Their primary responsibilities in this effort are to ensure resource allocation (staffing and funding), to clarify priorities, and to drive cross-functional cooperation. In this capacity, the sponsor must be an active participant in the program. They would rarely attend EAG meetings, but would instead be kept current through the EAG program director.

- The EAG Program Director

    o The EAG program director needs to be truly *domain independent*, and not favor one domain over another. Ideally, they are a direct report of the executive sponsor.

    o The EAG program director should be the only *full-time dedicated resource* on the EAG program team, with the exception of support resources like technical writers and project managers.

    o The EAG program director needs to have *excellent leadership skills* and the ability to keep a vision in the team's head of what they are trying to accomplish in order to keep everyone heading in the same direction. Directing architects is more than a little like herding cats.

    o The EAG program director needs to have *top-level interpersonal skills*, especially *conflict resolution* and the ability to bring discussion back from sideline issues. A good architect is someone who has strong opinions and a passion to communicate and convince. Unfortunately, this means that if you have the right people in the room, there's going to be a lot of drama. This comes with the territory. If they weren't passionate and opinionated, they wouldn't be good architects. If you find that consensus is coming easily, you probably don't have the right people on your team.

    o The EAG program director needs to be able to speak *both business and technical*. They may not be the equal of the domain experts, but they need to be able to understand the discussion well enough to guide it. The director can't be simply a meeting facilitator. You could get a project manager for that. The director needs to be able *to lead, to make decisions, and have the respect of both the business and IT*. The director may not be a domain expert, but they should be an expert in the concepts of enterprise architecture, the goals of the program, the "what," "why," and "how."

    o The EAG program director needs to be able to *work closely with the sponsor and other executives* to keep them informed of the progress and aware of the vision of the program. It's the job of the director to keep these executives engaged and committed so that they'll continue to support the involvement of the domain architects and enforce the decisions made by the team.

- EAG Program Domain Leads

    o Each EAG architectural domain needs to have an *official, recognized leader* to whom the other architects in that domain report. This domain architect can still be a part-time, matrixed resource, but must have the respect of the other architects in their domain, the leadership ability to help the EAG program director maintain control in meetings, and the initiative to keep domain-specific work products moving along between meetings.

- In many organizations, the domain leads have a *day job where they report directly to senior VPs in their area*. The business domain lead might report under the COO, but the technology domain lead might report under the CTO, the application domain lead under the CIO, and the information domain lead under the CDO/CAO. This reporting structure is critical to establishing executive sponsorship, prioritizing EAG work despite pressing daily demands, and enforcing EAG decisions.

- The business architect is the *single most important resource on the team, and the hardest position to fill*. They have to truly understand the business model, and be actively engaged in discussions at the highest levels on the business side. They need to have their finger on the pulse of the day-to-day business operations and be able to see which IT functions are working well for the business and which are not. They need to be engaged in business planning and be able to foresee future IT functionality needs and bring these to the rest of the EAG team for discussion. They need to be able to articulate requirements at the business level. We'll talk more about this when discussing the business domain, but you need to understand up front that this person will be the voice of "the business" to the EAG team. They will cast the business vision that all the other domains will be supporting. These are very special, rare people. Spend the time to find the right fit, because they can singlehandedly cripple the program.

- **EAG Program Architects**

  - Even at the largest organizations, you'll be hard pressed to get anything done with more than 5-8 architects per domain. The domain lead is just like any technical leadership position when it comes to the *size of the team* they can manage successfully.

  - Each EAG program architect needs to be able to *dedicate at least 25% of their time* to enterprise architecture and governance related activities without suffering ill-will from their managers

  - Each EAG program architect needs to be a *subject matter expert*, not someone who was included for political reasons. They need to be an expert in their IT field and an expert in the domain infrastructure of your company. This may be the most difficult part of building a good team, but this is one of those cases where it's important to put the good of the company ahead of the feelings of an individual, even if that person has worked at the company for decades. One or two ineffective people on the architecture team can destroy the effectiveness of the entire team - a team whose time is far too valuable to waste.

  - Each EAG program architect needs to be able to *put the good of the company over their own agenda*. They shouldn't decide architecture based on what keeps work flowing to their department. It's a good thing that your architects have strong opinions about how things should be done, but they need to be able to listen to opposing views and come together in a compromise that is best for the company, not just for their domain or the department of their day job.

  - Each architect must bring *strong opinions* about "how things ought to be done" and be willing to defend those opinions clearly and professionally. Yet, that architect must be willing and able to adjust their opinions with grace and good will based on the feedback from the team, putting the good of the business above the desire to win every argument.

o Not every developer has what it takes to be a good architect. You may have a software developer who is a true wizard when it comes to writing code, the best in the company. Nevertheless, that may not translate to the *ability to visualize what the infrastructure should look like five years from now*.

o I would want to make sure each of my EAG domain architects were well versed in the relevant best practices for architecture and governance. The technology architect should be familiar with TOGAF. The Application and Information architects should be familiar with the Zachman Framework. ITIL education would be a huge benefit for the business architects. In addition, all of your architects should be familiar with any regulatory standards (e.g. NIST CSF, HITRUST).

o There's a whole spectrum of planning horizons in your company, from who focus on a horizon five to ten years in the future, to those who focus on what is happening in the operational environment right now. An EA architect probably has a day job with a very practical, tactical focus at the scope of a single project, looking at a horizon two to three months in the future when the project will complete. They *need to be mentally flexible* enough to step away from that tactical mindset and function in the context of EA on a strategic vision that is more distant, and more idealized.

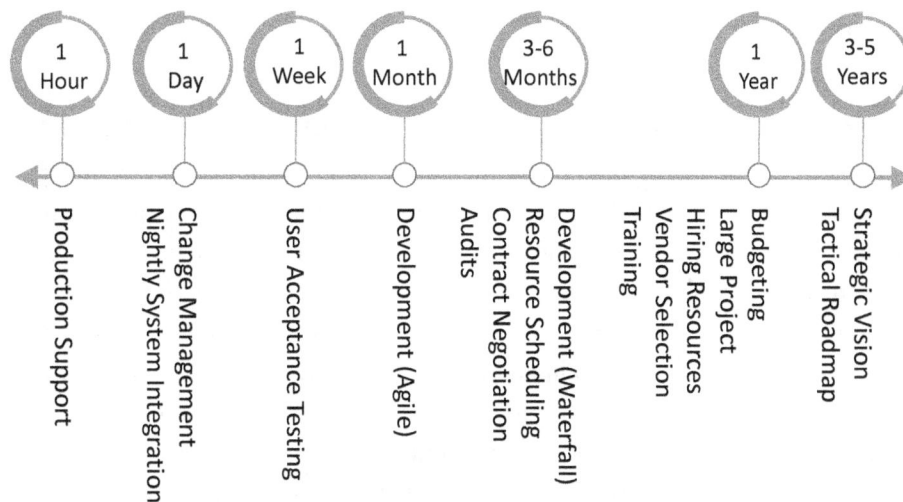

Figure 2.6 Typical Planning Horizons for Different IT Support Tasks

- EAG Technical Writer

  o The EAG technical writer is usually a dedicated, *full time resource* reporting directly to the director of the EAG program.

  o The EAG technical writer is responsible for *documentation consistency*. I would want them to have COBIT training as soon as possible.

  o The EAG technical writer is also responsible for the *enterprise architecture and governance repository*, where the various architecture and governance artifacts are collected, maintained, and communicated.

- **EAG Project Manager** (a role sometimes performed by the EAG Program Director)

  o The project manager is usually a dedicated, *full-time resource* reporting to the EAG program director.

- The EAG project manager is responsible for managing the work tasks involved with completing and maintaining the *enterprise architecture rollout*: the strategic vision and tactical roadmap. The business architect will assign priorities, but it's the project manager who's responsible for making progress toward completion of the gaps in the framework.

- In the same manner, the EAG project manager is responsible for managing the tasks and resources to complete the *executive governance rollout*: the tasks involved in creating and approving the policies, standards, processes, and roles. This completion involves both the breadth of the framework (documents for all functions in the framework), and the completion of the depth of the framework (documents for all information systems covered by the framework). If the SDLC documentation is performed separately by each information system, the project manager has the responsibility of tracking that each of those system-level documents are completed and handed over to the EA technical writer.

EAG program director

Because they are responsible for the EAG program and are independent of the EAG domains discussed in detail later in this book, I want to take just a bit more time talking about the EAG program director role.

Any architect worth their salt will have a good deal of experience-backed confidence, and a strong vision of the way things should work "if they had only asked me." You get all these large egos in a single room and things can degrade rapidly unless there is a strong, respected leader who can tell when an argument has passed from legitimacy into obstinacy, and can nip it in the bud while maintaining an environment of professionalism and mutual respect. This group of prima donnas will roll right over someone who is weak technically and can't call their bluffs or tell when the discussion has gone down a bunny trail. Likewise, a leader who can't or won't step in and command respect and order will find they're trying to herd cats that are all scampering in different directions based on their own agendas. The EAG program leader must be technically strong, professionally and emotionally mature, and must understand the true purpose of enterprise architecture. They must have a clear vision for the goals of the program and must be able to clearly articulate that vision. The EAG program leader needs to be charismatic enough to build team identity and excitement about the program's potential.

The director needs to be able to make decisions when necessary to move the architecture forward. The individual architects are the experts, not the leader. However, when experts can't agree and facilitation/arbitration isn't working, the leader needs to be able to step in and make a fair, informed decision. Leaders who can't make decisions suck the energy and morale right out of the program, making it ineffective. Leaders who appear to the team to be making biased decisions or decisions above their level of understanding are even worse that leaders who make no decisions at all, because they disenfranchise the members of the team. If no decision is being made, the architects will still hope they can influence the direction of the program, but if decisions are biased or being made by someone who doesn't have a clue, the architects see the program as already headed over the cliff. There's no reason to stay and waste their time watching.

In order to have the authority to make and enforce decisions, the EAG program director must also have the full support and assistance of the most senior management. To this extent, it's important that the EAG program director be positioned high on the org chart, where they have the full ear and confidence of executive management.

The EAG program director is also the one who is going to be responsible for recognizing that a resource assigned to the team is not working out, perhaps unable to see beyond their domain, work at a strategic horizon, or remain professional during stressful situations. They are responsible for returning these resources to where they can provide the most value to the company, allowing the EAG team to function smoothly and efficiently. This isn't easy to do. Make sure your director is someone who can and will make that call.

Let me describe one of the more effective and mature EAG programs I have been involved in.

I worked at a large mobile phone carrier for many years. The CEO of that company was often quoted as saying, "Our two most important assets are our people and our data." When that company decided to set up an EA program, they reorganized the entire IT organization so that the CIO had three senior vice presidents reporting to him, an SVP of Information Management, an SVP of application development, and an SVP of Technology. Each of these SVPs had a team of architects reporting to them, led by a director-level domain architect. They brought me in as the Director of Information Architecture, reporting to the SVP of Information Management. My peers and I were matrixed (a dotted line on the org chart) to a VP of EA, who actually reported to the SVP of Application Development. Ideally, we should have reported to a business-side executive sponsor, but fortunately, there was also a truly *brilliant* person from the business side matrixed in as the Director of Business Architecture. In a room full of the brightest minds in the company, I attribute the success of that EA program more to the business domain architect than to any other single person.

The EA program at that company put together a program that took what we felt were the best parts of Zachman, NIST, Spewak, and TOGAF.

From *Zachman*, we took the idea of a framework of domains communicating together at various levels of abstraction using agreed upon artifacts. We all took the Zachman classes and basically used the entire framework, except we didn't drill down more than two layers of abstraction on the "who," "when," and "why" columns, all of which fell to the Business Architect.

From *TOGAF* we lifted a large number of best practice policies and standards. Most of these related to our technology architecture simply because that's the most transportable across industries, but we were able to adopt some standards and practices from other areas of TOGAF as well. Many of the standards in TOGAF have been developed in response to national standards such as HIPAA, ISO 27000, COBIT 5, and NIST 800-53. The TOGAF model was at that time thought by our security office to be an excellent foundation from which to achieve regulatory compliance or standards body certification, especially those involving security.

From *Spewak, NIST, and others*, we took the concept of a hierarchy of supported decisions. The CEO set the vision for the company, typically in the form of "the five things we need to focus on this year are…"

The business decided what functionality was needed to support the company goals. The EA program took it from there, led by the Business Architect.

I'll discuss the individual domains in detail in later chapters. For now, let's return to our discussion of creating a hierarchical list of the IT functions that fall to these domains.

Creating the hierarchy of functions and functional areas

In general, there are two ways of taming complexity on any subject, depending largely on whether you're building something new or trying to get a grasp on complexity that already exists. Both involve creating a conceptual hierarchy with a small handful of concepts at the highest level of abstraction, each of which breaks down into more and more pieces as more detail is fleshed out. At the highest level, the picture needs to be simple enough for everyone to visualize and understand. This is your napkin drawing!

A Functional Framework for Architecture and Governance

	ORGANIZATION	BUSINESS				IT											
FUNCTIONAL FRAMEWORK	EA DOMAIN	BUSINESS		INFORMATION		APPLICATION			TECHNOLOGY								
	FUNCTIONAL AREA	AREA 1	Area 2	AREA3	AREA 4	AREA 5	AREA 6	AREA 7	AREA 8	AREA 9							
	FUNCTION	Function 1 / Function 2	Function 3 / Function 4	Function 5 / Function 6	Function 7 / Function 8	Function 9 / Function 10	Function 11 / Function 12	Function 13 / Function 14	Function 15 / Function 16	Function 17 / Function 18							
ARCHITECTURE	LONG TERM STRATEGY																
	ROADMAP																
GOVERNANCE	POLICIES																
	STANDARDS																
	PROCESSES/ROLES																

Figure 2.7 The Hierarchy of Functions within the Functional Framework for Architecture and Governance

So, how do you start building the hierarchy of functions in your own framework?

One approach would be to start by looking at a generic framework or one customized for another company or department, then modifying it as necessary to fit your needs. Don't be afraid, though, to make fundamental changes to that model where it doesn't reflect your operations. If your architecture team wants you to look at TOGAF as a reference model outside of technology and security, you'll be doing a lot of this.

Another approach would be to make a list of all the functions for which you're responsible, then start grouping them together in clusters of related functionality, somewhat like putting a puzzle together by first grouping together pieces by shape and color. Again, make sure you don't list projects and job titles; list actual functional responsibilities.

The difference between these two approaches really comes down to whether you're building the framework from the top down, or from the bottom up.

Top-down approach

As someone who came up through the programmer track, I can attest that learning a programming language is trivial. I once landed a job that required knowing a program language I had never used (FORTRAN), and learned it over the weekend before starting the next Monday. No programmer reading this is going to be impressed with that claim.

However, learning a programming language isn't the same as learning to program. The hard part of learning software programming, the part that takes years to master, is learning how to take a complicated problem and break it into smaller and easier problems. If you do that enough times, that one unimaginably complicated problem becomes several dozen (or hundred, or thousand) very easy problems. You start at the conceptual top, and work your way down to the implementation details. This is the **top-down approach**. As you may recall, this was the approach used by Zachman thirty years ago. Work out the highest level of abstraction first before dropping down to the more detailed layers. Don't get lost in the forest right at the beginning.

In this approach, you see whether the first level of abstraction suits your organization before digging too much into the detail below. This approach works well if you're struggling with being overwhelmed, and need to break the problem down into smaller pieces. It also works well if you suspect that you're going to have a lot of pushback from old-order managers and supervisors who are going to want to simply document the organization structure that exists today. It took a long time to reach the position they hold today, and they are good at it. They have no stake in what they perceive as starting over.

By starting with a high-level abstraction of functionality, you may have an easier time developing consensus than if you dive immediately into detail functions that are clearly someone's personal territory.

Bottom-up approach

In other cases, you may start with the details and organize them into larger and larger conceptual groups. As an example, I own a lot of books. I have bookcases everywhere my wife will let me put them; many of the shelves stacked two layers deep. In order to find anything, I had to create some kind of organization. Managing all the thousands of different books in my house has many similarities with managing all the thousands of different IT functions in your company.

Figure 2.8 A panoramic view of my inner sanctum

I group books together in ways that made sense to me: classics, science fiction, religion, Arthurian romances, books illustrated by certain artists. I have so many books by some of my favorite authors that I give them their own dedicated shelves. It makes more sense to me to keep these books together than to disperse them throughout my library by title or subject. Over time, the collection has rather arranged itself based on how the books are accessed and managed. I have yet to have grandchildren, but I have a collection of wonderful children's books on a low shelf in a sunny room. Rare first editions are kept in a protected barrister case in a room with no direct sunlight.

This isn't the Dewey Decimal System. You would no doubt organize it differently. My wife keeps *borrowing* my books based purely on the color of the covers to put together little decorating vignettes throughout the house. That's just wrong! My system works for me and my unique collection of books. It's grown into place over the years, and is perfectly suited to organizing the chaos that is my library.

In a **bottom-up approach**, your functional areas will likely emerge organically in this same manner. Starting with the details, group them together based on similar functionality and governance requirements, and then group the groups until the number of the highest-level groups is manageable.

In the bottom-up scenario, you start at the detail level, making a list of everything your organization does, in no particular order. Just toss in everything. We used to call this "green-lighting," where everything is just piled together with no particular order, precedence, or ownership. Just make lists:

- Think about what functions are performed by each division of the organization you're modeling.

- Look at timesheets and project lists for the types of functions that are being done, and derive function from those projects. Don't make a list of projects!

- Look at your strategic planning documents also – some of your organization's functions may be very immature or even non-existent today, but you want to make a place for them in your plan.

- Look at the detail level of the "sample" functional framework to jog your memory of things you might have missed.

- Look at frameworks such as ITIL to get ideas, but don't be married to their lists, which were originally created more than twenty years ago.

- Make sure you involve the business. The whole purpose of IT is to provide services for the business. It's often quite illuminating to ask the business what functions they believe you provide for them.

In keeping with my pursuit of "the big picture," a few years ago I decided to pursue a master's degree in theology. The seminary professors taught us to interpret scripture by first understanding what it meant in its original context, then to derive the universal "truth" out of that context, and finally apply that truth to today. Oddly enough, I find that training more useful than you might imagine when digging through frameworks from the past trying to understand what the framework was originally meant to accomplish, then extracting the timeless intent and interpreting it in today's context. It's less important that we reproduce how things were done in the past than that we reproduce the intent of those things in a way that is appropriate for today.

The typical real world approach

In reality, you won't use either the top-down or the bottom-up approach exclusively. You'll probably start with the standard top-level groupings we'll discuss in a minute, then start putting all your detail functions and setting them on the appropriate functional *shelf*. Every once in a while, you'll find a function that doesn't fit well in these high-level functional areas, and you'll need to adjust your structure a little at the top of the hierarchy; making a new shelf. Most of the time the top-level areas will come first and you'll file the details under them. Occasionally, though, you'll run across a detail function that will generate an entirely new high-level functional area. In the real world, building out the hierarchy of functions is an iterative process, both top-down and bottom-up depending on the moment.

I suggest making that list of your existing detail functions, then using the sample functional framework to organize those functions into a hierarchy, making modifications as needed along the way.

One thing you may struggle with is the temptation to list business functions, such as retail sales and advertising, rather than IT functions such as software development or hardware support. The purpose of the functional framework is to manage IT function complexity, not to manage the business. You need to ask yourself, "In the retail sales and advertising area, what are the IT functions?"

In theory, you can have as many levels as you need in the hierarchy of your functions. But in the real world, having too many layers just means that the hierarchy itself is too complicated. There's no need to keep breaking the problem down once the detail pieces are easy enough to understand and manage. I find that just two levels are about all that's needed in the framework itself. Any additional complexity can be fleshed out within the detail documentation rather than in the framework. In fact, that's the determining factor. If the "functions" are all going to end up using the same policy, standard, process, and role documents anyway, then there's no need to put any more detail in your functional framework. Leave the details for the document artifacts to spell out. There's no need to list a function for hardware support of retail sales and a separate function for hardware support of advertising if the hardware support standards, process, etc. are identical. Keep your framework simple!

While you should feel free to organize your functions into functional areas however seems best to you, there's a well-worn path that you should at least consider following before you start grouping your books by the color of the covers. The typical high-level functional areas that most companies will need to support are:

- Information lifecycle management functions, including:

    o Information collection functions
    o Information modeling functions
    o Information quality functions
    o Information security functions
    o Information analysis functions
    o Information delivery functions
    o Information end-of-life functions

- Software development lifecycle functions, including:

    o Software development request functions
    o Software development requirements gathering functions
    o Software development approval/prioritization functions
    o Software development estimation/budget functions
    o Software development project management functions
    o Software development architectural requirements functions
    o Software development technical requirements functions
    o Software development coding/unit testing/code review functions
    o Software development user acceptance testing functions
    o Software development system testing functions
    o Software development change management functions
    o Software development implementation functions
    o Software development support functions

- Software infrastructure lifecycle management functions, including:

  o Software request/approval functions
  o Software vendor selection/POC functions
  o Software acquisition functions
  o Software install/configuration functions
  o Software licensing functions
  o Software security functions
  o Software release management functions
  o Software end-of-life functions

- Hardware lifecycle management functions, including:

  o Hardware request/approval functions
  o Hardware vendor selection/POC functions
  o Hardware acquisition functions
  o Hardware install/configuration functions
  o Hardware licensing/inventory functions
  o Hardware security functions
  o Hardware release management functions
  o Hardware end-of-life functions

This is by no means an exhaustive list. It's just enough to show you how most of the IT functions you try to manage can be grouped into some high-level groups. You should at least consider using a structure along these lines before you try to reinvent the wheel. Many companies organize their IT management this way, but the functional framework concept will support other approaches if you feel strongly about it. The advantage of using lifecycles is that it's an overall concept that most everyone will understand. Arranging them this way gives everyone confidence that the framework is conceptually complete, and the functions don't overlap. Moreover, if you do decide one of your functions is missing from this list, it should be obvious where that function belongs.

Of course, your business may demand other high-level functional areas - other shelves for a unique collection of books. Most businesses involve managing people, not just data, hardware, and software. How are the lifecycles of personnel managed? In most companies, these functions are regulated to Human Resources (HR), where the person-lifecycle is managed through very specialized software that typically doesn't involve a lot of IT intervention. You manage the HR data, software and hardware, but you probably won't get directly involved in the business functions. On the other hand, if your company is a recruiting agency, a school, a hospital, or some other industry where a major component of the business itself involves managing a "person" lifecycle with specialized IT functions, you may need an entire functional area just for those. Just make sure that the IT support functions themselves do not better fit under another, existing functional area. Remember it's the IT functions we are managing.

Another common decision is to call out in a separate functional area those generic services that support many functions. You might, for example, abstract the print management functionality out of many applications into one managed function. You may decide to create a separate high-level functional area for functions that support other functions, a **systems services functional area**. You can have information services (master data management), applications services (print services), and hardware services (SAN virtual disk).

While this is acceptable, it isn't generally recommended, as will be discussed in detail in the IT domain sections later in this book. More detail just makes for highest level of abstraction more complicated and therefore harder to manage – which was the whole point of this exercise. You're aiming for a simple napkin drawing.

If you aren't going to manage those functions materially differently than other information, applications, and technology in terms of architecture and governance, then there is absolutely no value to cluttering up the napkin drawing. This framework exists to make IT management simpler, not to feed the ego of someone who wants to see their pet project called out for special attention.

How you organize your functional hierarchy is up to you. Do you want a separate security functional area that includes the functions for hardware, software, and information security all in one place? Alternatively, do you want a separate security function in each domain? Either answer might be correct for you, depending on how you'll manage the strategic vision, the policies, standards, and processes for security across these functional areas.

Odds are that your information, application, and hardware security functions will have separate policy statements and will be part of separate processes, in which case you would be better off separating out information security function into the information lifecycle functional area, and software security functions into the software lifecycle functional area. Remember, all the architecture and governance for these functions is going to have to be captured in documentation.

When trying to determine which functional area a function belongs in, ask yourself in which document it would make the most sense to place the architecture and governance. Information security includes defining data sensitivity labels (PHI, PII, PCI), and standards for masking, encrypting or de-identifying information appropriately for different roles in different environments. Software security focuses on provisioning and de-provisioning access to data, and technology security focuses on physical asset security[10]. Since the security-related policies, standards, processes, and roles for each domain will be different, I see no advantage to consolidating all the security governance into a single function.

In this case, your functional framework helps clarify your thinking about the functions you are managing, revealing that your security office must be staffed by experts from all the EAG domains. Placing the function of identifying PII data in the information domain makes it clear that the technology architects can't own all of the security-related functions. These kinds of realizations are why we use the functional framework, because it represents IT complexity in a simple, meaningful representation that helps clarify our thinking and discussion about managing IT functions. *This isn't a side effect of the framework; it's the primary purpose of the framework.* We'll discuss this topic in more detail under the security function in each of the domains in later chapters.

You shouldn't expect to completely flesh out your entire list of functions and functional areas before starting to use the framework. You should do the best you can, but acknowledge that there are some areas that will need more attention later. Your HR area performs many important functions like cutting

---

[10] This is, of course, an over-simplification. In many cases software components have been "hardened" onto a dedicated physical device, such as a router. In these cases, the software components may be best managed by the technology domain.

your paycheck, but it wouldn't be uncommon to leave that functional area at a high level or missing entirely until some point when IT architectural involvement is needed.

Despite all the insistence that everything starts with the business, you will almost invariably begin with your existing IT functionality when building your list of functions. After all, EAG came into existence as a response to the growing complexity of existing IT. As we will discuss in the chapter on the business domain, the business functions are added to the framework as the business asks for IT assistance. Even when you begin fleshing out your framework artifacts with IT functions, you need the business architect involved to keep the focus on business needs. All those existing IT functions were once business needs, and they *still* only exist to serve the business.

One good reason for documenting these existing functions is that it may actually be a regulatory compliance requirement. In many cases, if you're being audited, you will need to be able to "prove" that you have process controls in place. Auditors are used to hearing good stories about the processes you have in place, but will *always* ask for the formal documentation. We recently underwent a pre-audit in preparation for HITRUST certification, and most of the findings were documentation-related. You're going to have to produce the process documentation across your entire enterprise (and logs to prove those processes are being followed) or you will fail the audit. Most maturity models require process documentation before you can advance past Level 2.

It can also facilitate leadership transitions. Even the most gifted leaders will benefit from taking the time to clearly define and communicate how they do what they do. If the leadership truly is gifted, they'll eventually move up or out to other responsibilities, and the person who takes up the reins will have a much easier transition if everything is documented. Otherwise, the organization will soon be stumbling around in the dark, trying to figure out why it isn't as successful as it used to be. The lack of direction, in this case, is as much the fault of the predecessor's lack of communication as it is the successor's lack of vision.

As your business changes, you'll find a need to add new functions. Your list of functions and functional areas is a living document, with functions being added and dropped over time as needed.

A sample enterprise-level hierarchy of functions

The following sample framework hierarchy is a simplified example of what an enterprise-level functional framework might look like. I didn't even attempt to list any business functions, for reasons that will become clear when we discuss the business domain.

This sample functional framework includes many IT enterprise-level functions that are common enough across all industries that they should be meaningful and relevant to your organization. Again, this is just a sample, not to be considered complete in either breadth or depth. Remember to keep it simple. The goal is a napkin drawing, not a *Where's Waldo* poster.

This sample represents a perfect world where you don't have to worry about legacy architecture that doesn't function the way you would like. The functional framework is always conceptual. The real world details will, for the most part, be embedded in the governance documents, not visible in this functional framework.

Maybe all your development is outsourced – you don't own custom software development. Maybe all your software is "black-box" and you have no opportunity to manage data directly – you don't own that function. Maybe your hardware is all a cloud-based service – not a function you support. Regardless, these functions are occurring somewhere. You may not have a lot to document, but you'll still have policies that those who manage the outsourced functions for you will have to adhere to. You'll have standards (i.e. service level agreements), and you'll need to document roles and responsibilities. Many of the processes are completely outside of your responsibility. However, some support processes apply to that external work.

If I were working with a company to develop a functional framework for their organization, this sample framework is where I would start. On the IT side, what do you do that can't be described as one of these functions? I would expect there to be a few things that need to be added, but I would be very surprised to find that this basic functional framework concept couldn't easily be extended to include those functions. Again, the business functions in this framework are typically only those where active architecture and governance is still being developed. Even though this whole functional framework is focused on the business, when you're initially building out your framework, only worry about the existing IT functions you already provide for the business. You aren't ignoring the business – you're documenting what you already do for the business. That's still business-focused, if done correctly.

Enterprise Architecture and Governance Functional Framework

	ORGANIZATION	BUSINESS		IT				
	EA DOMAIN	BUSINESS DOMAIN		INFORMATION DOMAIN	APPLICATION DOMAIN			TECHNOLOGY DOMAIN
	FUNCTIONAL AREA	AREA 1	AREA 2	Information Lifecycle Management Functions	Software Lifecycle Management Functions	Software Development Lifecycle Functions	Software Services	Hardware Lifecycle Management Functions / Hdwr Svcs

Column functions (FUNCTION row):
- **Information Lifecycle Management Functions:** Modeling, Consuming, Ensuring Quality, Securing, Analyzing, Delivering, Aging/Archiving (End-of-Life)
- **Software Lifecycle Management Functions:** Requesting, Selecting Vendors, Acquiring, Installing/Configuring, Upgrading, Tuning/Monitoring, Auditing, Securing, Complying with Licensing, Decommissioning (End-of-Life)
- **Software Development Lifecycle Functions:** Requesting, Managing, Gathering Requirements, Estimating, Designing, Securing, Developing, Propagating through Environments, Testing, Implementing, Supporting
- **Software Services:** Printing, Reporting, Integrating using ESB, Managing Documentation, Automating Business Processes
- **Hardware Lifecycle Management Functions:** Requesting, Selecting Vendors, Acquiring, Installing/Configuring, Upgrading, Tuning, Auditing, Securing, Complying with Licensing, Decommissioning (End-of-Life)
- **Hdwr Svcs:** Virtualizing Servers, Virtualizing Disk

Row hierarchy (left column): FUNCTION HIERARCHY → FUNCTION

STRATEGY	LONG TERM VISION
	ROADMAP
GOVERNANCE	POLICIES
	STANDARDS
	PROCESSES/ROLES

Figure 2.9 Enterprise Architecture and Governance (EAG): Functional Framework

This functional framework isn't intended to be a mandate to which your enterprise must comply. It's included as a sample to help make the concepts clear and to give you some ideas about things you might want in your own framework. In this function framework example, I've included hardware and software services as separate functional areas as a common example of how you may wish to tweak the framework to meet the unique environment in your organization. These are discussed in more detail within the individual domain chapters later in this book.

A sample department-level hierarchy of functions

Of course, architecture and governance should be performed at the enterprise level. A company of any size and complexity that has no enterprise architecture and governance initiative is almost certainly well on its way to becoming overwhelmed by the complexity of the IT functions it needs to manage, not to mention being in significant danger of regulatory non-compliance.

If you don't have the power to make architecture and governance happen at the enterprise level, you can still find value in using a functional framework to manage the areas of the organization whose functions you *do* control. In a sense, your department is operating as if you were an enterprise with a lot of outsourced functionality.

Perhaps you don't manage the hardware or the network you use. That's not too different from a company that outsources servers to a third party cloud-based virtual server hosting service. In fact, I think we can all see the day where many of the function we have traditionally considered internal will more often be outsourced functionality. The hardware and software used to support the business is increasingly a virtualized commodity.

However, if you outsource functionality, you still have security policies, service level agreements for performance and availability, and processes for getting support when needed. This is true whether you're a company outsourcing functionality to third party vendors, or whether you are a department outsourcing functionality to other departments.

In essence, the IT domain functions of your department-level functional framework will look very similar to the enterprise example above. The main differences will be the amount and depth of detail that you need to go into when defining the architectural strategy and roadmap, and the governance polices, standards, processes and roles for the functionality that's outsourced.

For example, if you outsource application development, you probably want to have some governance for software development process, even if the developers are not managed by you, just to make sure that what you consider best practice is followed. The level of detail will be usually much greater if you are managing your own development, rather than managing outsourced development. On the other hand, you may be comfortable with a fairly self-directed agile development process internally, but want a much more formal process for management oversight of external development. Depending on the function, outsourced functionality may require more or less formal management than internal functionality.

The sample functional framework below is for a fictional enterprise analytics department within a larger company. This department is responsible for all data used analytically, including the enterprise warehouse and many application-specific data marts. Because the managed functionality is narrower in breadth, we can go into more detail regarding the functions without losing sight of the big picture. You can go into this level of detail at the enterprise level also, provided you have the ability to collapse the functional framework to a higher level for discussion and general planning purposes. For the most part, in an enterprise framework the lower levels of detail are of concern only to the architects in the domain owning the functionality.

This sample only has three levels of functional hierarchy. Yours may have more, but even the largest of companies seldom really need additional levels of abstraction. Remember that this is the framework on which your functions hang. All your functions need a place on this framework to hang, but each individual function need not be called out. For example, the second detailed task in the Software development lifecycle area of this sample framework is "Project Management." If you've ever been involved in project management, you know it can involve estimates, resource calendars, complex plans, baseline comparisons, and more. The important thing is that all those detail tasks have a place on the framework. The functional framework is only detailed enough to break down the strategy, the standards, and the ownership into manageably small chunks.

Later, when we discuss documenting the architecture and governance of each function in your framework, you'll find that there's plenty of room to go into far more detail in the documentation you hang from this framework. Keep your functional framework simple enough for people to grasp conceptually. If you add too much detail at this level, you'll be back to overwhelming complexity, and you've missed the entire point of this book.

Another opportunity you have with a departmental-level functional framework is to group the functions based on management responsibility. Again, functions are not derived from your organization structure. That said, in a smaller department within the enterprise, it's quite likely that when the dust settles, each function will be owned by a single manager. In your software development process, one manager may own business requirements and testing and another may own change management and operations. As long as the functions were derived independent of your organization structure, there is no harm in grouping them by manager on the framework. Indeed, there's a good deal to be said for having very clear lines of management responsibility using your functional framework.

Notice that, in this sample departmental functional framework:

- The function detail reflects the focus of the department (i.e. information management).

- The application and technology domain functions reflect that most third-party purchased software and hardware is managed outside the department. The only real management is in the support functions required of the outside area, and the compliance functions imposed by the outside area.

- In this example, I added some business functions to reflect initiatives that are still in the early planning phases, and have not yet become IT supported functions. This will be explained in more detail under the heading *Business functions* (page 78).

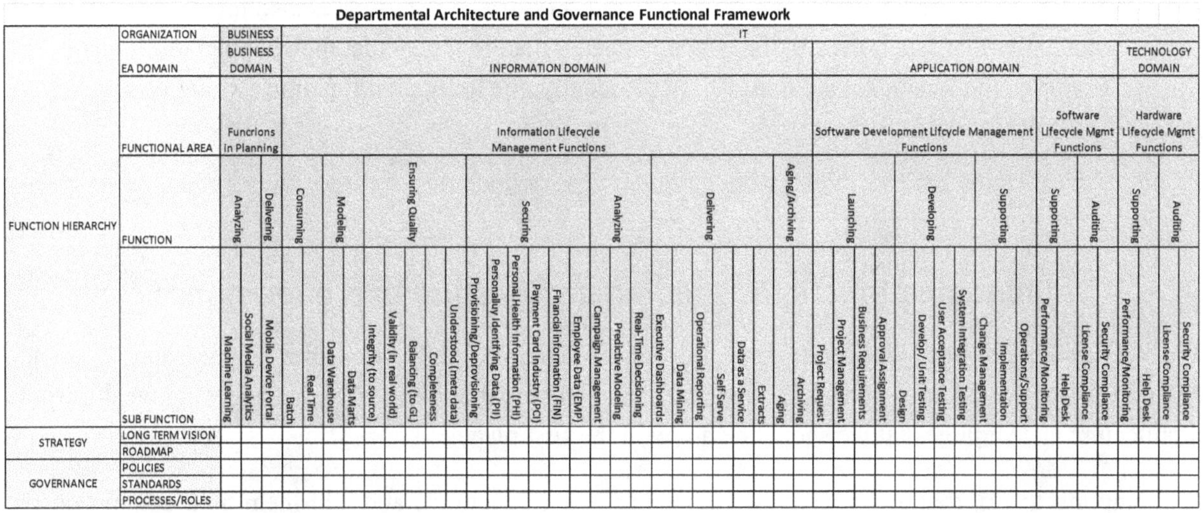

Figure 2.10 Departmental Architecture and Governance Functional Framework

Functional hierarchy summary

Your details will differ from these examples. That's to be expected, and those differences are perfectly fine, provided your framework doesn't violate the following core tenets:

- **Minimum Complexity**. These sample functional framework were trimmed a little for legibility, but your framework shouldn't be too much larger than these. If yours runs several pages, you have *far* too much detail. The goal here is to make the functional hierarchy simple enough to swallow, conceptually. If the functional hierarchy is too complex to easily visualize, then it's going to be too complex to easily manage, and managing IT complexity is the whole point.

- **Unconnected to Organizational Chart**. There is nothing on these sample functional frameworks about org chart positions. You might look at them and immediately know who in your organization owns some of these functions, but that ownership isn't mandated by the framework. If you have multiple rows for the same basic function, i.e. "Business Analytics for Department A" and "Business Analytics for Department B," then you need to merge them. "Business analytics for department A" is more than likely an org chart position and a sure sign that someone is trying harder to protect their personal territory than to help solve the problem of managing IT complexity.

- **Not about Architecture or Governance**. This functional hierarchy doesn't contain any functions for architectural or governance. Those will be captured in the cells underneath each function. It's just a simple functional description of the organization that the architecture and governance will have to support.

- **Functions are Verbs, not Nouns**. You can't point to a policy, form, database, application, or server and declare it a *function*. Those are just *objects*. A function is something that *happens*. "Securing Data" is a function – "Database Request Form" isn't. Admittedly, it is awkward to avoid nouns when they are so pervasive in our industry. However, it is also important to remember that functions are things that happen – not the things that they happen to. In this example, the functional areas are all verbs. Ideally, the individual functions would be also.

Managing functions – adding architecture and governance

We keep talking about architecture and governance. They're really two sides of the same coin, and should really be considered part of the same program. Governance is how we manage what we do, where architecture is deciding what we should be doing in the first place.

It's tempting to say that architecture and governance are functions, and add them as a column on the functional framework. This is the main source of confusion behind the meaning and scope of architecture and governance programs. When I talked with those companies[11] who were spinning up architecture and governance programs, the common thread seemed to be, "OK, I'm already managing all these IT functions. What is this new 'governance' function I'm going to have to do on top of that?"

---

[11] Mentioned in the Introduction

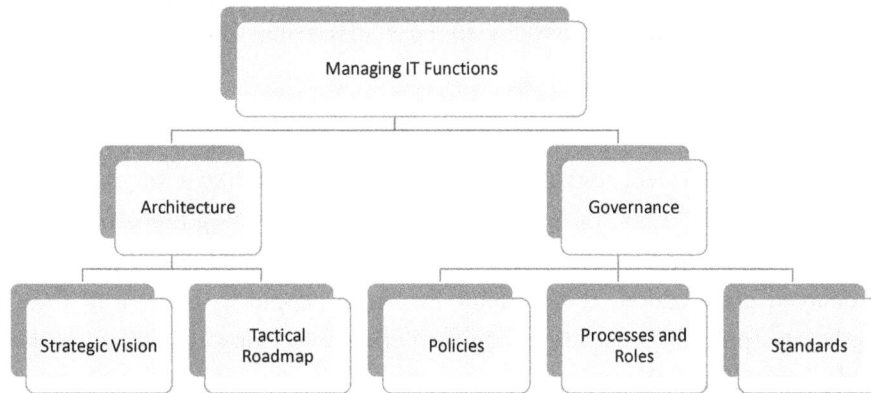

Figure 2.11 Managing IT Functions

Governance and Architecture aren't functions in your functional framework; they're how you manage those functions.

The most important thing you're going to do with this functional framework is to create a unified long-term vision for *all* of your functions. You are going to identify governance policies, roles, responsibilities, and oversight processes for *all* your functions. You are going to set up a way to create standards, review, and approve waivers, and escalate conflict for all of these functions. Architecture and Governance aren't something you do *in addition to* managing IT functions; they *are* the management of those IT functions. The good news is that you're probably already doing far more architecture and governance than you realize. Our goal is to organize it, simplify it, and bring it up to an enterprise initiative, not a departmental function.

Two kinds of people – focus on today's problems versus tomorrow's

There are two kinds of people in this world – those who are solving today's problems and those who are solving tomorrow's. You definitely need both kinds.

It's considered poor practice to have an architect as a lead developer on a project. Similarly, the manager of developers shouldn't also manage operations. It's extremely difficult to multi-task when the tasks are at different planning horizons. Absolutely the worst case example is when the same person is tasked with working on the 3-5 year horizon strategic architecture, and also tasked with supporting daily operations. I find this is most often the case where architects also function as system administrators.

In every location I've worked, there's been at least one architect who struggles with achieving the three-year planning horizon mindset. Even if they don't have actual responsibility for shorter-horizon tasks, their eyes keep drifting there. Perhaps it's the result of the roles they've come through in their career path. Perhaps it's a natural inclination for more immediate gratification. Regardless, these architects seem to always push for short-term expediency over long-term efficiency.

In my experience, a lot of friction within architectural teams is due to this very conflict. It's not that one of the architects is intellectually inferior, but rather that they keep reverting to a shorter-term planning horizon. In most cases, the architect keeps dropping to project-level planning horizons. This is where their vast experience has trained them to operate. Those same skills at delivering projects that have led to their rise to the architect position they hold today are now interfering with their ability to function in that role.

Even worse, I've had architects with an operational mindset who just want to be able to step in where there's an issue and make quick decisions. It's much easier to ride in like a knight on a white horse and save the day in the operational arena. In the long-term strategic planning arena, the battle is more of a marathon, and the victory and vindication can be a very long time coming. Some people just aren't suited to that kind of delayed gratification. It's difficult for these people to step away from the knee-jerk reaction to immediately apply their knowledge and experience to every immediate problem that comes up, and focus on the long-term problems.

Every project is going to be a compromise between the long-term ideal and short-term return on investment. In order to have those conversations and weigh the various choices at the project level, architects first need to articulate a vision of that long-term ideal future. The time for the compromise is not while creating that vision, but when working at the project level to guide individual projects toward compliance with the future vision. Inevitably, some people given an architect title will tend to design a strategic vision that has many short-term compromises built in because their experience tells them that these compromises will be needed. That tendency to compromise doesn't mean that these people are less valuable resources, but they may be *misplaced* resources. The same person who makes a second-string strategic architect may make an outstanding project-level technical lead. You need *both* roles.

Growing up, I was a big fan of the original Star Trek series. The crew of the Enterprise included Chekov, the navigator, and Sulu, the pilot. Have you ever thought about those two roles? Both involve flying the ship around, right. Why did they need two of them? What was the difference?

The difference is that the navigator sets the ultimate goal and the flight path to get there. They "lay in the course." The pilot, on the other hand, steers the ship around local obstacles, making sure they don't scratch the paint. The navigator is focused on the long range, and the pilot is focused on the short range. Both are critical occupations, neither one "better" than the other. It would be a mistake to put the hotshot pilot in the seat that's responsible for long range planning – a waste of their skill and experience just as much as it would be to put the navigator in the pilot's seat.

It's hard to tell ahead of time whether someone would make a better navigator or a better pilot, a better strategic architect or a better technical lead. However, when you do find that someone is misplaced in either direction, you need to make every effort to get them into a role where they can be successful and contribute the most value to your organization.

It isn't uncommon at all to have a full team of people with the word "architect" in their job title, and little or no strategic planning ever getting done. Instead, they're focused on the present, creating asset inventory lists, discussing production problems and active projects, not focused on the architectural horizon. Of course, you need people focused on both long range and shorter-range horizons, but not the same people. If you have architects who can't tear themselves away from shorter horizons, maybe those people should be moved back to positions where their skills and inclinations are needed. Then you can look for someone else to fill the architect positions.

Speaking for myself, I came up in the development track before I moved to an architect position. However, even as a developer, I was always the guy saying, "If they'd only asked me…" Every single promotion I've ever received has been the result of someone getting tired of listening to my suggestions, and giving me a chance to prove myself. If you can find a senior resource who really knows their trade, knows your infrastructure, and is always casting a vision for the future, citing industry pundits and sketching napkin drawings, you may want to consider them as a candidate for a strategic architect.

Architecture

Architecture is how you manage the future. "If you fail to plan, you plan to fail." No amount of day-to-day management oversight is going to fix your IT issues if you don't know what you are trying to achieve in the long term.

> *When there is no vision, the people perish.*
>
> Proverbs 29:18

There are two parts of architecture. The first part is creating the strategic vision. If you were to look into your crystal ball and see three to five years into the future, what would you want things to look like? Paint the picture of that future in your strategy documents.

The second part is creating a tactical roadmap from that vision. If you want your disaster recovery function to look like your ideal strategic vision three years from now, what are the steps that must be taken each year?

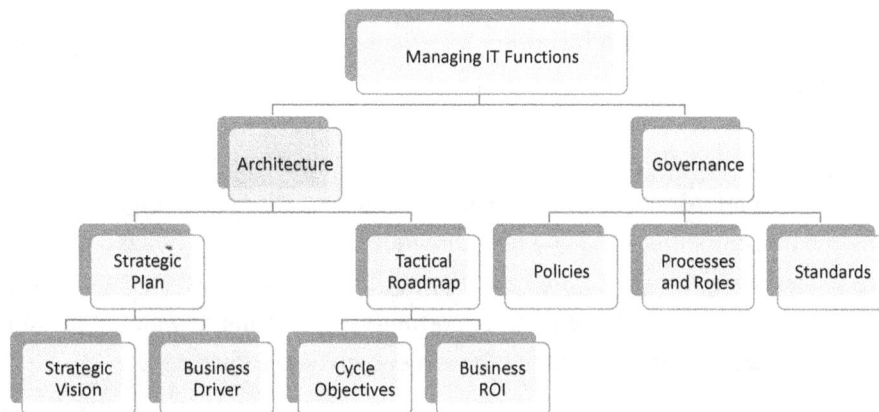

Figure 2.12 Architecture

You aren't documenting a utopian ideal. It's probably unrealistic to plan for a future in three years where all of your legacy applications with their functional limitations will be replaced by high-end, state-of-the-art products. That sounds more like the vision of the IT purist rather than the vision of an architect trying to support the business in the most efficient, productive way! Odds are that the limited budget you are going to have could be better spent in other areas. This reminds me of that childhood classic, "It's the Great Pumpkin Charlie Brown," where Linus talked Lucy into waiting in the pumpkin patch with him to see the Great Pumpkin rather than going door to door with the other kids. At the end of the movie, when all they saw was Snoopy, Lucy cried out, "I could have been trick or treating!" Don't let IT invite the business to the pumpkin patch if their time and money could be better spent trick-or-treating. *Focus on what's important to the business*, not the IT Great Pumpkin.

For some functional areas, you'll find that your solution is mature, and barring any major industry changes or breakthroughs in technology, the future has already arrived. Great! Document your architecture and check off the box.

For most other functional areas, your current solution is not all that it could be. Document your strategic vision for the future, and document the steps that it would take to get you there. You may not even know all the steps, but document the steps you do know. Each year when the budget cycle begins, you'll have a list of all the things that you need to accomplish in the next year to reach your eventual strategic vision.

Of course, each year both the strategic vision and the tactical roadmap will need to be revisited. Other business goals or regulatory requirements may need to be prioritized, pushing the strategy out. That's fine, so long as both the long- and short-term implications of the decision are carefully considered. The future is a moving target! Keep adjusting your aim.

Building and maintaining this strategic vision and tactical roadmap are very important responsibilities of your EAG architects and involve significant time to research, discuss and document. When the architecture program is first launched, you can't expect to sit down and write the strategic and tactical architecture plan for every single function. You may, in fact, never get to some of them. You will need, as an EAG team, to examine the gaps in your framework and assign them out in the order that makes sense, based on their potential impact on the business. Remember – it always comes back to the business. Where is a long-term architectural vision and strategic roadmap going to provide the most value to the business? Work on that one first.

Through an acquisition, I once ended up working for a large company that was in a growth market. The company had been founded from the very beginning as a consolidation of eleven different child companies. The internal architecture was appalling, a significant drain on expense and productivity, and everyone knew it. However, rather than addressing the architectural integration issues, the business decided (rightly, in my opinion) that they were facing a rare growth opportunity, and elected instead to invest in growing their customer base. They knew that they would eventually have to turn internally and reduce the expenses resulting from poor architecture, but they consciously elected to postpone that for about four years to take advantage of the growth opportunity. I chose not to wait out those four years, but I've often pondered how we would have tackled the project, given the chance.

Strategic planning
What is a strategic plan, in the context of a functional framework? It's a picture of what you want your IT infrastructure to look like in the future, together with a description of the value to the business of such a vision.

The strategic plan for your company needs to be broken down into manageable pieces. At the highest level of abstraction, you don't want some massive "city of a thousand planets." While that vision may be beautiful, it's too complicated to manage unless you break it down. Remember, the whole purpose of what we're doing is to manage IT complexity on behalf of the business. So break that massive world-vision down into separate visions for each of the IT functions in the list you built earlier.

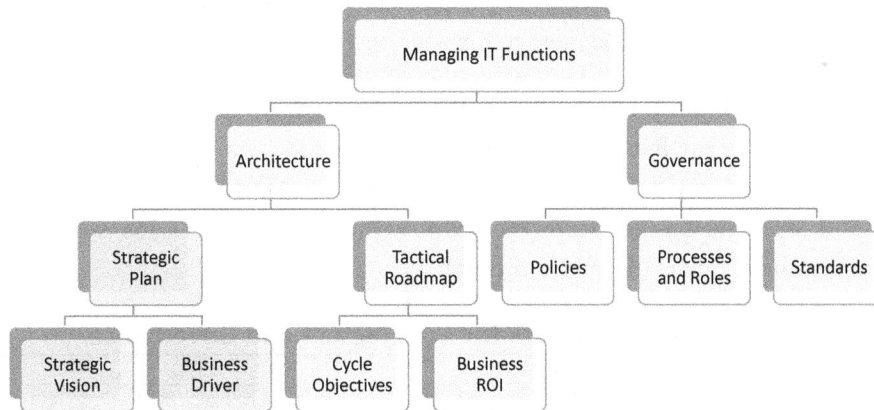

Figure 2.13 Strategic Plan

In some cases, the different functions are tightly integrated, and it might be tempting to create a single strategic vision for both functions together. Avoid that temptation as best you can or else admit that they aren't separate functions, but rather sub-functions of one higher level functions, and arrange your functional framework accordingly. A good example is the software development lifecycle (SDLC). There's really one long process flow consisting of project initiation, requirements gathering, design, development, and testing functions. If you think ahead to when you'll be writing the governance process documents, you know you don't want your SDLC processes spread across a dozen or more function documents. You're going to want a single document for all the SDLC processes and roles. That's fine for process documentation, but at the architectural strategy and roadmap level, you need to keep the functions separate: a strategy for the testing function and a separate strategy for the change management function, etc.

I've found this to be a good practice. Functions can be combined once you reach the governance documentation, but it always seems best to keep the architecture for each function separate. You can have the strategic plans for multiple functions in a single strategic plan document, as long as each function has a distinct and separate strategy spelled out in that document. They are still separate strategies, even though they are collected into a single document. The Appendix contains a sample template for capturing both the architectural strategic plan and the tactical roadmap.

The strategy doesn't have to be in detail, but it does need to be recognizable. You don't have to name specific vendor products, but you do need to name the components with vendor agnostic labels that identify the component's purpose. Your plan needs to contain more than vague future wishes for an IT function: "It will be faster," or "It will be more scalable." If you don't know how you are going to approach making the function faster and more scalable, then you don't yet have a strategy. The strategy needs to be clear enough to guide future decisions in the right direction without being cluttered up in design details.

I've heard of some major manufacturers who claim to have fifty-year strategic plans. Maybe that's possible on the business strategy side, but I think we would all agree that it would be a waste of time to try to predict what our IT infrastructure will look like fifty years from now. IT capabilities change far too rapidly. If you have a solid grasp on the plan for the next five years, you may want to expand your IT strategic planning out to eight or ten years. However, you had better have a better crystal ball than mine! Most companies have been pretty much winging it strategically up to this point, and just being able to plan your IT infrastructure three to five years down the road is plenty to take on for now. Even that much vision will create significant strategic advantage for your business.

IT is incredibly complicated, but it has the power to transform the business, making a real difference in people's lives. It's changing the human experience, and we get to be a part of it! The opportunities for architects today are unprecedented. With that power, though, comes great responsibility. We are casting the vision that will steer the business into the future. Our architecture is the star that steers the IT functionality of the entire company through the rough waters that lie ahead!

A Functional Framework for Architecture and Governance

FUNCTIONAL FRAMEWORK	ORGANIZATION	BUSINESS		IT													
	EA DOMAIN	BUSINESS		INFORMATION		APPLICATION			TECHNOLOGY								
	FUNCTIONAL AREA	AREA 1	Area 2	AREA 3	AREA 4	AREA 5	AREA 6	AREA 7	AREA 8	AREA 9							
	FUNCTION	Function 1	Function 2	Function 3	Function 4	Function 5	Function 6	Function 7	Function 8	Function 9	Function 10	Function 11	Function 12	Function 13	Function 14	Function 15	Function 16	Function 17	Function 18
ARCHITECTURE	LONG TERM STRATEGY																
	ROADMAP																
GOVERNANCE	POLICIES																
	STANDARDS																
	PROCESSES/ROLES																

Figure 2.14 The Long Term Strategy within the Functional Framework for Architecture and Governance

One critically important part of each long-term strategy is to *document the business case*. Why is this so important? Is the strategy "good for the business," or is the strategy merely a desire for architectural purity, or the desire to play with the latest IT toys, regardless of the return the business will receive from the investment? You need to document the business driver stating why this vision of the future will benefit the business, justifying expense.

Unlike the business return on investment (ROI) that we'll discuss in the tactical roadmap, the business driver for the strategic vision can be fairly generalized. The driver isn't a dollar amount; it's just a description of how this vision benefits the business. "Increased customer satisfaction and reduced churn." "Expense reduction through resource consolidation." "Significant reduction in risk of a security breach."

IT architects will be tempted to skip the business justification as self-evident, and jump straight to the fun of shaping the vision for the future. You can't skip documenting the business justification. *If you can't articulate in a very compelling way why the architectural investment will benefit the business, then you're just playing games and wasting time.* This is a business, not a science project.

Tactical roadmap

The other half of architecture is the tactical roadmap. As Arthur Ashe once said, "Success is a journey, not a destination. The doing is often more important than the outcome." IT governance demands an architectural destination. But real business value is realized through the tactical roadmap journey. The vision isn't an IT project and won't generate business change. The tactical roadmap is how change happens. It's where the rubber meets the road.

The strategic plan is a vision for where you want to be in three to five years. Unless you're pretty close to that vision already, though, it will be hard to know what steps you should be taking. This is where the tactical roadmap comes in.

The tactical roadmap consists of a series of **cycle objectives**, which represent the steps you need to take in each of the foreseeable budget cycles. For each budget cycle, you'll list the objectives that need to be funded, and how that business investment will be justified.

Say you have a vision that all your inter-application operational communication will be based on web service calls within five years. Your strategic plan will paint the picture of what that world looks like, what the pieces are, and how they interact. It will articulate how that vision of the future will benefit the business.

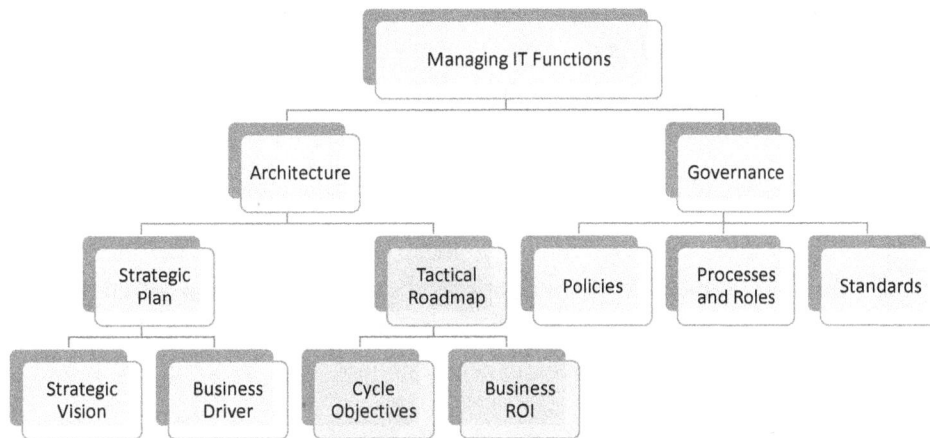

Figure 2.15 Tactical Roadmap

However, you aren't anywhere close to that today. You have a few ancient applications that have no SOA interface, you don't have an enterprise service bus (ESB), or more than a handful of point-to-point services. That vision is a long way from where you currently stand.

No problem! Just break the vision down into steps. This is what software programmers do, right? Break big, complex problems down into lots of smaller, easier problems. There are two ways of approaching this, and you'll need to do both.

Figure 2.16 The Roadmap within the Functional Framework for Architecture and Governance

Justifying tactical IT projects

The first way to break down the vision into steps is to make year-by-year goals as best you can without knowing what the business will have you working on. If you were guaranteed a moderate budget each year, what would you do first that would bring immediate business value while taking a step toward the long-range goal? What would you do after that?

You might start with a first year goal of taking what's currently a nightly batch file transmit of data between a source system and a call center solution, and replacing it with a handful of point-to-point data services. That would reduce latency, reduce disk usage, reduce the risk of data breaches, and reduce the chance of the call center application using the source center data inappropriately, because the data owners would now be in charge of filling the data request.

I once worked for a major telco where the customer information in the call center and the customer information in the store POS were separate repositories, synced nightly in a batch process. One day a married male customer of ours was allegedly caught cheating on his wife. He immediately called our call center and changed the PIN required to access the history of all the calls made from his phone. About four hours later, his wife walked in to a retail store, gave the salespeople the old PIN, and had them print out all the available call history detail. Our company ended up paying the husband's divorce settlement because we had inappropriately given access to the information critical to the judgment against him. That one mistake cost more than it would have required to make the infrastructure changes necessary for both the call center and the store systems to share access to the same single copy of customer information. This wasn't just some internal IT science project that IT was asking the business to fund; this was a priority for the business, affecting both real expense dollars and the company's reputation in the marketplace.

So, if replacing that batch synchronization with real-time lookup services is your roadmap for year one, then the next year you might want to call that same data services from another source application, and, now that you have a service that's called by two enterprise-critical applications, invest in a starter Enterprise Service Bus (ESB).

And so forth. Figure out how big of bites you need to take to get the vision implemented in the timeframe you have planned. Just remember that each year's goals must provide incremental business value to justify that year's expenditure. You'll occasionally find visionary business leaders who are willing to invest large dollars over multiple years, on faith that spend will eventually result in value. However, this is rare, and usually only after you've proven yourself on several single-year projects.

Most businesses can be convinced, if you've done your homework and documented the potential return on investment (ROI), to lay out some cash on faith that you can make a difference, but they will want to see that difference within the same fiscal year, before you come asking for more money the next budget cycle. Rarely, you might be able to go two years, but don't count on it. You have to make each year's budget count for the business. This is why we use a year-by-year planning increment in our tactical roadmap, to coincide with the budget cycle.

Hijack business projects

The second thing you'll do to progress your strategic plan is to carefully watch what projects the business requests each year. You may not get advance notice on these. If you're quick on your feet, though, you can find projects that the business really wants and are going to fund anyway. You need to make those projects take your infrastructure a small step toward your strategic goals in a way that won't break the ROI for the business initiative.

This is *important*, and the key to a long-lived, productive enterprise architecture and governance program. Many EAG programs produce a long list of internal IT projects that set lofty IT-centric goals and are shocked to find that the business isn't excited about funding them. An IT-centric EAG program is seen as a drain on the business, taking money away from what the business wants to accomplish. On the other hand, an EAG program with a comprehensive vision for the company's future, that is willing to work within the constraints of existing business initiatives is seen as valuable to business.

I once presented this functional framework concept in a breakout session at an industry conference. On the last day of that conference, a Gartner industry analyst gave the keynote speech. In front of the whole conference, he called my name and asked me to stand up. He told everyone that he had attended my presentation, and wanted everyone to share his takeaway about hijacking business projects. I was very flattered, of course. I would love to have talked with him about his thoughts on the rest of the functional framework, but I can say that he was definitely an enthusiastic supporter of the idea of rolling out your IT vision within business-funded projects.

Seriously, this may be the single most important concept in this book. *Hijacking business projects is far better than asking for business dollars to fund an IT agenda.* A good architect must have a bit of pirate in their blood.

Perhaps there's a business request for a new customer portal, or for new functionality in your customer service application. As long as you're going to have to design and develop new functionality, you might as well make it comply with your long-term service-oriented strategy, right? Maybe the project can't afford to implement a full ESB, but you can start creating point-to-point services and take a small step in the right direction while working on the things that are most important to the business. That's better than letting the project take steps in the wrong direction, taking your infrastructure further from your strategic goals. Enough small steps and you'll eventually get there.

What about the things that IT wants to do but aren't real business priorities? Guess what? If these things aren't important to the business, you shouldn't be focusing on them! Now, that said, there are times when there may be technical issues that *should* be important to the business but they don't yet realize it. In those cases, it's your job to convince the business of the impact. If you can't convince the business of the priority of these pet projects of yours, then you need to reconsider your own priority and timeline. The business doesn't exist to fund IT projects; IT exists to support the business. You work for them, not the other way around. Your job is to support business priorities, not to go off on your own, taking business dollars away from the things that are important to the business.

The difference between these two approaches is that the first are IT-generated projects, while the second are business-generated. Even though the IT-generated projects are justified by an estimated ROI, those projects aren't necessarily aligned with the primary goals of the business for that year. You'll have to work hard to justify money for each one of them because with the limited resources available, every IT project reduces the amount of resources available for business projects, reducing how much value you are bringing to the business, in their opinion.

Therefore, if you can catch those real business projects and tweak their approach just a little bit, you'll have a lot more success reaching your strategic goals. Rather than being seen as a drain on business resources, you'll be seen as a valuable partner who adds value to important business initiatives.

An architect can, to some degree, be blissfully ignorant of the real world when creating the long-term strategic vision. In fact, in many cases it helps to be just a little blind to the reality of internal politics and sacred cows. After all, the cost of building of the long-term strategy is mainly limited to the architects themselves. The strategy is just a vision, not a real project. The long-term vision costs the business very little.

However, when it comes time to create your tactical plan to implement that long-term strategy in real-world projects using either of the approaches above, you need an architect who has deep experience in the real world of your company. You need someone grounded in reality who knows what's going to be possible and how big of a task it's really going to be. Otherwise, you end up with tactical roadmaps that are unrealistic flights of fantasy. This last is very common in organizations where the architects are full-time direct reports of the EAG program rather than matrixed resources with real day jobs.

Every step in the journey must make business sense. At a minimum, you should be able to articulate how the **business return on investment (ROI)** will exceed its cost within a reasonable amount of time. Ideally, the ROI will be realized within the scope of your planning cycle. If your strategic roadmap has year-by-year goals, then this year's investment should be realized before next year's investment is requested.

If at all possible, you should plan on going further and showing why this investment of time, money, and resources will provide more return than any of the other projects the company might have invested in. At a minimum, however, the business case should be shown to at least pay for itself, justifying the resources that are being dedicated to the project.

Naturally, it's likely that it took most of that fiscal year to design, build, test, and implement the solution, so it's a little harsh to expect it to pay for itself in the first revenue cycle. You might easily argue that the ROI will be seen in the second cycle instead. As long as the expected ROI timeframe is documented from the beginning and the business accepts that investment risk, you've done your job.

Let me present one caveat. When you claim an ROI, you are committing to building a solution where that ROI can be measured. Whatever it is you say you are improving, you need to build metrics into the requirements, along with the appropriate governance controls to ensure that they are collected and reported.

You don't have to give all of that monitoring detail in the strategic roadmap. Just realize that you are committing to it down the line. *Don't you dare claim an ROI you have no intention of monitoring.* It's inexcusable to claim that the cost of measuring the ROI is too high; that the business should just trust that the investment was sound. If the project was one that was requested by the business, not by IT, then the responsibility to justify the spend with ROI is on the business, not IT (though IT should still build in any metrics required to measure the business' stated ROI). However, if IT initiated the funding request, then IT must justify the drain on business resources, and must be able to show proof during the next funding cycle that the investment paid off.

Information systems in architecture

One of the key concepts you'll see throughout this book is an information system. An **information system** is a collection of people, applications, and technology that work together in a system to create and maintain information. Most of your major applications are going to be considered information systems. An information system is an ecosystem within the corporation that can be thought of as one of the high-level components of the corporate infrastructure.

Each information system has an owner, who should be on the business side, not an IT resource. The business owns the information system and makes decisions about how it will be used and enhanced. The infrastructure supporting the system is owned by IT, but the system function is a part of the business.

Many regulatory bodies require that you maintain a complete list of information systems in the enterprise in order to ensure compliance reaches throughout your infrastructure. This list of information systems and their owners is usually created and maintained by the EAG team.

For the most part, your architecture is performed function by function at the corporate level, not application by application. Some of those functions may indeed be implemented on a single application in the infrastructure, but the focus of the architecture is on the function's place in the enterprise, not its place within an application. You may have three separate print management systems today, but the strategic vision will normally either be equally applicable to all of them, or will include all of them as separate components in one architectural vision. You wouldn't expect a separate long-term strategic vision for each application if they perform the same function in the framework.

Governance

Your IT Governance encompasses how you manage IT functions day to day. It's how you create, document, update, communicate, monitor, and enforce the policies, standards, processes, and roles that will be used to manage your IT functions on a day-to-day basis. Governance isn't the same as architecture. Architecture is managing your future vision. Governance is managing what's going on in the real world today.

My first real job was working as a lifeguard. I was well trained and in good shape, but I have to admit I was a terrible lifeguard. Sitting in the sun for hour after hour, day after day, my mind wandered. I was about to graduate from High School and facing the grim reality of a future where I was going to need a real job to pay my own way through life. So, I would get to thinking about things, planning, working things out in my head. I would *not* be watching the swimmers. I still don't understand how the other lifeguards were able to stay alert and watchful hour after hour without losing focus. The architect roles plan for the future. The governance roles have to stay alert and focused on what's happening right now. Having a great plan for the future is no excuse if someone drowns. Your governance people are your company's lifeguards.

Governance of IT functionality can be thought of as three things: the policies, standards, and the processes and roles you use to manage the IT functions on behalf of the business.

Policies	Explain the *why* constraints on the functions, the high-level mandatory requirements that the whole enterprise must comply with.
Standards	Explain *how* we comply with those constraints.
Processes and Roles	Explain *who* does *what* for each function and when that occurs. Technically processes and roles are two different things, but it's almost impossible to document one without constant reference to the other. They're so deeply intertwined that there's no business value to separating them.

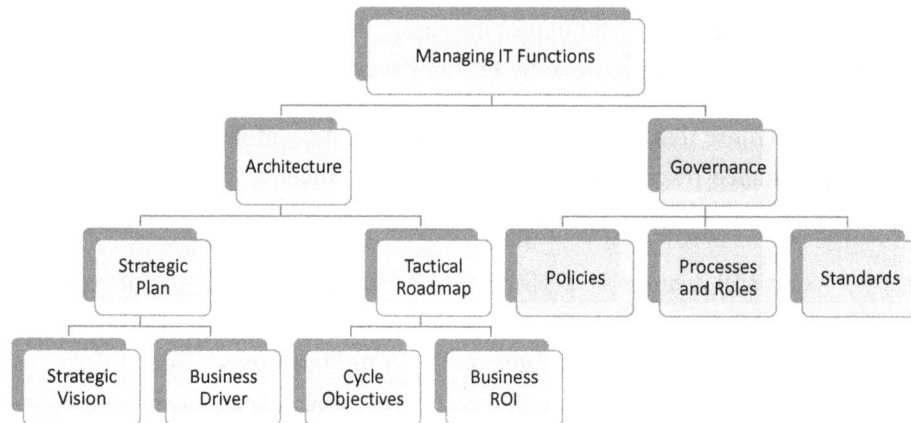

Figure 2.17 Governance

Consider the following example:

- Policy

    o **Corporate** — "Every network-attached device must have a unique identifier."

- Standard

    o **Desktop Services Standard** — "Desktop services will generate a unique identifier for each network-attached device using the asset management system and place an asset tag sticker with that number on the front panel of the equipment."

    o **Data Center Standard** — "The manufacturer's serial number will be used to uniquely identify each asset on the data center floor."

- Process and Roles

    o **Desktop Services Processes and Roles** — "All network attached hardware in the workstation environment must be installed by Desktop Services technicians, who will generate and record a new asset id and tag the equipment before removing it from the storage area…"

    o **Data Center Processes and Roles** — "Before standing up new network attached hardware in the data center, the data center technician will record the manufacturer's serial number in the asset inventory system…"

Obviously, your actual documentation content will be much more formal, and will contain a great deal of additional information. In reality, the policy above would no doubt include verbiage about regular asset inventory, etc., but this example should clarify the distinction between the various governance document artifacts.

Using a functional framework, the EAG program team can easily produce reports showing the percentage of the IT functionality that is actively managed by architecture and governance. Which functions have been brought under governance? Within each function, which information systems are participating? Which are not? If you want to show the value of enterprise architecture and governance, you must be able to show the degree to which the program has penetrated the business.

Part of the governance program must include:

- Where are these documents located and how are they accessed?

- How often are they reviewed by architects for compliance?

- If the documentation is found to be non-compliant or incomplete, what is the process by which it is rejected and resubmitted, and how is that enforced?

- What is the frequency which they are reviewed by the document author for any necessary updates?

- What is the process for requesting clarification or enhancements to the documents?

- Any governance document has the potential to require exceptions to be granted from time to time. How are those exceptions submitted and to whom? What are the criteria for accepting or rejecting exception requests, and how are those decisions communicated and archived? Is the exception permanent, or for a limited period of time? All of this is part of governance.

- If each information system fills out their own copy of a document, how is it determined that the repository contains documentation for the complete list of information systems? Where is the master list of information systems?

Information Systems in Governance

Policies, as we will see, are very short, straightforward mandates at the corporate level. Policies are never defined separately for each information system (see page 55). However, other than these corporate policies, all the other governance document artifacts are quite often created and maintained separately for each information system, though this need not be the case. For example, the standards, processes, and roles in the application security provisioning function may be the same for all information systems. In that case, you would probably want to consolidate them and only have one document at the corporate level.

The goal is to minimize duplication, leveraging the same governance documents for as many information systems as possible. Where the governance standards, processes, and roles are unique and different, you should not hesitate to create multiple documents, provided they use the same template and are stored in the same enterprise repository.

In fact, this is a practical way to help determine the boundaries between information systems. If you have a whole suite of individual .NET applications that are all developed using the same processes, migrated through test environments using the same processes, provisioned using the same processes, and supported by the same operational processes, then they can and should be grouped into a single information system, all sharing a single set of governance artifacts.

Executive versus operational governance:

The realm of governance (which includes policies, standards, processes and roles) is broken down into two major components.

1. **Executive Governance** is where the powers-that-be create, capture, communicate, monitor, and enforce the policies. This is the body that decides how the company will operate. This includes handling requests for waivers or modifications. This executive governance is usually staffed by the enterprise architects, possibly supplemented by executives and subject matter experts (i.e. HR or Legal) when needed. Policies, which are corporate mandates, may also need to be ratified by the executive leadership team, though they do not necessarily participate in the authorship.

2. **Operational Governance** is where the IT functions are managed day-to-day using the processes and roles that were defined by executive governance. These are the people who execute the process, not the ones who create the process. Several industry authorities[12] today refer to executive governance as simply "governance," and refer to operational governance as "stewardship."

Executive defines, and operational executes. This isn't a new concept. COBIT divided the management of IT into four areas, though they gave those roles different names. The terminology you use isn't important. What's important is that all of these roles exist, and the responsibilities are clearly defined and documented.

COBIT 4.1 2007	Other Industry Pundits	Functional Framework
Plan and Organize	Governance	Architecture
Acquire and Implement	Governance	Executive Governance
Deliver and Support	Stewardship	Operational Governance
Monitor and Evaluate	Governance	Executive Governance

Table 1- Executive and Operational Governance

In their capacity of creating a cohesive array of governance documentation defining how the work will be performed, the executive governance team can be thought of as a governance **Center of Excellence (CoE)**, or a **Competency Center**. They are tasked with creating a body of governance documentation that is consistent across the enterprise, complete in breadth (all IT functions) and depth (policies, standards, processes, and roles). If the creation of governance artifacts is delegated to individual information systems, then those departments become individual centers of excellence.

For example, you might allow the analytics resources to document their own standards, processes, and roles for creating external-facing customer reports. These might include guidelines for font, color scheme, headers and footers, disclaimers, standards for sensitive information, and processes and roles for developing and testing. In that case, the BI Analytics team is your analytical reporting center of excellence. These governance documents will still be subject to review for compliance to corporate

---

[12] For example, Informatica. See white paper Holistic Data Governance: A Framework for Competitive Advantage.

policies and architecture, but within those broad constraints, the BI Analytics team operates independently as a center of excellence.

This kind of distributed executive governance is very important to your ability to manage IT efficiently at the corporate level. Your EAG team will not be able to develop all the detail in every governance document. Moreover, if they did and simply handed those documents out as a mandate, they wouldn't be enthusiastically received. But if the EAG team gives the information system team the basic governance document templates and some training on how to flesh out these templates, granting the team freedom to self-govern within the guidelines of the corporate policies as their own center of excellence, then most teams will be more than happy to build the governance artifacts for you. They will probably implement harsher controls over themselves than you might have handed down, had you the time to write the documents yourselves.

Two kinds of people – micromanagers versus enablers

There are two kinds of people in this world: those that micromanage every little thing, and those who point things in the right direction and turn them loose.

If you've been out in the workforce for more than five years, I'd be willing to bet that you've seen, if not worked with, manager/supervisors of both types. Some managers seem to think it's their job to hold their employees under their thumbs. I've seen supervisors that want their salaried employees to clock out and back in when they go to the restroom. In general, I find that these same supervisors have no knowledge/ability to manage the work their employees are actually doing, but they are masters at micromanaging the details that don't matter.

I think this comes down to leadership style and the type of work being managed. If you're managing a call center where a lot of high-turnover hourly people need to be in their seats answering phones, then maybe you do need to be fairly heavy-handed in monitoring people's whereabouts. However, if you're managing salaried professionals working on projects that span weeks or months, it seems rather degrading to treat your employees like schoolchildren.

When I purchased the house I live in now, my wife and I had to go to an abstract and title company to sign all the papers. The person who stepped us through the process was *very* condescending. At one point, she pushed a page over to us flagged for our signatures. She watched us sign in silent anticipation, and then was delighted to tell us we had done it wrong. She made a big show of tearing the page up into many little pieces, sighing heavily, and printing another copy, which we then signed with our full middle names. Several years later, we closed on a house we were buying and flipping for our daughters. We made sure to ask for a different title company, and were on the lookout for the paper that needed the middle names. However, this person took the time up front to explain the process, and why different forms needed different kinds of signatures. As she handed us each page, she explained what the form was, and what kind of a signature was needed. It was a much more pleasant experience.

I think there are some people who just delight in being "big brother," managing using fear and intimidation, eagerly waiting to demonstrate their total power. That sounds dramatic, but I swear I have no other explanation for the behavior of these IT management "brownshirts." If I were their employee, as soon as I could find a different job, I would. The better I am, the sooner you'll lose me, leaving you with a team of beaten-down, low-skill, low motivation employees. There are very, very few times when that sort of management style is appropriate.

Other managers are true leaders. They cast a vision and lead by example. They encourage their employees, and trust them to do their jobs. Yes, they'll occasionally find someone not pulling their weight, and if a private chat doesn't fix things up, maybe that person needs to be let go. However, you don't address the one person who's slacking off by cracking the whip over the entire team. If you extend trust and someone on the team betrays it, then you don't want him or her on your team. Your job as a manager is to build a *team*, not a slave labor camp.

Our job in an EAG program does include the creation of some rigid rules. However, most of the time what's really needed is a vision. If the people using your policies, standards, processes and roles understand the overall vision, odds are they'll do the right thing. If they won't, you need to let them go. Our role isn't to be *Big Brother*, laying down the law and cracking the whip. If you have people on your EAG team who like to use that approach, get rid of them, no matter how good they are. Instead, put together a team that will make "the right thing to do" easy to understand and easy to accomplish. Most people who have to perform these functions will do the right thing if they know what it is. Most of the rest of us are just lazy and will do the right thing if you make it easy.

If you want to make the management of IT functionality simpler and more efficient, don't set yourself up to be the governance dictators. *Make the right thing to do obvious and easy, and you'll be a lot closer to IT functions that seem to manage themselves.* What's really going on is that you are distributing ownership of the IT management to your team, making your own job easier.

Policies

The first governance row in our functional framework is for policies. A policy is a rule that the company wants to enforce. Individual information systems may take different approaches to comply with the corporate policy, but comply they must.

A Functional Framework for Architecture and Governance

FUNCTIONAL FRAMEWORK	ORGANIZATION	BUSINESS				IT												
	EA DOMAIN	BUSINESS				INFORMATION				APPLICATION						TECHNOLOGY		
	FUNCTIONAL AREA	AREA 1		Area 2		AREA3		AREA 4		AREA 5	AREA 6		AREA 7			AREA 8	AREA 9	
	FUNCTION	Function 1	Function 2	Function 3	Function 4	Function 5	Function 6	Function 7	Function 8	Function 9	Function 10	Function 11	Function 12	Function 13	Function 14	Function 15	Function 16	Function 17	Function 18
ARCHITECTURE	LONG TERM STRATEGY																		
	ROADMAP																		
GOVERNANCE	POLICIES																		
	STANDARDS																		
	PROCESSES/ROLES																		

Figure 2.18 Policies within the Functional Framework for Architecture and Governance

Standards, processes, and roles may be defined at the corporate or the information system level, but policies are *always* defined at the corporate level. Governance policies (i.e. security mandates) defined at the corporate level should apply to all information systems. If they don't they're not polices. Other layers of governance, though – the standards, processes, and roles – can be defined system by system.

If you find that you can't generalize policy verbiage to the entire organization, then it probably contains too much detail. Standards and processes must support the corporate policies, but you may allow different departments to create their own custom standards and processes, so long as they document and publish them in a consistent manner, and so long as those custom implementations don't violate the corporate policies.

The policies will largely be written by the EAG domain architects working with subject matter experts such as HR or legal. These policy documents will often contain a verbatim copy of regulatory or compliance verbiage. You should consider creating global templates for all the governance documents: policies, standards, processes, and roles, so that all the various artifacts are consistent in style and complete in scope. You can initially populate your framework with pre-existing artifacts, but you'll eventually want to convert them to comply with the enterprise standard templates. I strongly recommend you engage a technical writer to develop those templates and manage the document repository where the governance artifacts are stored. I also suggest you examine the COBIT standards before trying to re-invent the wheel. In many cases, enterprise architects are also information system resources, and may also be writing those departmental standard, process and role documents while wearing one of their many hats.

Corporate policy documents are a compliance requirement for many standards and certifications. As stated previously, auditors are used to hearing companies speak in glowing terms about their policies, standards, processes and roles, but will *always* want to see the actual documentation.

A sample template for corporate policies can be found in the Appendix. It contains the following:

- A header that identifies the location of the policy within the functional framework. It specifies the function area, the relevant function within that area, and the policy name for that function.

- A purpose statement that describes what the policy is intended to do (i.e. names the regulatory requirements or business decisions it supports).

- A scope statement that describes what parts of the company's assets and staff are subject to the policy.

- A detail section that each requirement in the policy.

- A timeline section that describes when the policy will take effect.

- A section describing how to ask questions and request exceptions.

- A section describing how compliance will be monitored, by whom, and what measure is considered acceptable.

- A section describing the consequences of non-compliance. This refers to the consequence to the employee who violates the policy, not the consequence to the company.

- A communication plan describing who will be responsible for giving training, and who needs to receive the training, and how often.

- A revision cycle section explaining who must review the policy, how often it must be reviewed, and who must approve changes.

- A footer section giving contact information and revision dates.

I wish I had time and space to go into each of these sections, but, to be honest, most of them are pretty self-explanatory. But I do want to take the time to stress the importance of the compliance monitoring section, because I find that's an area where many EAG programs fail to provide the value they should. There are several different models for measuring the maturity of a process, including COBIT, which we've already discussed, and CMMI (Capability Maturity Model Integration). All of these maturity models align very closely, as shown in Table 2.

Level	CMMI Maturity Levels (paraphrased)	COBIT Maturity Levels (paraphrased)	Gartner - April 2006 (paraphrased)
0	UNAWARE – No activity	NON-EXISTENT – The enterprise does not even recognize that there is an issue to be addressed	
1	INITIAL – Process are disorganized. Any success is dependent on key individuals and cannot be repeated in their absence.	AD-HOC – The enterprise realizes issues exist, but there are no standard processes. Any management of processes is on a case-by-case basis.	CHAOTIC – ad hoc, undocumented, unpredictable.
2	REPEATABLE – The existing process (whether right or wrong) is at least documented. May be very different across the organization.	INTUITIVE – similar processes are followed by different people, but there is no formal training or communication of standards.	REACTIVE – Managed at the project level, but no enterprise standards.
3	DEFINED – The process has been standardized to follow best practices in the larger enterprise context.	DEFINED – management processes are communicated through training, but any deviations are unlikely to be detected.	PROACTIVE – enterprise mandated process management consistency.
4	MANAGED – The process is monitored, and data is collected and analyzed to ensure compliance.	MEASURABLE – Management monitors compliance with process management standards, and takes action where there are issues. Little automation.	SERVICE – IT is treated as a service provider, with defined and measured process service level guarantees.
5	OPTIMIZED – The process feedback data is used not only to ensure compliance, but also to continually modify and improve the process itself. Improvement is defined by business impact.	OPTIMIZED – Processes have been refined into best practices using integrated and automated collection of process metrics in a process of continual improvement.	VALUE – IT is a strategic business partner, continually improving the process based on measurement of metrics and strategic planning.

Table 2 - Maturity Model Comparison

You can see that these various maturity models are *very* similar, almost identical. Looking at this table, it should become evident that *some sort of automated outcome measurement is required for mature governance*. You must build that measurement into your template, so that you measure compliance by default, not by exception.

In order to do this, you need to define the metric, how that metric is measured, and what the acceptable measure is. The metrics should be chosen based on the value to the business, not purely on their adherence to an IT ideal. You may have some metrics that seem more operational, such as compliance with service level agreements (SLAs), adherence to privacy and security policies, and data accuracy, integrity and completeness, but, since every operational policy and process is intended to provide business value, even these operational metrics should be relatable to some business value, albeit indirectly. If they provide no business value, why are the policies in place? Business value may come from many different aspects, including minimizing exposure to penalties for regulatory compliance, reducing fraud risk, expense reduction, improving the efficiency of an operational process that provides business value, increasing revenue, or increasing customer satisfaction.

For example, suppose you create a policy to eliminate redundant physical copies of customer information outside your **Customer Relationship Management (CRM)** system of record. In this case:

- The metric is the number of copies of customer data.

- This number might be measured using automated tallying of the extracts that are distributed (pushed or pulled) from the system of record, assuming that each extract will be physically instantiated somewhere. There are much more sophisticated ways of detecting data propagation, but this approach will suffice as an example.

- The acceptable measure in your environment at this time might be four: the operational system of record itself, a copy in the analytical data warehouse, a copy sent to a government-required reporting agency, and a copy in a commercial campaign management system that does not have the ability to integrate with the system of record at this time.

- The actual measure may be more like twenty or more.

Remember that *you can't manage what you don't measure*. If your policies don't include a description of how you'll measure compliance, then you probably won't mature beyond level three in the model shown in Table 2. That doesn't sound like an EAG team that's on top of their game.

Here are a few guidelines for your policy metrics:

- Your metric should measure something that has *real business value*, not just an indicator of architectural purity.

- Your policy should state *not only what is measured, but how often and where* the measurements are to be stored. In order to monitor compliance at an enterprise level, there must be consistent, automated, and centralized collection of data.

- Your metric should be **SMART.**[13] SMART is an acronym developed back in 1981 by George T. Doran[14] giving guidelines to designing good objectives:

  o **Specific**. The metric should be very clear and unambiguous data point that indicates progress.

---

[13] Some pundits now use SMARTER, adding Evaluate and Reevaluate, recognizing the need to constantly review the metrics you are measuring for value and effectiveness.

[14] Doran, G. T. (1981). "There's a S.M.A.R.T. way to write management's goals and objectives". Management Review.

- o **Measurable**. The metric should be something that has an objective value.
- o **Assignable**. The policy should identify who is accountable for the metric being collected. The other roles should be detailed in the process documentation.
- o **Realistic**. The metric must be something that can be realistically collected, without undue resource cost.
- o **Time-Related**. The policy must specify when and how often the metric is to be collected.

- Choose your measures to show *ongoing value*. Governance is a program, not a project. It has no completion date. Don't choose metrics that imply that it does.

When creating policy documents, keep in mind that every policy is a business policy. Whether or not you will comply with regulatory guidelines is a business decision, not an IT decision. Nike released the Air Jordan sneakers on September 15th of 1985. On October 18th of that year, NBA Commissioner David Stern officially barred Michael Jordan from wearing the shoes during games because the red-and-black shoes didn't match the color scheme used by the rest of the Chicago Bulls. Jordan was fined $5000 a game, which added up to $410,000 in fines over the 82-game regular season. This was almost two-thirds of Jordan's $630,000 salary. Nevertheless, Michael Jordan continued to wear the shoes, and Nike reimbursed him for every fine, because the media controversy acted as free advertising, generating millions of dollars in revenue. Most of the time, your company is going to want to comply with all the relevant regulatory guidelines, but there will still be cases when the business may decide that non-compliance makes more business sense. Even security policies are, in the end, business polices, not technical ones.

In some cases, corporate policies require other subject matter experts to approve waivers and modifications and perform regular reviews. Your legal department will need to review compliance policies. HR will want to review any policy for which non-compliance can result in termination. There will be modifications, and the policy document should make clear who all will need to review any changes, a list which should include those other subject matter experts. All governance documents are living, breathing artifacts that will require maintenance and review over time.

Standards

Standards can be defined at the corporate level (i.e. which fields are considered PII), but are more often at the information system level. As long as each information system's standards support the corporate policy, this is perfectly acceptable.

If you don't want to allow this departmental flexibility, then, by all means, spell out in a corporate standards document what the corporate mandate for all departments will be.

The Standard templates section of the appendix contains a template that assumes that each function in the framework has a separate standards document. In the software development lifecycle functional area, this means a separate standards document for application design, application testing, and change management.

A Functional Framework for Architecture and Governance

FUNCTIONAL FRAMEWORK	ORGANIZATION	BUSINESS				IT												
	EA DOMAIN	BUSINESS				INFORMATION				APPLICATION						TECHNOLOGY		
	FUNCTIONAL AREA	AREA 1		Area 2		AREA3		AREA 4		AREA 5		AREA 6		AREA 7		AREA 8		AREA 9
	FUNCTION	Function 1	Function 2	Function 3	Function 4	Function 5	Function 6	Function 7	Function 8	Function 9	Function 10	Function 11	Function 12	Function 13	Function 14	Function 15	Function 16	Function 17	Function 18
ARCHITECTURE	LONG TERM STRATEGY																		
	ROADMAP																		
GOVERNANCE	POLICIES																		
	STANDARDS																		
	PROCESSES/ROLES																		

Figure 2.19 Standards within the Functional Framework for Architecture and Governance

This function isolation isn't required, but is a good idea for standards, as it helps prevent the creation of huge, overwhelming documents. For the most part, any one standard applies to only one function. Furthermore, most resources will only be working in one or two functional areas. Our goal is to make IT functions simpler to manage, and separating out the standards by function makes them much easier to work with, provided they are all easily accessible in a repository whose structure aligns with the functional framework. That said, if you're starting from nothing, you might initially keep the standards for each function as separate sections in a single document per subject area just to prevent the creation of dozens of small documents. As soon as they begin to grow unwieldy, however, I would break them into separate documents by function area.

When you first put together a functional framework, you'll no doubt have many existing standards documents for many different functions in many different departments, using many different documentation styles. Your first step is to collect those artifacts and get them into the architecture and governance documentation repository just as they are. All of those separate documents should be retained in the document repository, of course. Each standards document should contain all the standards for that function. If a COBOL developer need to research design standards, there should be only one document they need to read.

Therefore, it is appropriate to identify these standards by the framework function, or even by information system. However, that's the smallest level of granularity that should be acceptable. If you decide to create a separate standards document just for the application design function within the larger software development lifecycle, and you decide to create one application design standard for the Java information system development, and a different application design standards document for the mainframe COBOL information system development, that's perfectly fine.

Once you collect all your existing standards into the EAG repository, your next goal will be to make the EAG repository copy of those documents the system of record, deleting them from their previous location. In order to accomplish this successfully, you will need to be able to convince the current document owners that they can still manage the document. Authorship will still be theirs. The only thing that's initially changing is the location of the document. The only oversight that will be imposed is a review by the relevant domain architect to make sure that the standards do not violate any corporate policies or best practices. If the architect reads in a document that passwords are passed as parameters in unencrypted service calls, they will likely push back, changing the standard to comply with corporate policy. In cases like this, change the standard immediately. Identify which existing applications violate the revised standards, and bring them into compliance. It may be necessary to grant temporary, limited-time waivers until the changes can be made, but the standard document should be changed immediately. This review and approval process can't begin until the documents are in the managed EAG repository.

Your third goal is to convert any pre-existing standards to the consistent enterprise standards template. A technical editor is probably the best person for this job. Converting to the new template does make all the standards more consistent in style, but, more importantly, it makes them more consistent in scope and completeness.

As a rule, your standards will include definitions of IT-centric terms and logic. Definitions of business terms belong in a data dictionary component, which is part of the data quality function of the Information Domain.

Processes

Your processes are the documentation for what you do (or *should* do) every day. The process documentation should describe the flow of tasks and the conditions under which the process advances or retreats from task to task.

A Functional Framework for Architecture and Governance

FUNCTIONAL FRAMEWORK	ORGANIZATION	BUSINESS				IT													
	EA DOMAIN	BUSINESS				INFORMATION				APPLICATION						TECHNOLOGY			
	FUNCTIONAL AREA	AREA 1		Area 2		AREA3		AREA 4		AREA 5	AREA 6		AREA 7			AREA 8		AREA 9	
	FUNCTION	Function 1	Function 2	Function 3	Function 4	Function 5	Function 6	Function 7	Function 8	Function 9	Function 10	Function 11	Function 12	Function 13	Function 14	Function 15	Function 16	Function 17	Function 18
ARCHITECTURE	LONG TERM STRATEGY																		
	ROADMAP																		
GOVERNANCE	POLICIES																		
	STANDARDS																		
	PROCESSES/ROLES																		

Figure 2.20 Processes and Roles within the Functional Framework for Architecture and Governance

Write this process documentation so that it can serve many purposes:

- The process documentation serves to document the duties and responsibilities for each role, and should be useful for onboarding new resources, reviewing HR job description accuracy and resolving ownership disputes.

- The process documentation should include information about how to handle exceptions, especially emergency production issues. Who has the authority and responsibility to do what? Moreover, what must be done afterward to review or approve the fix as permanent?

- The process document should serve to document your process to auditors. It could include, for example, your CMMI or ISO 9000 certification, or proof that your security initiative is foundationally integrated into your entire process. If a process is intended to support specific corporate policies that should be explicitly spelled out.

- The document should identify the author and the roles that must review the document on a regular basis and who approve any changes. Processes tied to regulatory compliance should be reviewed annually. Who is responsible for the review, and how/where are the results tracked?

- If a situation arises where an information system is not going to be able to comply with the process, how are waivers requested? Where are the approvals/rejections documented?

- You can't manage what you don't measure. The process documentation should explicitly define what metrics are needed to measure the effectiveness of the process, who is responsible for collecting them, where are they stored and in what format, and who is responsible for reviewing them. Metrics may measure the maturity of the process, and they may measure the ROI of the cost of the process provides the business. This includes contractual service level agreements, both for services that you provide to your customers, and for services your vendors provide to you. If there is a service level in a contract, your process needs to make explicit how it is measured, who is responsible for getting it done, and what is done with those measurements.

Bear all this in mind when building your process documentation templates.

Roles

It's critically important to your governance program that you clearly document the all the roles in each process. You'll find that it's often going to be the case that everyone will easily agree on *what* needs to be done, but bloody political battles await the person who dares say *who* is going to be responsible/accountable/consulted for that work. A failure on this task pretty much guarantees a dysfunctional, unsuccessful organization.

In addition to formal written documentation, it's usually helpful to include a visualization. This often takes the form of a "swim lane flowchart" showing how the various tasks fit together into the larger process, with a "swim lane" for each role. The flowchart, however, typically only documents the role actually doing the work. The written documentation should go into more detail, spelling out the responsibilities of all the roles.

You may recall an earlier discussion of the distinction between executive governance and operational governance (see Governance, page 55). All of these roles should be included in the process document.

Make sure you name the role, not the person. You don't want to have to change your documentation every time an individual person changes roles. If a person wears many hats, they are probably performing many roles, and they should document each role separately.

There are several standards for documenting roles and responsibilities. You're welcome to use any method you like, so long as each role and its responsibility are clearly articulated. For myself, my "go to" standard for documenting roles and responsibilities is the **RACI method** developed by those COBIT gurus. Using this methodology, you would include in each task of your process the following roles:

- Who is **responsible** for actually doing the work? Depending on the task, this may be a developer, an analyst, a call center operator, or an executive. This may be more than one individual.

- Who is **accountable** for verifying that each individual task was completed correctly? The testers are not accountable for the development task; they have their own task in the process. Accountability for any given task should be assigned to only one role.
- Who must be **consulted** as a subject matter expert, although they may not actually be responsible for doing the work? This is two-way communication.
- Who must be kept **informed** (i.e. one-way communication) of the progress and outcomes?

There are several variations of this standard to accommodate the need to document unique and unusual responsibilities such as:

- Processes where multiple approvers have veto power over a task
- Processes where some roles must explicitly *not* be informed about the task progress and outcomes, such as blind study research trials
- Processes where other roles may assist the role primarily responsible
- Processes where additional roles are required for quality or testing responsibilities

I encourage you, however, to keep your roles as simple as possible. The goal here is to simplify the management of IT functions. Don't create roles just to match an org chart if those roles needn't be called out separately. Yes, you may have teams to test user interface compliance, security compliance, or other functions. However, you should list those as responsible roles on separate testing tasks in the process, not some new role in the development task.

There are several ways to document these roles.

- You might document the RACI roles within each task in the process
- Alternatively, you might use swim lane UML to identify how the tasks flow from role to role
- Or you might create a single RACI Matrix for all the tasks in your process (see diagram below)

I like to include a swim lane UML diagram showing the process flow, but I don't think you can use that a technique alone. It's a great way to visualize the process tasks and roles all in one flow diagram, but it's used only to document the person who is doing the work. Go ahead and include a swim lane, but make sure to use one of the other techniques to document the other roles in the process. Personally, I'm a big fan of the RACI matrix shown in Figure 2.21.

As you can see, roles are complicated. There are many roles for each task, and many tasks in each process. That being the case, you'll often find that there is a high-level role accountable for each process as a whole, a **process owner**. Various roles may be accountable for the different tasks in your software development process, but there's probably one high-level development manager who ultimately owns responsibility for the process as a whole, the *owner* of the operational governance SDLC process. The accountable roles for each of the functions in the process typically report to this process-manager role, either as a direct report or in a matrixed, dotted line relationship. These roles and relationships role should be documented as well.

You should be able to look through the RACI matrix and see that all the *accountable* roles report to the process owner. If the relationship is other than a direct report, explicitly spell this out in the process and roles governance document.

It is this manager's role to oversee the day-to-day operation of this entire process. That process owner must give day-to-day direction regarding relative priorities and tactical decisions to the roles accountable for the individual tasks in that process. If the process manager is going to be successful in managing the operational governance, these relationships must be clearly defined. You are not going to be successful in managing for IT functions on behalf of the business if the team isn't working together under a single clear vision and reporting structure. You can document the RACI roles for each task until you are blue in the face, but if the roles accountable for those tasks are working under different relative priorities and reporting structures, you're going to have inefficiencies and differences in priorities, which will lead to disagreements and infighting. Don't skip this step.

The various task *accountable* roles need not be direct reports. A matrixed reporting relationship is just fine if the controls are defined clearly. The manager of the application development process may report to the CIO, while the DBA roles actually report up to the CTO. The analysts and testers on the team may report up to the COO. If you can, for a moment, imagine the functional framework with the IT functions subdivided into domains, functional areas, functions, processes, and tasks. Some roles will fall to teams of many individuals. Some individuals will have many roles. The high-level managers can probably look at the functional areas and draw a line around the part they are accountable for. Mid-level managers and supervisors may need to go down to the individual functions to identify their responsibilities. Front line employees will have to go down to the individual tasks within the processes to define their responsibilities. At some level, every person in your company who is supporting these IT tasks in some way should be able to draw a boundary around their area of responsibility.

Maintenance Crew KPI RACI Chart

Tasks	Maint Supervisors	Maint Analyst	Maint Planner	Maint Technician	Maint Supert	Rel Specialist	CMMS Proj Engr
Inputting Failure Data	A	C	I	R		C	C
Work Order Completion	R	C	C	C	A	I	I
Work Order Close Out	C	R	C		I	I	A
QA of Failure Data Input	C	R	I	C	I	C	A
Analyze Failure Reports	C	C	I	C	A	R	I
Maintenance Strategy Adjustments	C	I	I	C	A	R	R
Implementing New Strategies	R	I	R	C	A	I	I

Responsibility	"the Doer"
Accountable	"the Buck stops here"
Consulted	"in the Loop"
Informed	"kept in the picture"

Figure 2.21 RACI Matrix example for Hardware Maintenance. Each task should have all four RACI roles assigned.

You are documenting roles, not documenting your org chart. That said, a good org chart should align with the work that's actually being done. If you find that multiple high-level managers share responsibility for the same IT functions, you should probably rethink either your functional framework or your organization chart. If your company is large enough to have several major information systems all under development, you may have development managers in each system. However, there should be some coordination between these departments.

If your goal were to simplify the management of IT complexity, why would you manage these very similar departments separately and independently? Who is going to make the inter-department priorities and tactical decisions? For example, if one application decides that their test system will be a de-identified subset of production, how is that going to affect the other departments' ability to perform system integration testing? If your goal is cohesive, comprehensive, coordinated IT functional capability, why would you deliberately choose to make the management of these IT functions isolated and uncoordinated?

Likewise, if you find that one mid-level manager or supervisor is responsible for individual tasks scattered almost at random through the functional framework, you may have an org chart poorly aligned with your work. Wouldn't it be better for that role to be accountable for tasks or processes that have a similar focus? Operations, security, and change management are all highly formalized processes, all with an immediate focus and no necessary separation of duties. One person can easily manage them. Conflicts arise if the same manager is accountable for all of those functions and software development, which has a longer planning horizon and must be kept separate from operations. This is one reason why it's critical to create the functional framework as a list of functions performed by the organization, rather than a list of verbs for each position on the org chart.

Most of the high-level processes we describe in our sample functional framework take the form of *lifecycles*. There is a flow from one process to another through the various stages of the lifecycle. Software development begins with project initiation, design, development, and testing, and ends with production implementation, support, and decommissioning. Each stage of the lifecycle has many tasks. The early stages (e.g. project initiation and architectural design) have relatively long planning horizons. As you move into development, the planning horizon drops to months or weeks. Testing may involve iteration cycles counted in days. Production support deadlines can be counted in minutes.

Wouldn't it make sense if your organization chart reflected this same flow? Managers and supervisors may be responsible for many tasks, but those tasks are all related, with a similar planning horizon focus and no separation of duty conflicts. I've actually seen organizations arrange seating assignments based on process flow so that resources are co-located with other individuals who are working on the same stage in the lifecycle. It sounds extreme, but actually worked remarkably well. Do you think the requirements analysts need to communicate more with the developers, or with production support? Why not locate people to facilitate the necessary communication instead of discourage it?

Defining clear roles using a functional framework prevents political infighting where more than one person believes they should be in charge of the same function. Defining clear roles using a functional framework highlights those functions where no one is really responsible. But one less intuitive way in which the functional framework really helps is in calming the fears that will inevitably occur when you make changes. If you just make an announcement that responsibilities will be consolidated and streamlined, most of your staff will immediately translate this as code for downsizing, and will live in fear that their position will be going away.

This fear can lead to morale issues, obstructionism, and nay-saying. Most people really don't care about the welfare of the organization as much as they do the gainful employment that comes with their little empire. I've found that articulating change using the functional framework helps to give the necessary context, and to clarify the ambiguity of what the future holds. Lay out those lifecycles and show how the responsibilities line up. Usually, many new roles will be created, generating new opportunities, not staff reduction.

I once worked in the enterprise business intelligence organization of a fortune 500 telecom company. When we set aside for a moment the roles and responsibilities we had always operated under and just considered the functions of our organization, it became clear that the functions followed the life-cycle of the work. In that organization, we had business requests that came in and had to be broken down into clear requirements. Next the architects who maintained the strategic vision and standards would look at the requirements and define an approach that guided the project in the direction of our long term goals, then we had developers and project managers who oversaw the work and progress, and we had testing and change management functions to move the work from development to test and into production. And finally there were functions related to post-production support. These functions described the daily work performed by the organization. Unfortunately, they did not describe the org chart we had been operating under. We had organized the list of functions in our framework along the life-cycle of the work, but when we started color coding which manager was responsible for which functions, the chart looked like a floor covered with confetti after a particularly epic New Year's Eve party. And it was immediately apparent to everyone that the constant recurring arguments, bickering, and infighting we had accepted as inevitable actually could be mapped directly to these overlapping or unassigned responsibilities.

It was actually surprisingly easy to agree how the functions should be organized and assigned because everyone could easily visualize the change in the framework. It was easy to see that, while things were moving around, nothing was moving out. Indeed, it became obvious how many gaps we needed to fill, creating new opportunities. Nearly every manager lost some part of the responsibility they had previously thought fell to them, but nearly every manager also gained responsibilities. The resulting organization structure grouped functional responsibilities in a much more consistent, logical way. Managers were more focused and felt more ownership for "their part" of the project lifecycle.

This change, of course, also shifted around some of the front line resources, but by clearly communicating the new roles, the analysts, architects, developers, testers, and operations staff felt reassured and anchored, rather than adrift in a sea of incomprehensible change. They too felt a new sense of purpose and ownership that had been somewhat lacking before. I realize that this sounds like a fairy tale, but our employees went out of their way to give us glowing feedback on the changes we had made.

Clear definition of roles and responsibilities, and clarification of the relationship between roles is critical to the successful management of IT complexity. Oftentimes, the awkward and ambiguous roles we create are the biggest contributor to IT management complexity. After all, the *roles* are where the office politics are found. IT functionality is complicated enough without adding needless organizational confusion on top of it. Use your functional framework to tame IT complexity by clearly defining roles and responsibilities.

CHAPTER 3

The Business Domain

Despite Spewak's formative ideas about the importance of business-centric architecture, ratified by NIST, TOGAF and others for the last thirty years, many enterprise architecture and governance (EAG) programs begin as purely IT initiatives, with IT-only executive sponsors and IT-only architects. It's been my experience that these IT-centric initiatives are, at best, severely limited in the true business value they bring to an organization. Truth be told, most of these initiatives are outright failures.

For at least thirty years there have been well-defined best practices dictating that everything IT does needs to be in support of the business. The project priorities in the IT area should be a direct reflection of the business priorities. Unfortunately, years of evidence clearly show that, left to themselves, IT does a *very* poor job of determining what's best for the business.

If you find that business units are setting up their own development teams because IT isn't meeting their needs, then IT has already failed, regardless what IT believes they are doing.

Even seemingly IT-centric initiatives such as security and expense reduction should only be a priority to the IT department to the extent that they are a priority to the business. Fortunately, security and expense reduction are definitely a priority to most businesses.

Coming from the IT side of the house, I know we tend to plan a year's IT projects based on the combination of business objectives and IT-driven objectives; I've done it myself. This is, however, very bad practice. If you can't convince the business that your "internal" projects are a priority to the business, then you probably don't need to be working on them. If you took your car to a mechanic for one problem and they found something else that they believed must be fixed, they may well be correct, but it's still on them to convince you of the need before they begin spending your money to fix what you didn't ask to be fixed.

The **business architect** who will represent the business to the IT architects is a very special person. Granted, the vast majority of the folks on the business side of the house are very competent at what they do, but most have only a vague understanding of the underlying infrastructure complexity that makes it all possible. You need to find that special person who really "gets it." You don't want a business person on your EAG team that doesn't really understand what's going on, but trusts that you do. This kind of "token" business involvement is less than useless; it's actually a waste of everyone's valuable time. If the business architect isn't actively *driving* the strategic alignment of the entire enterprise across all domains, then this strategic alignment of IT and business is unlikely to occur. A business architect who "trusts IT to do the right thing" is ensuring that IT will do the right thing for IT, not for the business.

Instead, you need to find a person who truly understands the enterprise business model, the business process, and the IT infrastructure. The business architect needs to be involved in the business-side executive-level strategic discussions about competitive pressures where the high-level business goals are set. The business architect needs to not only understand the business today, they also need to understand the direction executives are steering the organization toward for the foreseeable future; not only *where*, but *why* that direction is an executive priority.

This business architect also needs to have the skill set and authority to sit in a room full of IT architectural prima-donnas, cast the initial high-level vision of the present and future business needs, and guide the architectural and governance teams to align with this vision. This doesn't mean that they run the EAG program, but it does mean that they create the business vision from which the other domain visions take their cue, much like Spewak's vision of the business conducting the symphony being played by all the various IT instruments. If the other domains begin to drift away from business priorities, the business architect needs to be able to recognize this and raise a flag, reminding everyone of the goal.

Business Architecture in an EAG program

In addition to the general requirements for architects discussed earlier, the business architect has many responsibilities in the enterprise architecture and governance program. This role is both the most critical and the most difficult position to fill in the entire EAG team – even more critical than the EAG program director. Unlike the IT domains, which generally bring a lead architect along with a swarm of domains specific architects, the business domain lead architect will typically serve with only one or two supporting business architects. I'm not sure why this is the case, or whether it's a good or bad thing. Perhaps this is because the business architect role mainly involves giving direction to the other architects, while the IT domain architects are also responsible for communicating direction and giving oversight to the IT teams they represent.

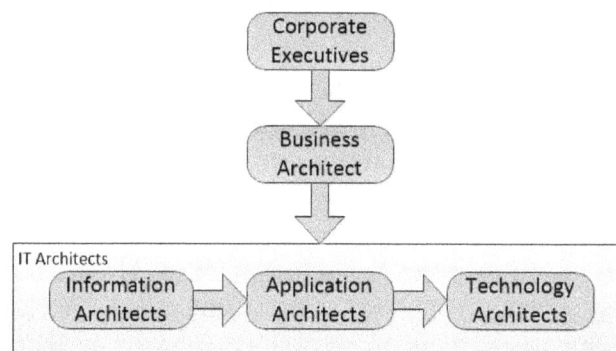

Figure 3.1 Architecture and Governance Flow

Communicating business objectives to IT

The business architects are responsible for communicating both long-term and short-term business objectives to the EAG IT domains in terms that IT can understand.

The business architect isn't expected to have the skills and experience of the IT architects, and isn't expected to do their job. The business architect isn't there to do IT architecture work. They are there to tell *what* needs done, as well as *when* and *why*. They are not there to tell IT *how*. Likewise, they need to be able to push back when the IT domains try to impose their own beliefs about *what* the business should want, and *why*.

The business architect may communicate, for example, that the executives have decided that the company needs to implement a specific new customer workflow to address customer satisfaction issues, or that the company needs to offer a specific new product or service to address an offering from a competitor. The business architect will give details of the *what* and *when* and *why* for these requirements. The business architect may create use case diagrams and swim lanes describing the desired functionality from a business perspective, but the business architect isn't expected to create the IT-level process flow diagrams explaining *how* the functionality will be implemented.

In a functioning business, there are many, many existing business processes; a new EAG team cannot begin documenting them all. For functionality that meets the current and future business need, this is a waste of time, and not a business priority. *The scope of EAG is to manage IT as it supports the business, not to manage the business itself.*

There will be new business processes to develop, or existing functionality to address. These gaps can be taken on by the EAG program. The business architect should introduce them as a requirement, and the IT domains can add architecture and governance details.

The business architect should direct the priority in which gaps in the functional framework are addressed by the architecture and governance team. The business architect should determine whether some regulatory body's requirements are of a higher priority than some desired business functionality. For example, whether performing a required penetration test of the client portal is more important than extending the portal to mobile devices, given resources to only do one or the other. The mobile device support may have the potential to drop churn, but noncompliance with the security mandate could result in a loss of license, huge fines, and lost customer trust. Even security functions are prioritized based on business impact, not by technological idealism, or even by legal mandates.

Communicating IT concerns to the business

The business architects are also responsible for communicating IT concerns back to the business executives in business terms the executives understand.

This may be IT feedback regarding business initiatives. For example, IT might need to give feedback to the business that the desired functionality will degrade performance beyond SLAs, or that it might create risk of a security breach. If possible, IT should supply not just a problem, but a solution as well. "We recommend that you do it this way instead…"

IT feedback may also come in the form of a warning about something that wasn't even on the business radar. Perhaps a vendor is dropping support for hardware or software used in the current environment, or business growth is reaching capacity on a particular infrastructure component. Again, if possible, IT should present not only a problem, but a solution as well.

Whenever any architect faces a problem, I advocate communicating the problem using the following template:

- Brief description of context (i.e. the project or system in which the problem was found)

- Description of problem

- Description of impact

- List of subject matter experts (SME's) involved in the discussion

- List of all alternatives discussed, even those quickly rejected, with pros and cons of each

- Recommendation of one of the alternatives, with justification. This often takes the form of a combination of short term (interim) and long term (strategic) recommendations

This is common sense, and is probably the path the discussion actually followed, but is seldom the way things are documented for communication. The lists of SME's and alternatives, in particular, save many subsequent questions about "Did you consider approach X?" or "Did you talk to expert Y?" This approach to documenting the problem is especially helpful when questions arise after some time has passed. Used consistently, this approach breeds confidence both with the upstream executives and with the downstream people who will be implementing the decision that the architect team does indeed practice an open-minded discussion with all the involved experts, considering all possible alternatives before making a decision that's best for the company as a whole. This confidence is critical to the long-term success of the EAG organization.

I use this basic outline even when discussing day-to-day issues with my team via informal emails. "The way I see it, we have three options…" But if I were performing a formal recommendation for senior executives, I would want to use an EAG program template. Really, this is one of those little things that can make a huge difference. I challenge you to try it.

Oversight of IT to ensure business compliance

The business architect isn't just responsible for delivering business requirements and walking away. They need to be an integral part of the architectural discussion in order to respond appropriately if the team turns down a path that doesn't align with the business goals.

For example, given a business problem of centralizing customer contacts and offers in order to provide a more unified, coordinated customer experience, the IT architects may begin to take the discussion in the direction of a custom development project that includes ground-up re-working the campaign management solution and the customer service application. This may be IT hubris or it may be a legitimate misunderstanding of the nature of the business requirement. If this level of effort isn't justified, it's the business architect who needs to pull the discussion back, perhaps clarifying the objectives and priorities. "The existing campaign results and SLAs are fine. We just need the output integrated into a prioritized list of action items, available during any customer interaction on any channel."

This oversight scope includes the EAG discussions and the enterprise architecture and governance document artifacts they produce. Once the EAG decisions are made, the business architect isn't typically involved in each of the individual IT "day-job" projects where those decisions are implemented unless their assistance is specifically requested.

Designing business solutions

The business architect role of communicating the *what*, *when*, and *why* isn't limited to typing up a couple paragraphs. They are the architect of the business functionality and are responsible for producing the formal EAG documents.

Suppose the business has identified that poor customer support is causing customer churn, and that one of the leading complaints is that the customers have to read off their account number and verify their social three or more times as they are passed through the customer service process. "I just gave the last guy that information. Why do I have to give it to you again?" Don't you hate that?

The business architect doesn't just say, "Fix this." They construct the desired customer flow. The customer shouldn't even be asked their account number in tier one, which includes general public questions about mailing addresses. At tier two, ask the customer for their account number and verify their identity using one or more security questions. Retain their account number for the duration of the call. However, if the call terminates for any reason and the customer calls back, the call center should perform these identity verification steps again.

The business architect will design the entire interaction from a business perspective, preferably including lots of flowcharts and visualizations to clarify the vision for the desired business process. They shouldn't get into detail about specific applications, technologies, or how to interchange data between systems, but they should make the desired business process very clear.

This may well be an iterative process as the IT architects push back on various details. Perhaps the system handling the initial tier 1 call is the only one which can currently collect the information and pass it to all the other systems. The IT architects may then push back and say that they can meet the business requirement of a single ID verification with the current infrastructure, but it must be collected by tier 1 customer support. The IT architects can suggest other alternatives such as switching to a different call management system. This may seem unjustified to IT, but the business may actually see the problem as serious enough to justify the additional expense. They may not, but it's a business decision either way – not an IT decision. This is why I recommend you document all the alternatives, even the ones that were rejected. The point is that the problem and its resolution is an ongoing, interactive discussion between the IT and business architects, not a note slipped under the IT door by the business.

Participating in vendor selection

Too many times, IT goes out and selects a vendor product (hardware, software, or service) without involving the business until the contract is signed. This is seldom a conscious choice. More often, the IT architects are simply the ones who meet with infrastructure vendors on a regular basis. The discussion often gets started without the business involved simply due to the nature of vendor interaction with IT professionals.

But this needs to be avoided. Always keep in mind that IT exists for the sole function of supporting the business, not the other way around. Any selection of vendor hardware, software, or services should involve the business architect, who *may*, in turn, bring in specific business subject matter experts. "We need to involve the management of the call center in this discussion of their processes." A vendor selection *begins* with a list of business requirements, and ends with the IT requirements necessary to support those business requirements, not the reverse.

Every IT function begins with the business, but most of them are eventually turned over to IT to manage, even though the business is still definitely in charge. This is certainly true of vendor selection, which will be discussed in much more depth within the application infrastructure lifecycle *acquisition* function (page 175).

Business functions

In the functional framework, there is an area for business functions. This is a little misleading. The functional framework is all about managing IT complexity on behalf of the business using architecture and governance. It's about managing *IT functions* that support the business, not managing the business functions themselves.

So why is there a place for business functions in the functional framework? This isn't an extraneous or irrelevant topic. The concept of business functions is critical to the success of your functional framework.

If we consider the functional framework an IT-internal initiative, it will probably fail. It will fail because IT-focused initiatives never provide business value. Only business-focused initiatives provide business value. Every IT function in the information, application, and technology domains exists to support the business and provide real business value. If it doesn't, then you need to stop performing that function. Remember, "This is a business, not a science project." The focus of the functional framework is on the business. It's only focused on IT to the extent that IT supports the business.

You established your existing IT functions years ago, long before you built your functional framework. At that time, they met a business need. But over time, IT begins to take on a life of its own. IT professionals come to believe that their IT functions justify themselves. Remember that IT is never justified other than to the extent to which it is providing real, ongoing business value.

Now that you have a functional framework, there will still occasionally be a need for new business functions. Operating within industry regulatory compliance boundaries, the corporate executives will decide the top few annual objectives for the company. These will trickle down through business departments and surface as specific business changes: new or enhanced product or process functionality.

New business initiatives begin, from an EAG standpoint, as business domain functions. The business architect will introduce the business requirement, spelling out the desired product and functionality. These functions show up under the business domain of the functional framework.

The business architects may have several initiatives they are working on that aren't quite ready to turn over to IT architects, and it may take some time before they work out the desired business functionality.

When they're ready to discuss the functionality with the other domain architects, the IT architects discuss the objective with the business architect and together work out a high-level IT infrastructure approach that seems to provide the best value to the business both immediately and as a part of the long-term strategy. While this usually takes place in a joint working session, NIST and Spewak would clearly insist that the information requirements supersede and drive the application requirements, which supersede and drive the technology requirements. Remember that this is an agile process, and all of the architects are interacting together to reach consensus quickly. You'll need to take the more detailed requirements offline and restore them later, but you should be able to quickly figure out the high-level desired functionality in a collaborative setting.

For example, earlier we discussed a hypothetical business function to create and manage a unified view of all customer offers, data collection campaigns, next-product-to-buy campaigns, and globally or market-specific promoted products. The business wants the experience to be, that when a customer calls in to the call center, the agent can see, in a single list, all the offers, promotions, and campaigns for this customer prioritized by business value on one screen. The items on this list come from many systems across the company. The call center agent needs to be able to accept an offer and jump straight to a streamlined fulfillment process. The agent needs to be able to decline an offer, and have that noted so the customer isn't hounded again when they call tomorrow. The offer is to be suspended, though, rather than deleted; it will re-activate after a certain time, perhaps for a limited number of recurrences. The design needs to be such that it can, in the future, be rolled out to the web and mobile self-serve channels.

Before the business architect was ready to discuss the process with IT, there was an extended period when the business architect was working with the business executives and strategic planners. During this analysis, the project was a *business domain function* in the functional framework.

The business architect may give brief status updates to the EAG team while their internal design work is in progress. When the business architect finally unveils this new desired offer management functionality, the information architect is going to be thinking about master data management. They want to make sure that these various offers can be combined from multiple systems in a way where we know that customer 123 in System A is the same as customer 456 in System B. The business requirements describe a data model of certain entities, attributes, and relations. All of those offers exist today:

- Where are they? What is the system of record for all the information components?

- Is one of those source systems going to become the system of record for all offers, or is there going to be a new repository where they are collected?

- Are there requirements to update the offer data in the source systems when offers are presented?

- Is there a requirement to collect response data on these offers?

- Is any sensitive data involved? What existing information policies and standards would apply?

- Do we need to review or enhance those policies and standards?

All the architects will first need to address these high-level information architecture questions under the guidance of the information architect, supervised by the business architect. When the high-level information domain requirements are sketched out, the focus will shift to application architecture:

- What are the software infrastructure components?

- Will this be a build or a buy?

- If build, what changes need to be made to existing applications?

- How are we going to be able to click on a single list of offers consolidated from multiple systems and launch the correct system-specific fulfillment process? What is the business process logic?

- Are there software policies or standards that apply, or need to be reviewed or created?

- What is the workflow? What are the integration points?

- Will there be a separate application on the call center workstation, or will this functionality be integrated into an existing application?

- How is security provisioned and de-provisioned?

Architects will work out these high-level application architecture approach requirements, within the constraints of the parameters that came out of the business and information discussions.

When the high-level software approach is hashed out, it's time to work through the hardware architecture issues:

- Where will all of this run?

- Will this utilize new or existing infrastructure?

- Are the current platforms suitable for the additional load in terms of resource bandwidth, support tier, and user licenses?

- How does this impact our disaster recovery strategy?

- What are the technology domain security requirements for authorization and authentication?

Again, the technology architects will lead the discussion of these issues, given the constraints that have been passed down.

The result isn't a detailed design that can be handed to a developer to begin coding. It is the high-level architectural approach. Many, many questions remain, but the approach is sufficiently documented to guide the development teams. Most approach documents I've seen seldom exceed five pages for any one architectural domain. Some are mere paragraphs directing the developer to the target domain component. This isn't a detail design document. You have lead developers for that.

At this point, what began as a business function is now broken out into one or more IT functions spread out among the IT architectural domains. The business function drops from the functional matrix, and IT domain-specific functions appear. The business justification and business approach documented by the business architect become the foundation of the architectural strategy document for the other domains. You can see in this flow the wisdom of the business domain architectural approach recommended by NIST and Spewak thirty years ago. Imagine a technology-dominated EAG program tackling this effort. The discussion would have begun with server requirements, asset inventory, and security. All of those things are important, but you don't have the context to make these decisions until you first know the information and application functions that the technology will be supporting.

Having the architecture in place doesn't necessarily mean the work begins immediately. What should in fact be happening is that the business architect is getting the most important future needs to the team for planning long *before* the project starts, so that when the starting gun is fired, the architectural planning work has already been done and construction can begin immediately.

This complete high-level process of taking a business function and expressing it as a series of domain specific IT functions may take place in a conference room in an afternoon, or it may be months in the making, with many domain-specific breakout work-sessions, vendor discussions, and proof of concept trials. Most new ideas will be desired as soon as they are conceived. A good business architect will have their finger on the pulse of the executive leadership's musings, and will introduce business functions with as much lead time as possible – even if they're still only probabilities rather than certainties. How many times have you been handed a business project that is needed in a couple of months, and find that the business has actually been discussing it for a year before bringing you in the loop? Your business architect is your ticket to the show.

Some of these projects may end up being set aside if you realize that the IT costs outweigh the business value. Some may be set aside because business drivers and priorities change. Some will make it to fruition, and the EA team will have a plan in place that provides immediate business value, fits the long-term strategic vision, and complies with domain policies and standards. This process of proactively addressing the architecture of likely business functionality needs is one way a functional framework minimizes the effort of developing and maintaining complex IT infrastructure in support of the business.

CHAPTER 4

The Information Domain

Intuition is useful in business. But...it isn't enough.

The Wall Street Journal, October 23, 2007

From the first discussions of enterprise architecture, information management has been the lynchpin of every major strategy to gain control over the increasing complexity of managing IT functionality. Spewak and NIST, TOGAF and Zachman, all began with the management of information.

I use the term *information*, not *data*. Originally, the terms were interchangeable, but two factors are changing that:

- First, as the discipline matures, we've realized that there's a great deal of difference between simple, raw data like transaction amounts, and complex, derived data liked predictive analytic outcomes. To call them all *data* would miss important nuances that are critical to understand in order to manage all types of information successfully. See page 95 for more details.

- Furthermore, another group of professionals who specialize in the visualization of data on screen or page has taken to calling themselves **data architects**, creating LinkedIn groups and conferences under that name. That's a very useful specialty, but things get confusing when both trades take the same name.

To avoid any ambiguity, the practice today is to use the term information to describe the full range of business data, from simple to complex, both at rest in physical repositories or in flight using batch files and web services. We refer to this area of IT as the information domain. Information management refers to the architecture and governance processes we use to administrate this domain. The people who set up these management structures are information architects. We try to only use the term "data" when discussing the simplest type of information: raw data created and maintained by operational processes in order to provide core business functionality.

In this book, you'll find a great deal more discussion of the information domain than of the application or technology domains. There's a reason for this. As I said in the introduction, I'm not trying to teach anyone how to perform any of the functions in any of the domains. I have to assume you know, or have people who know how to perform these functions: how to model data, how to develop software, how to upgrade hardware, and so forth. The purpose of this book is to tell you how to coordinate all those different efforts into an EAG program that checks two key boxes:

- Spans all the information systems you support (i.e. how to model data at the enterprise level, rather than project by project)

- Integrates with all the other functions (i.e. how your data modeling function needs to integrate with your data security function and application development function)

In the discussion that follows, we aren't going to try to teach you how to perform the basic functions; there are already whole books dedicated to each with far more information and expertise than I can provide. Instead, we are going to focus on the aspects of each IT function that need special attention when you take those efforts from isolated silos of expertise and make them instead components of an enterprise architecture and governance (EAG) functional framework that spans all functions and all information systems in the enterprise.

In that context, I have more to say about the management of information than about applications or technology. Although the entire focus of computer technology in business is to improve the efficiency of managing information, most companies have been focusing on the hardware and software, not the information that the hardware and software was supposed to be supporting.

The information domain is the weakest link in corporate IT today. Many companies have great EAG programs in place to manage hardware and software, but still practically ignore information management as a discipline.

This is why I feel driven to speak at such length in the pages ahead about the information domain; because *most of us are doing a poor job of it*. There are far more gaps to address in the information domain than the other two domains put together.

Information architecture in an EAG program

In the context of enterprise architecture and governance (EAG), information architecture suffers from a bit of an identity problem.

Unfortunately, information architecture is still often treated as an IT-centric initiative. When you focus on data for data's sake, you're missing the bigger picture. Information is only as valuable as the business processes and decisions it improves. *The ultimate goal of an information management program is to generate the greatest return from corporate information assets.*

In an EAG program, the information architecture *should* be second only to business architecture. Once the business has identified a problem or goal, the first questions shouldn't be about the hardware the solution will sit on. Your first questions should target the information required by the business. These could include:

- How should the data be represented in the enterprise logical data model (entities, attributes, data type and length, relationships, and constraints)?

- What's the data volume?

- What's the system of record for this data?

- Is any of the data sensitive?

Only after you understand the information needs should you consider the application requirements needed to collect, maintain, and deliver the information and the technology needed to support those application requirements.

As late as the 1990's, very few companies formally recognized information as an independent domain equal to the application and technology domains. The application domain rolled up to the CIO, and the technology domain rolled up to the CTO. However, the information domain, if it existed at all, was usually subservient to one of those two in the org structure. In some cases, the developers in the application domain might perform their own information architecture functions within the scope of the project they're working on, or might employ a dedicated project-level data modeler. In other cases, the DBAs in the technology domain might serve as data modelers. However, in all these cases, information management was a project-level tactical function, not an enterprise-level strategic one.

I once worked for a large company that developed banking software. One of the products I was responsible for was a **Customer Relationship Management (CRM)** system that was the *golden copy* of the customer name and address information across all our product lines. When developing features for this product, each project followed the same flow:

1. The business would give us requirements for new functionality.

2. The data modelers would model the required data through several layers of abstraction, eventually producing an updated physical model. This physical model was instantiated as both DDL to create tables, and XML to give to the application developers.

3. The first team of application developers would create simple data maintenance CRUD (Create, Read, Update, and Delete) services. These simple data access and maintenance services are commonly and collectively known as **Data as a Service**, or **DaaS**.

4. Then a second team of developers would develop front-end applications which orchestrated those DaaS services together into complex business process services (**Software as a Service**, or **SaaS**).

5. A third team would then expose the functionality to our users through a web-based user interface.

6. Technology architects would address issues with the Enterprise Service Bus (ESB), network access, firewalls, server capacity, and the like.

In this example, the business gives the initial direction, but, true to Spewak's vision, everything else is driven by information.

Even today, this isn't often the way things work at most companies. I think the reason for this has to do with how companies were organized and how they functioned before the advent of EAG. Data had been around for thousands of years and was considered just *part of the business*. However, when computers came on the scene, we suddenly needed specialized roles to manage all the new hardware and software that came with them. Suddenly all the interest was focused on the shiny new computers, not the information those computers existed to support.

I liken this to someone who buys an expensive sports car, then keeps it locked up in a garage where they can admire it, enhance it with more powerful parts and keep it polished. The purpose of a car isn't to sit in the garage; a car exists to take you places you want to go. The business doesn't exist so that IT can assemble the latest technology; the technology is assembled to manage the information assets of the business. *Without information, hardware and software have no purpose.*

Unfortunately, for most IT organizations, the Information Age isn't about information. From the beginning, the IT department was *supposed* to be all about the information, never the computer. The term Information Technology (IT) described the original intent that all this technology existed to support information.

Until recently, the process flow at most companies was that a business request would be routed straight to an application developer with no real guidance regarding enterprise information standards and interoperability. The developer pretty much had free rein to implement the information in any way they thought best. Many of these developers were talented, intelligent people who wanted to write the best code they could for their company, but they were hampered by:

- Lack of experience with information management disciplines
- Lack of an articulated enterprise vision for information
- Lack of guidelines regarding how to best manage information
- Lack of communication with developers from other teams across the enterprise
- Lack of time and money to spend worrying about the bigger picture

As such, any consideration of information architecture was left to the hardware and software professionals. Information Management seldom rose above project-level planning and scope. A data modeler (if they existed at all) reported to the project developer and implemented the project team's decisions.

Although most companies followed established best practices and defined information architecture as a separate domain of EAG from the very beginning, many remain under the assumption that information architecture is a sub-function of the application or technology domains. They did not create an organization structure with a separate domain for information. This has been changing since 2000, slowly at first, but accelerating each year as companies realize that the central purpose of information management had somehow been lost. Somehow, IT had become all about the hardware and software.

Consider this. Every organization, regardless of size or industry, has a finance function. There's some person in the organization whose responsibility includes protecting and optimizing the value of the organization's financial assets. This person is usually the CFO, a direct report to the CEO, and often sits on the board of directors. Likewise, every organization has a similar role that is responsible for technology assets, the CTO. While the financial assets do rely on supporting and enabling technology, the financial assets aren't a technology domain responsibility. In the same manner, the human assets of a company rely on the technology infrastructure, but HR isn't a technology domain responsibility.

The growing recognition of the importance of information assets has led to the establishment of a dedicated C-level executive role to manage information assets, the **Chief Data Officer (CDO)**. The

CDO manages the information assets. The **Chief Analytics Officer** (or **CAO**) manages the things that are done to those information assets to provide insight and make decisions. It took thirty years, but the work of NIST and Spewak is finally beginning to bear fruit in the boardroom.

Why now? I believe that the progress we have seen in the steady rise of the influence of the information domain within enterprise-level IT management is due to *more* than thirty-year-old books and theories. Whether or not they've acted on the knowledge, most companies have recognized the need for enterprise architecture and governance for at least two decades now. But only in the last five years has mainstream IT culture suddenly become interested in information architecture. What's going on?

I believe the answer lies in looking at how corporate competition has evolved over time.

Information as a competitive differentiator

I believe businesses today are feeling more pressure than ever before to manage their information assets strategically to create a competitive advantage. I see this as the inevitable evolution in the nature of competition in the information age. I have a theory. I believe that every industry follows a standard evolutionary path.

Phase 1 - competing on infrastructure

In the early stages of any industry, companies compete by building out infrastructure. During this phase, financial institutions are rushing to build branch banks on every street corner, car manufacturers are building car lots and showrooms, and telecoms are buying up the rights to put up cell towers. During this phase, you aren't so much competing against other companies as you are staking your claims on the unwashed masses.

I imagine this phase of competition as a reenactment of the great land rush in Oklahoma. On April 22 of 1889, an estimated 50,000 people waited at a starting line for the noon gun that would release them to rush out and claim up to 160 acres of some of the most valuable land in the United States. Regardless of how you feel about the morality of the Indian Appropriations Act parceling out this "unoccupied" land, this vivid image of a rush to stake a claim is a perfect picture of the earliest phase of competition in every developing industry.

If you have a young niece or nephew just beginning to pursue a degree in computer science who comes to you for advice, this is when you would advise them to focus their studies on technology and infrastructure. "Learn as much as you can about security, LAN/WAN and NAS/SAN." "Get your Cisco certification and buy a wheelbarrow to take all your money to the bank." You want to work in the technology domain.

Technological advances can still return a company to this phase of competition overnight. When 4G cellular service technology became widely available and the Feds opened up bidding on the new frequencies, telco carriers suddenly found themselves in another land rush to stake out their claims to 4G tower locations across the country.

Figure 4.1 A land rush in progress

Phase 2 – competing on feature/function

At some point, though, the infrastructure rollout saturates the marketplace. There's a branch bank and car lot on every corner and no more cell tower licenses are available for purchase. No unclaimed customers remain, so you have to figure out how to steal customers from your competitors while protecting your own customer base. At this point, companies begin to compete on feature/function and it becomes an *application development arms race*. At one time, the only way to access your bank account was to drive to a branch during business hours, park, get out of your car, and walk in to talk to a teller. Then one bank began offering drive through windows where customers didn't have to get out of their cars. All the customers would leave the bank across the street and rush over to take advantage of this cutting edge feature. Remember those amazing pneumatic chutes? The bank they left would not only have to even the playing field by getting drive through windows, but they would then have to one-up the other bank by rolling out ATMs. And so on. ATMs, telebanking, internet banking – each bank would have to bring out some attractive new feature function in order to up the ante and regain the competitive advantage.

This is the point where you tell your niece or nephew to get into application development. "Learn C++." "Learn HTML." "Learn Java and you can name your price." Companies are always willing to invest their money in the people who are most critical to the work that will make the company competitive. Steer them toward the application domain.

At this point in the competitive landscape, the infrastructure just gets you in the game. You have to have it, but it isn't a competitive differentiator. No matter what your industry is, you need to ante into the game with technology before you can increase the bid with feature/function. At some point, the technology playing field is level, and you *must* turn to feature/function to remain competitive.

As with technology, there are times when new functionality becomes available and disrupts the industry. Companies who thought they were past all this suddenly find themselves competing over feature/function again. Blockchain, for example, is a disruptive game changer. Once the functionality overcomes the performance and scale issues facing that technology today, companies in every industry will find themselves fighting to roll out blockchain-enabled features that will differentiate them from their competition.

However, you can't depend forever on your ability to keep coming up with *the next killer app*. At some point, the feature/function landscape becomes a level playing field. My little community bank has a great internet banking site. How do you remain competitive? Do you desperately throw your corporate investment into finding the next killer app? Or do you change tactics once again?

Phase 3 – competing on information

Eventually, in every industry, the focus shifts again and companies begin to compete on information. *It's not enough to know your product; you have to know your customer*:

- You must know more about your customers and prospects than your competitors and you must know it faster.

- You must be able to apply that knowledge to generate business decisions.

- You must offer individualized products and services that appeal to your target market while maximizing your profit.

- You move from one-size-fits-all to products and services customized for a customer segment of one.

This is the point when you would encourage your niece or nephew to learn data modeling, or learn statistical analysis. "Whatever you do, do it in the information domain because the future is in information, not application or technology." Forbes consistently lists data scientist salaries well above the highest developer salaries[15] and Harvard Business Review recently named "data scientist" the sexiest job of the twenty-first century.[16]

Companies are outsourcing more and more these days. Hardware and software infrastructure are quickly becoming cloud-based virtual commodities. Application development is being outsourced to offshore contractors who do great work for a quarter of what you'll have to pay locally. In any stage of competition, businesses are going to try to hang on to those skills that they perceive as enabling their competitive differentiators. If a company believes that the key to their success is their ability to cleanse, integrate, and mine information, then that's where they're going to be offering the most competitive salaries in an attempt to attract and retain the best people.

When I was working in the telecommunications industry, I thought it was very interesting to compare the advertising strategies of the big carriers:

---

[15] http://bit.ly/2Dkullu.
[16] http://bit.ly/1F4PkTo.

- Verizon focused their advertising on technology. Consider their advertising message, "Can you hear me now?" They very intentionally focused on telling the public that Verizon had the best network infrastructure. They were competing on technology and infrastructure. A phone was a piece of hardware.

- Sprint and AT&T had advertising that seemed to focus on feature/function. You could watch the game, manage your stock portfolio, and listen to music all on one device. They were competing on applications. A phone was an application platform.

- Alltel's campaign focused on customer-centricity and flexibility. Rollover minutes, discounted rates on calls to your friends and family, and no fees for early termination. Their tagline – "Come and get your love" – was intended to communicate that they will treat you like a person, not a number. A phone was a social connection. If I traveled to the other side of the country, I would see exactly the same Verizon commercial that aired back home, but the Alltel commercials would be completely customized for the local region. Alltel was competing with information.

Today, information is the key to competition. You must have a strong information architecture team and you must build an information-centric IT infrastructure to ante up. Companies that don't have strong information management programs are steadily losing ground in the market, wondering why everyone else seems to be playing a different game.

Phase 4 – What's next?

I don't know what the next phase of competition will look like. The future will certainly bring more disruptive technological advances like the coming flood of internet connected devices or quantum computing, and there will be application breakthroughs like blockchain that create new opportunities for companies to differentiate themselves and grow their customer base. Those aren't new phases of competition so much as brief returns to a previous phase until the playing field is level once more.

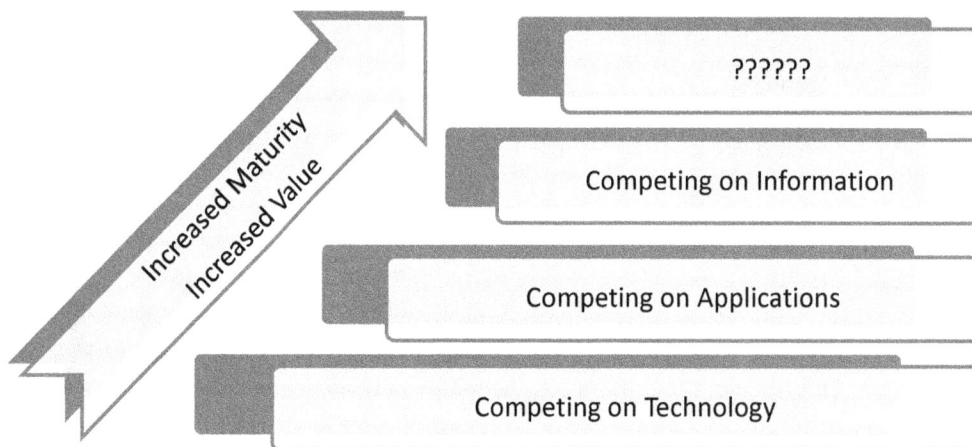

Figure 4.2 Each Phase of Competition Builds Upon the Last

If technology infrastructure were required before we could begin competing on application feature/function, and applications were required before we could begin competing on information, then it would seem that the next phase of game-changing corporate competition would be built on top of well-managed information. Personally, I have my eyes on artificial intelligence and machine learning. I think they're much more than a new application. They're a completely new kind of competitive advantage.

However, like all the previous phases of competition, each new phase will require a solid mastery of what's come before. Whatever comes next, you won't be able to jump on board until you first master competing on information. I can't predict the future, but I *can* predict that it's going to require rock-solid information management.

Recommended Reading:
Competing on Analytics: The New Science of Winning, by Thomas H. Davenport and Jeanne G. Harris, 2007, Harvard Business School Publishing.

Two kinds of people – knowledge sharers versus knowledge hoarders

There are two kinds of people in this world: those who think knowledge is more valuable when shared, and those who think knowledge is more valuable when withheld.

We've all seen people who are undisputed experts at what they do, yet still become a serious bottleneck in your organization because they can't seem to pass their knowledge and experience on to others. They insist that it will be faster for them to do the task themselves than to take the time to teach someone else, especially when the less experienced person will inevitably make mistakes which the more experienced person will then have to spend even more time correcting.

Architects don't spring forth fully formed from the forehead of God. Every architect started in another role. This is a good thing – you don't want someone in an architect role who has no real-world experience and expertise. Architects should always be prepared to share their knowledge and experience. The primary responsibility of an architect is creating and communicating a shared vision. It's a teaching position as much as anything else.

It's quite common for a developer to do a great job *applying* their expertise, but be very poor at *sharing* it. In a developer position, it would certainly be better if your senior resources mentored others, but they can provide value to the company even if they have zero communication skills. But an architect that can't mentor others isn't an architect at all – just someone who wants the power and pay grade but isn't willing or able to do the job.

Some people seem to have more difficulty letting go of control than others. In the end, it may come down to an issue of trust. Do you trust the people who are supposed to do that job to get it done without your help? They may struggle with it and cause you additional work for a while, but eventually they'll catch on. This is better for everyone. Not only is there more bandwidth and backup for critical functions, but the day-to-day stuff can be handled by the people who are actually being paid to do that job, allowing the architect to focus on the tasks they are being paid to focus on.

For myself, I'm far too easily bored to keep all that knowledge close to the vest. If I don't make it easy for someone else to do this job, then I'll be stuck with it forever, and I'll never get to do the exciting new stuff.

Trends

Before we begin discussing how to manage the business' information at the enterprise level, it's important to understand a couple of trends that are shaping *how* we manage that information.

The coupling of operational and analytical

The functions that comprise the lifecycle of information are, at a high level, the same for both operational systems which process data in many small transactions (**Online Transaction Processing**, or **OLTP**) and for analytical data marts and data warehouses that process many rows at a time in a few large batches (**Online Analytical Processing**, or **OLAP**). While operational systems are responsible for the day-to-day *operations* of the business, they are, in the end, little more than data maintenance applications, adding, updating, and deleting records. The resulting data produced by these systems is the raw, unrefined source material for analytical systems.

That sounds as if I'm saying that the operational systems are trivial to develop, and the true work is happening in the analytical systems like the data marts and the data warehouse. In the information domain, there's some truth to this. Other than the initial data modeling, the bulk of the complexity of developing an operational system lies in the business logic, which is the responsibility of the application domain. Honestly, very few systems have ever been purely operational or analytical. Most of our core operational systems have always had some form of reporting and analytics. In fact, there has been a little-discussed trend in the last fifteen years to break down the barriers between operational and analytical. We're blurring lines.

Back in the day, there were recognized best practices in place to keep operational systems separate from analytical systems. The operational system *was* the business. It was dedicated to transactional performance and availability. Analytical systems were seen as just the opposite: poorly performing resource hogs not critical to business operations. All analytical functions were deliberately separated from operational functions so that they didn't impact the *critical* business systems. Analytical systems were typically lower tier environments, often without redundancy and failover, with large scheduled maintenance windows when the analytical systems were completely unavailable. The performance expectations were quite low, and the system itself wasn't considered mission critical. Often analytical systems weren't even part of the disaster recovery plan because, in the days before competing on information, the business could get along quite easily without analytical platforms until things got back to normal. Because of these factors, you didn't want your analytical processes to be in the middle of an operational process flow. Operational processes could feed data into an analytical process, but you didn't want an operational process depending on the output of an analytical process.

But over the years, as companies have had to rely more and more on analytically derived information to compete, the analytical systems have become much more closely coupled with the operational. We no longer deem it poor practice to intertwine the two in the same process flow, provided both are designed with acceptable performance, availability, and latency.

One example of the power of this trend is in making real-time decisions. At the telecom company where I worked as an EA architect, we were investigating the potential of combining operational and analytical information into a real-time offer generation solution. Our enterprise architecture team looked at several commercial products and made a recommendation to the business executives. The solution, with hardware, software, and the development necessary to integrate it into our environment was going to cost upwards of three million dollars. We made a compelling case for the business investment, but before signing the check, the executives wanted us to put together a proof of concept (POC).

At the time, if one of our customers called our automated support line and chose all the correct menu options to navigate to the "I hate your company and want to drop my contract" selection, they got routed to a call center in San Antonio, Texas. In that call center, every time the phone rang it was someone who was in a very bad mood and hated our company. The call center had a very high turnover and none of the operators lasted long enough to be trusted to make decisions about granting bill credits or discounts on a new phone. At best, they could put the customer on hold while they went and asked their supervisor to investigate. At that time, the call center was able to save about 1000 calls per month. "Save" in this context meant that the customer hung up without dropping their service. They might call back tomorrow, but in this call, they were saved.

To demonstrate the power of real-time decisions, we spun up a little project where one Java developer wrote some code in about two weeks to combine analytically derived information like profitability, customer segment, and risk score with real-time information entered by the operator to auto-generate a pre-approved decision. If the customer was calling about a problem with their phone, they've been a profitable customer for ten years, and are only two months away from the contract renewal date when we would have given them a brand new phone for renewing their contract, then just give them a new phone! Tell them to go down to the store and pick one out, on you. If they weren't a profitable customer, then thank them for their business and give them the phone number of our competition.

We defined about five different decision rules for things like billing issues, network problems, and competitor offers. We figured that almost all of these people were going to leave the company anyway, so there was very little risk to implementing the solution. With a development investment of only 80 hours, the POC cost the business very little.

Two months after implementing the POC, the number of saves had increased from 1000 to 11,000 customers a month, almost all of which were permanent saves. This little two-week POC was saving 10,000 additional customers per month! At that time, the way the telecom industry worked was that if a customer signed a two-year contract, the company would subsidize about $300 of the cost of a new phone. The company would go in the hole $300 in order to bring a new customer on board, on the premise that they'll remain a customer long enough to eventually break even and become profitable. There are lots of subtle costs for replacing lost customers, but at the very least, it was going to cost that $300. So saving 10,000 customers a month translated to an easily demonstrated reduction in $3 million dollars in expenses – every month! All for a POC developed by one developer in two weeks. *This* is the power of combining operational and analytical information. *This* is competing on information.

We got the funding. Nevertheless, they never did let us take down that little POC. It became a permanent application, with many enhancements over the years.

In the discussion of information lifecycle functions later in this book, we're going to combine the discussion of operational and analytical functions. For the information lifecycle, the functions you perform on analytical data are a superset of functions you perform on operational data, so the discussion may appear a little analytics-heavy. Get used to it. If you haven't realized it yet, go back and read about the three phases of competition again (page 87). The entire IT industry is racing to compete on information. Knowledge is power, my friend!

Data monetization

Data monetization has been gaining more and more attention in recent years, changing the way we think about and manage information assets. InformationWeek (January 2016) claims that, for many companies, data is their single most valuable asset.[17] If so, then how much is data worth? If data is a corporate asset, does it belong on the financial statement alongside hardware assets and cash reserves?

There's no doubt that information has monetary value. Companies buy and sell information every day. There are very successful companies whose entire business model is based on buying and selling information.

Unfortunately, **Generally Accepted Accounting Principles (GAAP)** doesn't currently specify how to measure the value of information as a corporate asset. However, while there's no standard, there's also no specific ruling against the practice, and many companies are already listing information as an asset on their corporate balance sheets.

If we treated data as a corporate asset in the same sense as financial assets, the business would be much more concerned with where data assets were located and who was using them for what purposes. How are we investing in those assets to improve their value? How are we leveraging those assets to increase revenue, reduce expenses, and grow the company? Data monetization is changing the way we think about information assets and how we manage information-related IT functions.

The companies that are changing the way we do business are the ones who are thinking about data differently, such as Google, Amazon, and Facebook. It isn't a matter of collecting data for data's sake. It's a matter of understanding the problems facing the business, and knowing how to use *information* to solve those problems. Information only has value to the degree that it impacts your company. If it isn't being used by the business, information has no actual value.

In the context of this book, in order to efficiently and effectively manage the complexity of IT functionality on behalf of the business, it's important that you realize that the business' data is a valuable asset that IT is helping to manage. The functional framework will help us to not forget the information lifecycle functions in the press of other demands.

---

[17] http://ubm.io/2BJHbZd.

Unfortunately, for most organizations, making information a true corporate asset is a major cultural shift. But that shift is coming whether you're ready for it or not. An IT organization that is truly serving its business will help, not hinder this transformational shift.

Information lifecycle functions

In the last couple of decades, most companies have realized the strategic importance of being able to use their data competitively and are trying to put together an information management program for the enterprise. Frankly, companies who haven't realized the importance of their information aren't surviving. Information management "is the gas powering the operating model's engine, enabling organizations to more effectively communicate and reach their specific goals."[18]

The information domain of the functional framework addresses the infrastructure necessary to compete on information, breaking down the complexities of managing information into a series of simple functions.

At the detail level, there's no one functional framework that can be dropped in to every corporation's information management program. Different organizations will have different drivers for data security, accuracy, latency, and for how information is delivered. They'll have different requirements for data volume and performance. Different organization will begin their journey with the components of their functional framework at different levels of maturity. In most cases, the real world includes accommodating a legacy infrastructure that will impact one or more components of the functional framework for years to come.

Throughout the remainder of this book, in the discussion of all three IT domains, I am not attempting to replace or even summarize the many very fine resources available on each separate IT function. Instead, we'll discuss these functions from the standpoint of how they must be coordinated and configured in order to fit into the overall vision of a company's IT management program. We have to assume you already know how to perform these functions. This book will focus on the higher-level task of integrating these practices with other functions in a larger picture that spans functions and spans departments across your organization in a coordinated enterprise strategy for managing IT complexity, as dictated by your functional framework. Knowing how to perform a function within the scope of one information system is one thing. It's another thing to manage that function across information systems, and integrate that function into other functions. The rest of this book will focus on these latter challenges.

In one sense, the central purpose of this book has already been achieved – the introduction of the functional framework. The rest of this book is really just my attempt to highlight some of the areas where I think IT is struggling today, and illustrate by example how the functional framework helps clarify and organize the thought process, simplifying the process of controlling the chaos that is IT.

So, let's talk about the information domain of the framework. First, what's the best way to organize information management functions? Or, for that matter, the best way to organize functions within any domain of the framework? We want a framework that checks the following boxes:

---

[18] http://bit.ly/2DyXXit.

- A framework that is reduced to *an easily graspable concept*. Everyone in the organization should be able to easily sketch and understand the EAG napkin drawing.

- A framework that is *flexible* enough to adapt to changing requirements, best practices, and technology.

- A framework whose organization that *reflects the real-world*, to instill confidence that the framework encompasses the complete picture. The framework shouldn't look as if someone loaded a random list of functions into a shotgun and blasted them onto a wall. The organization should reflect some tangible, familiar concept. The organization should be meaningful.

You can use any organization of information management functions you want, but I find that the most easily grasped, flexible, comprehensive organization is to arrange the information domain functions so that they reflect the management of an *information lifecycle*. Just like hardware and software assets, information has a lifecycle that begins with creation/acquisition, and includes integration, inventory, and management of updates, security, and so forth, until the information asset reaches an end-of-life.

Figure 4.3 The Information Lifecycle

If you had organized your information functions alphabetically, the organization wouldn't be a reflection of the real world. There's no way you could be confident that you had captured all the functions, and if you did later discover a function you had missed, it could just as easily go in several different places in the organization depending which of several interchangeable words you used to describe it. The information lifecycle organization, however, is an easily grasped reflection of the real world. Looking at the organization, any big gaps would be readily apparent, and the proper place of any missing function would be pretty obvious. That's the kind of organization structure we are looking for.

The information domain functions don't just happen – you have to manage them as an information lifecycle. How? You manage them by setting up that lifecycle of functions in your functional framework.

Before we go much further, let's dig a little deeper into the meaning of "information" that we touched on briefly earlier in this chapter. What is this information we are managing? Information comes in many flavors. One categorization that's going to be very useful for the purpose of the discussion in this book is the following breakdown:

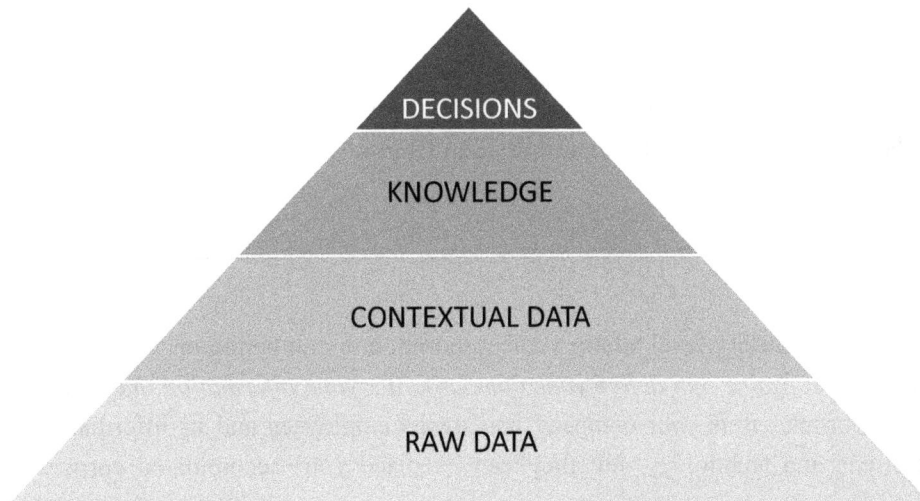

Figure 4.4 Types of Information

Raw data is the names, addresses, account numbers, purchases, etc. that you manipulate during the normal course of operating your business. It's the core information you collect, generate, and maintain in order to operate your business every day. It doesn't include data collected purely for analytical purposes.

Contextual data is information that puts the raw data in context. This information is often purchased (i.e. retail demographics), but it can also be collected directly. Like raw data, contextual data is just basic facts. The main difference is that contextual information isn't critical to *running* your business; it's critical to *running the business smarter and more efficiently*.

An insurance company wouldn't normally need to know a person's education level in order to pay an insurance claim. Education level just adds context that the business finds useful, perhaps as a predictor of lifestyle or attitude. For the insurance industry, then, education level would be contextual information, not raw operational data. For a university, a person's education level may indeed be raw data needed to run their business, perhaps a pre-requisite to certain courses. Gender may be core business data to a health insurance company, necessary to pay certain types of claims, but gender may be contextual data at a banking institution, whose checking and savings products are not gender specific.

Contextual data is appended to raw data, but isn't derived from it. Things like income level, marital status, education level, age, and gender are contextual if they aren't included in your operational raw business data, and have to be acquired and appended.

Knowledge is information that is derived from the raw and contextual information. Customer profitability scores, churn risk scores, and customer segmentation. An enterprise-wide unique person identifier generated by a CDI/MDM (Customer Data Integration/Master Data Management) tool would be derived knowledge.

Decisions are actions taken based upon information. Examples of decisions include generated customer offers, equipment renewal orders, automated account blocks for suspected fraud, or patient risk-based outreach lists. Decisions are actions based upon raw data, contextual data, and knowledge. We then feed the results of these decisions into applications such as vendor order management processes or employee work queues.

The information lifecycle function *Enhancing information* (page 130) will discuss these different types of information in more detail, but I wanted to introduce them now because the terms are necessary to the discussion of the modeling and consuming information functions.

Modeling information

If you've reached the maturity level where your corporation is competing on information, then *it's not your servers or your software that define your company; it's your information and what you do with it.* The two most important assets your company has are its employees and its information. Vendors can replace applications and technology, but they can't replace your accumulated corporate information assets.

When introducing the information domain earlier, I said that I would be giving it the most attention of the three EAG IT domains, because, despite thirty years of best practice insisting that IT architecture and governance must *begin* with information management, it's the least-well managed domain within most companies today. I'm going to spend most of the discussion of the information domain talking about data modeling for the same reason. You can't manage what you aren't tracking. If you want to manage enterprise information, you have to understand it, and that *begins* with data modeling.

Previously, when discussing data monetization, we talked about information assets being as important as financial assets. Just as you would for your financial assets, you want to keep track of your information assets: where they are, how they are being used, which are returning value, and who has access to them. Tracking your information assets begins with data modeling.

Data modeling is the name given to the processes and techniques that are used to document information assets. Modern data modeling techniques have been around since 1970. They bring clarity and understanding to the information structures within database repositories and web services, and optimize those structures for efficient support of information access.

This book isn't intended to teach or replace *any* of those techniques. Instead, this is a discussion of where those data modeling techniques fit into your overall program to manage IT complexity at the enterprise level. Assuming you know the techniques of data modeling, what else do you need to be thinking about when you ramp data modeling up from a project or departmental effort to an enterprise-wide function, part of a holistic effort to manage all aspects of your IT infrastructure across the enterprise?

In 1989, The National Institute of Standards and Technology (NIST) introduced the idea of an **Enterprise Logical Data Model (ELDM)**. The ELDM wasn't about making a data model for any one repository. Instead, it was about building a conceptual data model for all the information across the entire enterprise. The ELDM was the centerpiece of NIST's concept of a three-tiered modeling approach.

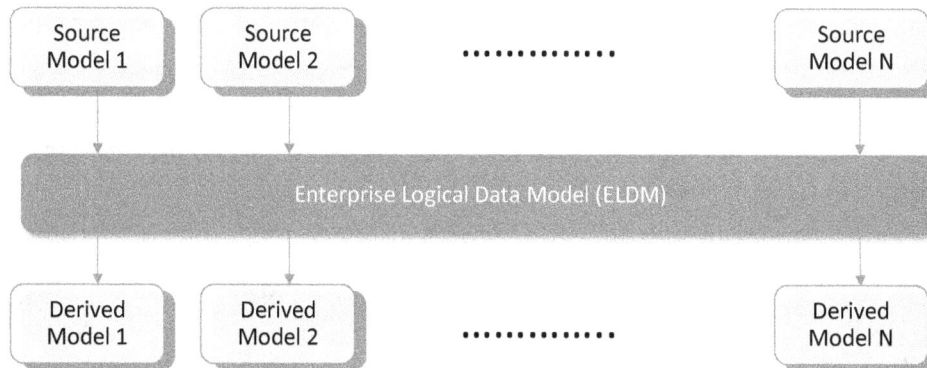

Figure 4.5 NIST Enterprise Logical Data Model

In this approach, the enterprise data architect would first gather all of the pre-existing source data models, including both internal and external applications. From those disparate sources, and from discussions with the business regarding how they conceptualize the company's information assets, one master data model of the company's information would be created and maintained.

The ELDM was never designed to be a physical repository. Its purpose isn't focused on a single project or information system, but on the enterprise. It's a single data model that shows how the business understands the entities and attributes in single holistic picture, as if all the applications shared one, single, all-encompassing enterprise database. The intent was that this ELDW would let you design one logical model making modeling decisions in one place rather than repeatedly in each repository.

If you try to manage all the different data models in your company separately, it's simply too overwhelming, and conceptual differences will be introduced that will cause ongoing problems until they're resolved. By creating one master data model in one place, when you need to implement a model for a project or system, you simply derive it from the ELDM, copying out the subset that you need. There are some segments of our industry today which call the ELDM a **Target Information Model** (or **TIM**), but I think that's misleading, as the intention is for it to become the source, from which many targets are instantiated. I prefer the original ELDM terminology. Of course, the sources and targets of the three-tier NIST model are source and targets only in terms of model building, not information flow.

These derived models will still need modification in order to support application-specific data needs. However, we can do most of the business-related modeling in one consistent model, using consistent terminology, relationships, constraints, and reference data.

Of course, creating a master model of the entire enterprise is a *huge* task, one that would take many years to complete. This dedicated effort is unlikely to ever be justified in terms of business value. The *architectural* goal is an enterprise logical model. b Raw data is the names, addresses, account numbers, and purchases that you collect during the normal course of operating your business. It's the core information you collect, generate, and maintain in order to operate your business every data. It doesn't include data collected purely for analytical purposes.

Contextual data is information that puts the raw data in context. This information is often purchased (i.e. retail demographics), but it can also be collected directly. Like raw data, contextual data is just basic facts. The main difference is that contextual information isn't critical to running your business; it's critical to running the business smarter and more efficiently. But like all strategic goals, we implement that goal over time, in a series of stages consisting of smaller projects that align with business priorities and provide immediate value. Start your enterprise logical model with the entities needed by active business projects, and add to it over time. Like all of IT, the ELDM should only be implemented as it provides real business value, not as an end in itself.

In a company where the technology domain dominates the decision-making, you may find that the data modeling function is the responsibility of the technology team DBAs. There's no real thought to enterprise data modeling. The modeling that does occur is very technology-centric, with a scope suited to the technology domain focus on server performance, efficiency of disk space utilization, etc. The technology domain isn't focused on enterprise information management; they are focused on managing pieces of technology.

In other cases, people only model data within the scope of an application development project. In these cases, data may be modeled by the application developer. However, application developers are also not focused on information. Their focus, and rightly so, is on the implementation of business logic in their applications. They aren't going to make the information easy to manage; they are going to make the applications easy to write. Document databases like MongoDB are especially well adapted to this mentality.

But enterprise information architecture isn't supposed to be a sub-function of any of the other domains of enterprise architecture. It requires the attention of resources with specific training and a focus on information assets.

I've been a fan of IBM's Rational Data Architect (now renamed Infosphere Data Architect) for many years. From the beginning it had these features:

- The ability to work with multiple data models at once, rather than individually, in isolation.

- Two completely different models could be mapped to each other. This let you reverse engineer the repositories in your legacy sources into models within the tool, and, when you built the enterprise logical data model (ELDM) in another model, document which element in the ELDM model maps to which element in each of these information system models. Between derived models and mapped models, all of your information across the enterprise can map to a single ELDM. The tool didn't work with a single model at a time, but allowed you to work, simultaneously, with all of the models and with the relationships between them. You could easily use this to trace inheritance back to see where specific ELDM attributes originated.

- Likewise, when you derive new implementation models from the ELDM, the tool could document how they map, so that all the data elements these derived models tie back to the same master ELDM information concepts. You could perform impact analysis when you make a conceptual change to the ELDM in order to identify potential impacts in the derived information system repositories.

- The tool could be used to generate both DDL (for implementing physical repositories) and XML (for implementing data services), resulting in consistency of information representation and exchange throughout the enterprise. It was designed from the beginning to exchange these structures with the application development tools and the technology team database management tools using the Zachman model artifacts.

- The data model could be shared between multiple data modelers and data architects. Most major modeling tools these days have the capability of allowing multiple modelers to work on the same model at the same time, but this is usually separately-purchased functionality. Typically, this works like a code repository, where the modeler makes changes locally, then checks them in to a central repository, where they are merged and distributed.

When this suite of products first came out, it was the only major data modeling tool to have these features. Since that time, other data modeling tools are also adopting more of an enterprise data modeling approach, allowing the modelers to work with multiple models at once, coordinating, and mapping the data attributes across them.

These functions separate an application-level or project-level data modeling tool from an enterprise-level data modeling tool. If you want to implement an information management program to help your enterprise manage complexity, you have to start thinking at the enterprise level of abstraction, eliminating silos of redundant, inconsistent data modeling effort. If you aren't managing your enterprise data with an enterprise logical data model, then you'll be overwhelmed by the effort of trying to manually:

- Maintain consistency across physical repositories

- Document the data dictionary over and over within each of your information system models

- Make the same modeling decisions over and over again within each of your information system data models

- Deal with inconsistent, locally-managed reference data

- Maintain consistency across information exchange structures, and consistency between exchange structures and the physical repositories.

- Attempt to manage data at the enterprise level using tools that manage it at the application level.

The data modeling function must integrate with the:

- Data quality function, so that new entities and attributes created in the model can also be added to the metadata repository

- Security function, to identify sensitive data elements consistently across information systems

- Software development functions, to coordinate and simplify the integration of information domain data structures and application domain business logic

The functional framework is a great tool for considering one IT function in light of all the others.

Big data

A big data repository, also known as a **data lake**, is an array of servers working together as a single distributed solution, using very low cost, commodity hardware and software. It can be used to store both structured and unstructured data. You can use many different tools to manipulate data in a data lake. Some of these tools are similar to tools for relational databases. Other tools are unique to data lakes. Big data repositories are finding their way into more and more business solutions as the products continue to mature.

Why mention big data in a chapter on data modeling? Because *big data repositories (by their very design) don't require data modeling.* When the data is initially inserted into a relational database, the data structure must be defined. With a big data repository, modelers just pour raw data into the lake. It's up to the consumer to interpret the data when the data is read. We describe this difference as "schema-on-insert" versus "schema-on-read." This difference will impact your long-term vision for enterprise data modeling (and information delivery, data quality, and data security).

There are pros and cons to both approaches. Relational databases typically run on much more expensive hardware and software, and require significant time and development effort to integrate new types of data. However, once the data is loaded into a well-designed data model, it has a great deal of integrity and can be safely, easily and efficiently consumed by end users who aren't necessarily data experts using many off-the-shelf business tools.

A data lake, on the other hand, is orders of magnitude faster to on-board new types of data. The cost to the business of adding new data is very low, and the time required is almost negligible. One of the major challenges of such a solution, however, is how well the data can be trusted and how easily it can be integrated. It's up to the user to collect, collate, and interpret the raw data. It is unwise to turn the average end-user loose in a data lake for ad-hoc reporting. When users who are not data experts use poor-quality data to make business decisions, there exists serious risk.

Think of the differences between the two as the differences between using an encyclopedia and using the internet when writing a scholarly paper about an historical event. The encyclopedia set is vetted by experts, but has limited information. It can take years to add new information. On the other hand, lots of lay people (who are not experts) are constantly adding things to the internet. The internet has a lot more information, is almost constantly updated, and it costs a lot less than an encyclopedia, but you really have to use a lot more judgment when dealing with the information. You have to know how much you can trust the different sources it contains and may need to work harder to integrate the different styles of content.

Big data solutions like data lakes are growing more and more broadly useful each year. If you aren't working with them already, you will be soon. It's an amazingly useful technology, but I don't think big data is ever going to completely replace relational databases, at least in the foreseeable future. Relational databases are simply too useful at cleansing, analyzing, and reporting data with defined attribute properties and relationships.

The following two business cases for big data are common, given the current state of technology:

- Big data can be used to offload the kinds of work that relational databases don't do well, such as working with free-form text or very sparsely populated, dynamically defined data elements.

Relational databases do many things very well, but they don't do everything. There have always been some types of transforms and types of analysis that are better done outside of a database, and the results plugged back in when the outsourced work is done. There have always been some kinds of data that are difficult to store in a rigid schema. Analysis of free form text or of data streams that dynamically define new elements on the fly is better done in a big data solution.

- Big data can serve as a fast-to-fail proof of concept (POC) environment for testing new ideas without going through the delays and overhead of moving data that may never prove useful into a more rigorously designed relational repository. If the idea proves valuable in the POC, then it can be hardened with the data model and data quality inherently found in a relational database. Big data can be a development sandbox for expert business users to trial new ideas. Just be aware that you need to limit the users to those who truly understand the data, and limit the rollout to the development environment only, not to production.

Today, relational databases are the clear default for supporting business solutions, with data lakes being used primarily for tasks that relational databases don't do well. Some industry experts foresee data lakes gradually becoming more and more the default platform for data storage. Vendors who sell applications for big data platforms certainly have a vested interest in convincing you that this is true. These pundits believe that there'll be a tipping point where data lakes will become the default, and relational databases will only be used for the things that data lakes don't do well. Moreover, the list of things that data lakes do well is growing every year. Even heavy-duty statistical analysis tools such as SA, R, and MADlib already support Hadoop big data natively.

However, my opinion is that the future will be less a choice between the two technologies than a merging of the two technologies. One of the primary challenges of using a data lake in a production environment is the lack of a defined schema. We're already seeing products like Hive allow the imposition of relational database constraints on data lakes, blurring the distinction between the two. More than likely, big data and relational database technologies will merge over time, with the result containing features of both.

It wouldn't be unusual for database vendors to adopt and incorporate emerging technologies. Several modern relational databases have the following features:

- Can be configured as either Symmetric Multi-Processing (SMP) or Massively Parallel Processing (MPP) (see page 228)

- Can have some tables in the repository defined as row-based and other tables as columnar (see page 230)

- Can leverage solid state disks and in-memory implementations

- Are rolling out implementations that leverage arrays of low-cost commodity servers

The major relational database vendors have consistently realized that no one underlying technology is going to be ideal for all purposes. Rather than lose revenue to another vendor, these databases assimilate the technological advances into their own infrastructure. If big-name database manufacturers begin losing significant revenue to big data solutions, how long do you think it will take them to begin incorporating big data functionality? I predict that relational databases will expand their infrastructure once again to include big data functionality, just as we are seeing big data expand its functionality to include things like relational table modeling. As the two technologies grow, I believe they will inevitably merge. I predict that all the major database vendors like Oracle and IBM will be purchasing big data companies and their intellectual property within the next five years, in the same way they've acquired and incorporated columnar, in memory, and XML web service technology. In the future, I predict that some data will be schema-less, and other data in the same repositories will have all the formal constraints of today's relational databases.

I also predict that the current big data hype will deflate as it comes face-to-face with the cold, hard reality of supporting large-scale, real-world business systems rather than niche solutions targeted for the sweet spot of the current state of big data technology. As more relational capability is adopted by big data platforms, the commodity nodes in a data lake will function very much like nodes in a relational MPP environment such as Teradata, Netezza, or DB2 DPF (see page 228). As an MPP database solution, data lakes will need to find a way to overcome the same kinds of challenges that MPP relational databases face. An MPP solution is excellent at operational and analytical operations over a single table and over tables where related data can be guaranteed to be collocated on the same node. However, the solutions don't perform nearly as well in situations where data in two different tables that aren't co-located must be united (see in depth discussion of this in the hardware domain chapter, page 228). Other emerging technologies that distribute data over an array of servers (including NoSQL databases such as MongoDB) have this same co-location challenge, making the technology difficult to use for large-scale enterprise analytical applications.

Regardless of what component lies at the center of your infrastructure, both big data and relational databases are here for the foreseeable future. You need to determine at the enterprise level how they will be used. What are your policies for big data? How do you secure sensitive data in a schema-less data lake? Perhaps the most important to deal with immediately, what kind of review and approval is needed before standing up a data lake? I've seen individual departments stand up data lake and NoSQL solutions with no other justification than that the solution let the application development teams bypass the use of DBAs and data architects entirely, and let their developers create corporate applications without any information management oversight. Get a handle on your big data strategy *before* it becomes a problem, or it'll quickly be out of your control.

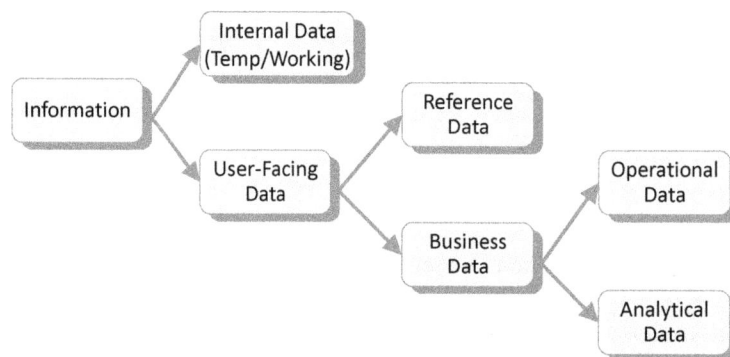

Figure 4.6 Information Zones *Within* a Repository

Zones of information within an enterprise repository

Most application repositories, whether operational or analytical, have several zones of information, though they may not be formally recognized as such. Figure 4.6 demonstrates one way in which information zones within a single repository might be defined in order to create policies and standards specific to different types of information.

You can use this same classification in repositories across the enterprise, allowing you to make your architectural and governance much simpler and more consistent. Thinking about information zones in this way allows you to make fewer, broader, more consistent decisions about architectural vision and governance standards, resulting in reduced complexity, greater uniformity, and increased efficiency.

The following table contains a few simple policies, showing how the division of information into zones reduces the amount of documentation and ensures consistency.

Information Zone	Modeling Technique	Naming Standards	ELDM	Security
Information				
Internal/Temp inherits *Information* policies and standards	Varies based on need. Does not need to be normalized.	Naming standards need not be followed, as data may still reflect source	Not mapped, unless sensitive	No end-user access. Should not accumulate historically.
User-Facing inherits *Information* policies and standards		Must follow naming standards	Content must be mapped to ELDM	Must use label-based security
Reference inherits *User-Facing* policies and standards	Non-normalized		Structure also mapped to ELDM	Should only be changed through the master data management process
Business inherits *User-Facing* policies and standards				All inserts, updates, and deletes must be tracked
Operational inherits *Business* policies and standards	Normalized		Structure should be based on ELDM. Should be grouped into logical subject areas.	Base data access at information system level for all non-sensitive fields
Analytical inherits *Business* policies and standards	Technique best suited for ease of use and performance		Structure need not map to ELDM	Base data access at data mart level for all non-sensitive fields

Table 3 - Sample of policy and standard inheritance for information zones

If you set up your architecture and governance around these information zones, then you have far fewer decisions to make than if you made your decisions table by table, repository by repository, and the result will be more consistent across the enterprise. With clear, simple guidelines, your development teams will have far fewer questions, and will tend to do the right thing without much oversight.

Layers of information across enterprise repositories
There is a sense in which data flows through these zones, from temp/working zones, to operational zones, to analytical zones. These zones don't exist solely within a repository; to some degree, they exist across the information infrastructure of the larger enterprise.

Data flows from repository to repository, being consumed, transformed, and enhanced along the way. In a large organization, there can be thousands of databases. Managing that complexity is impossible without some sort of organization – some way of grouping them into categories that can be managed similarly. You need a napkin drawing that explains your enterprise data repository strategy in a few simple terms. Unlike the application and technology domains, few companies have an enterprise-wide strategy for managing information. Oh, they manage information, but often this happens more intuitively than systematically.

Figure 4.7 represents an enterprise-wide organization of information structures. Note that this is the structure of information repositories, not the structure of application software or the hardware that supports them.

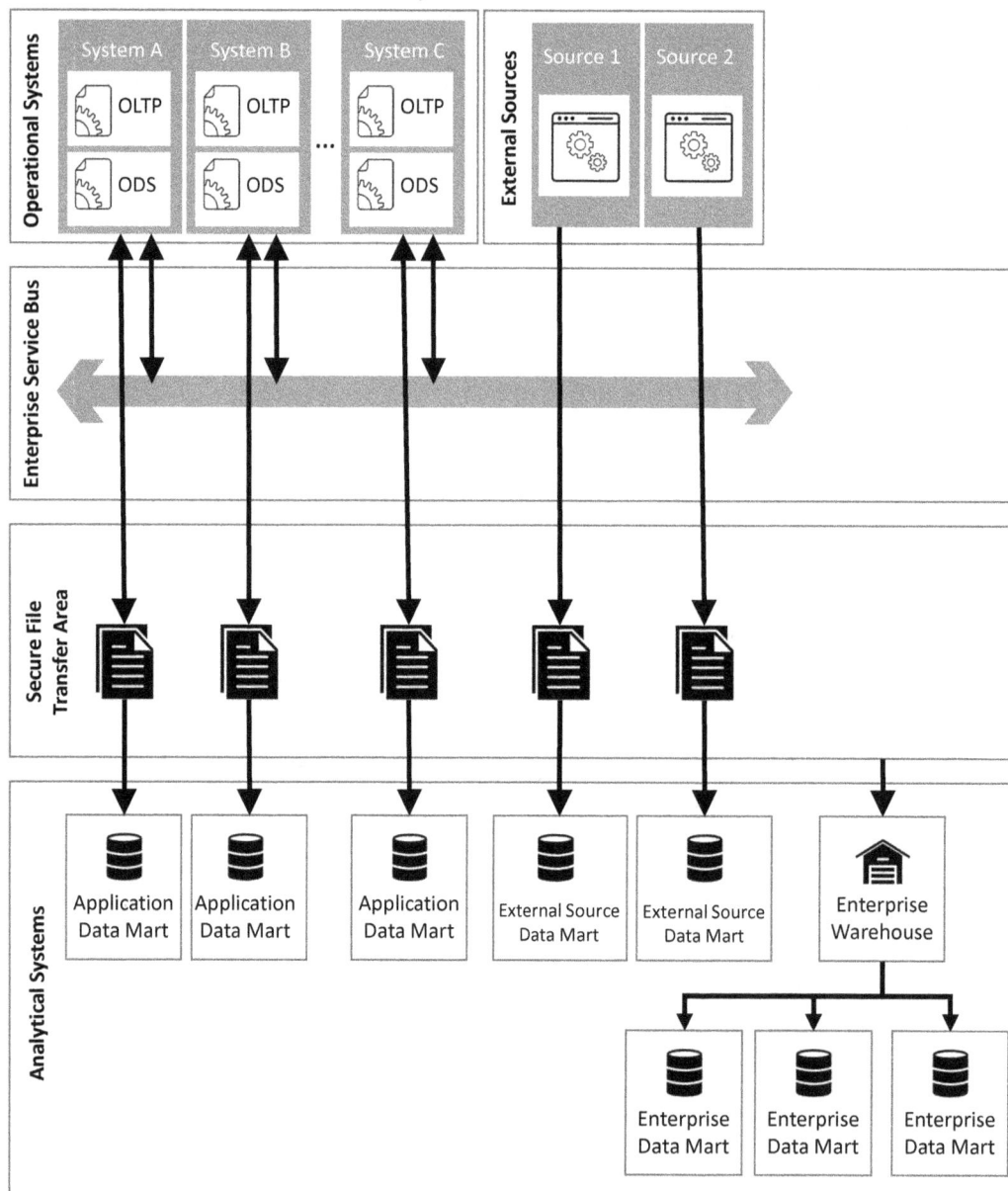

Figure 4.7 Enterprise-wide Information Management Layers

THE INFORMATION DOMAIN • 107

There are several layers of repositories in the conceptual picture. At the top are your operational repositories, where the raw data that runs the business is created and maintained. Beneath that are two transport layers for exchanging data between information systems. The first transport layer is the enterprise bus, over which data is exchanged using real-time web service *transactions*. The second is the secure file transport area, through which *batch* data is exchanged using files. At the bottom of the picture are the analytical repositories, the data marts, and the data warehouse.

The advantage of thinking of your company's information assets in these layers is, again, that you can make broad decisions for each layer, rather than have to plan and document repository by repository. In order to simplify and reduce the complexity of managing the company's IT functions, the EAG architectural vision for the information modeling function in the information domain of the functional framework should include some such high-level information model. All the repositories should be classified by layer, and all the tables within each repository classified by information zone, such as user-facing tables, reference tables, and temp tables.

The next few sections will discuss these information asset layers in a little more detail.

Operational layer

Operational Repositories contain the raw transactional data that runs the enterprise. This is the information created and maintained by customer systems, account systems, web portals, HR systems, and so forth. These contain business data that is maintained, for the most part, by inserting, updating, and deleting a single record at a time. From a data management standpoint, it doesn't matter if these repositories are within your firewall or are cloud-based services. These repositories are the **System of Record (SoR)** for the business data they create and maintain. In an integrated IT infrastructure, information systems will need access to all of the enterprise business data spread across dozens of applications, each of which is the system of record for some subset of the ELDM.

What you *do not want to do* is distribute complete copies of data throughout the enterprise so that each operational layer information system has its own local copy. This wastes disk space, network bandwidth, and developer time. It causes synchronization and data integrity issues. Each local copy of the data is another potential security breach, and another component that must be managed in a disaster recovery environment.

Instead, the information in these operational repositories should be exposed through service interfaces to your application infrastructure, a practice known as Data as a Service (DaaS). These data services allow the data to be loosely coupled, meaning that the data could be accessed in the same manner by any application that called the correct services interface, and that the application could access any data, provided the data was exposed using the same services interface. Loosely coupled data makes your infrastructure more flexible, easier to enhance, and faster to adapt to changing requirements. Loosely coupled data can be moved to a different data storage technology, or even to the cloud with no impact, so long as the service interface, security, and performance are sufficient. Any application you build or buy today should include the capacity to expose data through transactional web services. Applications should expose data not only internally to their own business logic, but also externally to the rest of the corporate infrastructure. Build or buy with this extra volume requirement in mind.

In some legacy software, the system data is housed in a proprietary storage format or is constrained in some other way such that it can't be accessed directly even though it is the system of record. In those cases only, you may be forced to stand up an **Operational Data Store (ODS)** – a copy of your source data with as little latency as possible, which can be used in turn to provide DaaS to the rest of your application infrastructure. The ODS serves as the services interface that the application is unable to provide. When the system forces you to set up an operational data store, that ODS becomes the **System of Access (SoA)** for operational reads, but the OLTP repository is still the system of record. An ODS typically only exposes read-only services to other applications. Any maintenance of the data must go back through the *real* source system, after which it will naturally flow down and update the ODS. Since most intra-application DaaS service calls are select statements, this approach works well for most business needs.

When evaluating any new third party software, one of the information domain requirements should be that the application exposes its data externally through services. No new application you build or buy should require an operational data store in order for other applications to access its information via data services. An ODS is only justified for legacy software in your infrastructure. Figure 4.8 shows an ODS in every operational information system. Hopefully, this won't be the case in your environment!

Information exchange layer

Ideally, information is exchanged between applications in only two ways:

- On a transactional basis, via data services
- In bulk, through secure file transfer

Your enterprise service bus coordinates the exchange of services. The secure file transfer area coordinates the exchange of files.

No single project is likely to want to bear the expense of setting up these areas of your information exchange layer. The cost and complexity is simply too much for one project to bear. Your EAG team will have to build this layer. This may be one of those cases where the EAG team must go request money for an IT-centric project. However, the information exchange layer isn't a case of IT wanting to play with the latest toys. These information transport areas provide significant value to the business in the long term.

Enterprise Service Bus

An **Enterprise Service Bus** (**ESB**) is a means of passing a very high volume of small chunks of transactional data through your network in real time, without having to stage data through files. ESB's support both software as a service (SaaS) and data as a service (DaaS).

It's possible to implement services without an ESB using a point-to-point architecture. While better than no services interface at all, a point-to-point architecture forces the source and target to handle a great deal of the overhead of configuring connection points, authenticating the service, orchestrating services into larger business processes and translating from one service protocol to another. You may implement point-to-point as a tactical step toward your strategic vision for managing your corporation's information assets, but you should make plans to move to a service bus as soon as it can be justified. The business isn't paying IT's salary so IT can develop software in-house that could have been purchased off the shelf for less money with more features.

Ideally, in a **Services Oriented Architecture** (**SOA**), all data will be accessed via services. This is true even for a software application accessing its own data inside the information system.

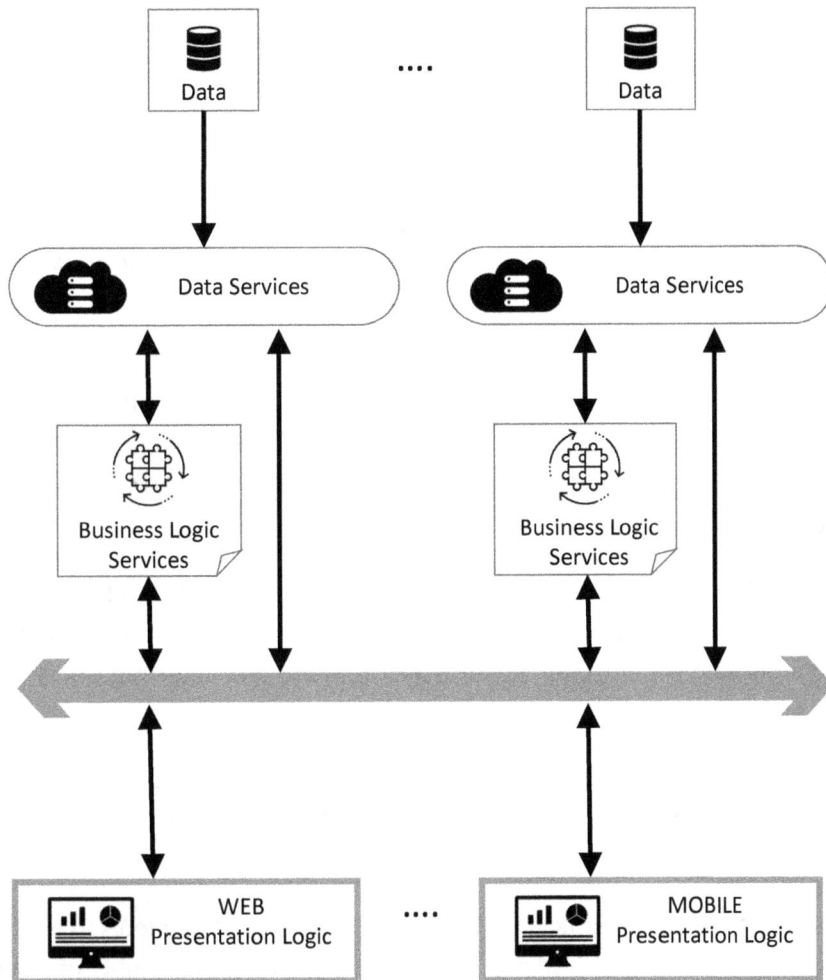

Figure 4.8 An Enterprise Service Bus

Accessing data via services is what creates the loosely coupled architecture that insulates the applications from changes to the repository implementation and vice versa. If a new field is added to a table, applications can still read data with the old service. Likewise, applications can be upgraded or replaced with limited impact, as long as the new/updated application supports the same data service interfaces. For example, you may initially develop a customer data hub in-house to assign a master ID to every customer (see page 168). As long as all of your operational systems access that information via services, you may one day be able to replace that homegrown functionality with a commercial product, provided you can translate your homegrown interface services to and from those required by the commercial software.

DaaS Services developed for one use are immediately available for any other information system that needs the same data. DaaS services initially developed for the web presentation business logic can be reused by the mobile device presentation logic. This speeds development time and reduces testing.

Data within these services should be modeled on your ELDM model. In a third-party product with a proprietary data model, the data services within the application will reflect the native third-party model. But in this case those data services should still be translated to reflect your ELDM before exposing that information outside the system. Your data modeling tool used to generate the ELDM should be able to generate both DDL to build physical repositories and XML to build data services. This way, you design the information once in the ELDM, then, from that ELDM model, generate consistent representations for various subsets of information at rest and in motion throughout the enterprise.

Most ESB appliance solutions today have the capacity to translate service protocols, for example, from SOAP to REST. One information system can expose data in one format, and, through the ESB, another information system can consume the data in another format. From an information management standpoint, one of the most useful ESB translations is the ability to take a database-stored procedure and translate that procedure name, input, and output into SOAP or REST services. This is a very useful approach for several reasons:

- You don't have to stand up dedicated web servers to support Java DaaS services developed in-house. You can create a simple stored procedure in the database and let the ESB translation tool expose it as a service. Fewer components means the solution is easier to manage, faster, and your disaster recovery plan is simpler.

- By forcing database access to go through stored procedures, you're limiting the type of data access that can be done, mitigating the risk of inappropriate access. You can grant a user access to a stored procedure without granting them access to the data in the repository that the stored procedure accesses.

- The stored procedure can be developed to include embedded logging, insuring that there's an audit trail for all service-based data access. Auditors like an architecture where data can't be accessed without generating an audit trail.

- When you alter the database structure, you use the same people and tools to modify table structures and to modify the stored procedure. This minimizes the number of resources needed to implement the change. You don't have to get a DBA *and* a Java developer to make the database change and the associated service change.

There are several considerations to keep in mind when building data services. Data services should be quite small in size. I once worked at a company with a very powerful ESB infrastructure, yet the system was always bogged down, performing poorly because the developers had coded a one-stop shop "get me everything I could possibly need" service, so that they only had to call a single get_account_info( ) service. Unfortunately, this account information included all the customer information, all the product information, and all the transaction information, all in one multi-megabyte service.

- Services should be designed at the same granularity as the underlying data. In the example above, it would have been better practice to implement a get_account_info( ) service that pulled the account-level information, and separate get_account_product_info( ) and get_account_transaction_info( ) services for all the child objects of the parent account information. If the information would be represented by more than one table in a normalized repository, it should probably be represented my more than one service in a service catalogue.

- In cases where you must retrieve a number of records at the same level, the services should not return all of them in one massive list. Rather, you should implement pagination. Typically, you would implement pagination as Get_list(key, starting_with). For example, Get_transaction_history(account_key, starting_transaction). Calling the service with 0 as the starting transaction would start with the latest. If the caller really needs the entire list every time, this should raise a red flag. Perhaps they're attempting to build a local copy of the data, which is never a good thing. Or perhaps they are performing some sort of aggregation or analysis which might be better done ahead of time in an analytical repository, with the results exposed as a fast, efficient service.

Secure file transfer area

Most companies will also have a secure file transfer area. Here data can be dropped by one source and picked up by another without risk of access by unauthorized people or systems. A dedicated team within the hardware domain usually manages this. The secure file transfer service is an important business function, which usually includes security, logging, multi-generations of backups, and is monitored against defined service level agreements.

Batch file transfer is rarely a good way to exchange information between two operational information systems. Analysts typically use batches to transfer data outside the network, or to transfer daily delta information between operational and analytical repositories.

Analytical layer

Analytical repositories are copies of data from the operational applications, possibly enhanced, transformed, and accumulated. Where your operational repositories are your systems of record, Forrester Research calls the analytical repositories the **System of Insight (SoI)**.[19]

Someday the analytical and operational worlds will merge. That trend has already started (page 92). However, until technology catches up, it's still considered best practice to separate the two most of the time. There are two acceptable analytical repository destinations for operational data, an application-specific data mart, and an enterprise data warehouse. We will also discuss enterprise data marts, but those are fed from the data warehouse, not directly from the operational source systems.

Application-specific data marts

Operational repositories are designed to support a very high volume of create, read, update, and delete (CRUD) transactions that access a very small number of rows. Analytical repositories, on the other hand, need a much smaller volume of transactions that access a much larger volume of records in read-only mode. Implemented in the same repository, analytical and operational functions conflict with each other, causing performance problems on both sides. Database block size, block free space, the number of indexes and constraints, and the entire hardware stack are configured differently for analytical and operational processes (see page 228).

Until technology matures to the point where the operational and analytical process can coexist in the same repository without conflict, it's acceptable to make an analytical copy of an application's data for application-specific analytical reporting. This **Application-specific Data Mart (ADM)** will be located on a separate physical database on separate physical hardware from the operation data.

The application-specific analytical data mart is usually a dump of a large part of the operation repository, with the minimal database structural changes. The database block size, free space, and indexes may be configured differently. The hardware stack supporting the analytical repository may be tuned differently.

---

[19] The Anatomy of a System of Insight: How Systems of Insight Turn Data into Action. Forrester Research, March 22, 2017. http://bit.ly/2mWPM5S.

However, the table and field names are typically unchanged, so that the same SQL queries can be run against the source system – albeit without the same performance.

The practice of keeping the data in the same structure as the source is mainly used to minimize the effort of building and maintaining the analytical repository, and the complexity testing its fidelity to the operational source. In some cases, it may make sense for the ADM to be created in real-time using a **Change Data Capture (CDC)** tool. The fewer structural changes between the source and target, the more stable these tools are. The one transformation I would recommend in this case is the generation of a record update timestamp, which can be very useful in determining which records have changed, known as the "delta."

The analytical repository may need some summary tables that are not present in the source operational repository. That's ok, provided the operational tables be brought into the ADM as-is, then separate summary tables built from them.

There should be only one ADM for any one information system. That data mart may be built and maintained by the application support team, or it may be built and hosted on their behalf by an analytics team. It's very common to know the enterprise analytics team as the "data warehouse team," but this team also manages dozens of applications-specific data marts. There are several advantages to this approach:

- Building and maintaining analytical data marts requires several specific skills distinct from those required to support operational systems. It makes sense to leverage the same set of analytical experts for many hosted data marts.

- Hosted data marts for several applications can share the same physical database, under different schemas and security roles. This allows the repositories to share more powerful physical resources, as well as shared services such as backup/restore, disaster recover, and security provisioning.

- The hosted data mart solution often serves as an end-of-life repository to preserve the application data after the application is decommissioned. If anyone shuts down the operational application, having an analytics team host the data mart eliminates the need to build and populate an end-of-life repository, and allows the operational team to immediately move on to other projects.

End users should never be allowed to join data across multiple application-specific data marts. In effect, that would serve as a mini-data-warehouse solution. Combining data from multiple operational systems into a single confirmed model with conformed reference data, balancing and integrity is an extremely laborious process, requiring a very specific skill set. Your information management strategy should include only one data warehouse, and enforce that all cross-application analytics occur there.

Even if data will eventually flow from the application-specific data marts to the enterprise warehouse, they should not share physical resources. Placing them together will impact database backup and restore times, as well as make your batch windows longer. It increases the size of the technology infrastructure needed to support the solution, which increases the risk of not being able to add CPU and memory to your warehouse solution because your hardware platform is maxed out. It also makes it difficult to manage the data mart and data warehouse at different levels of failover and redundancy, and creates a single point of failure if that one underlying hardware solution fails.

Enterprise data warehouse

The most important five words that describe the **Enterprise Data Warehouse (EDW)** are "there can be only one." The enterprise data warehouse is the one place in the entire company where all the enterprise information assets come together.

This is the closest you'll probably get to a physical implementation of the full enterprise logical data model (ELDM), though the warehouse model will probably be missing some components of the ELDM, such as HR. The goal isn't to build the entire ELDM; the goal is to consolidate an analytical copy of all the information assets needed to support the business requirement for enterprise analytics in one solution. The data warehouse may have some extensions of the ELDM as well, such as load dates.

As the IT industry focuses more and more on information, analytics becomes more and more critical to the success of your company. The enterprise data warehouse is the only place to perform enterprise-wide analytics. It has to be correct and trusted. It has to be current, and available. It has to perform well, and it needs solid tools to support various types of analysis.

Time was when a warehouse wasn't a critical component of an IT infrastructure at all, and many companies didn't even have one. Those that did have them didn't consider them strategic; and they were mostly an unplanned, gradual accumulation of data necessary for various projects. They were warehouses in name only; practically speaking, they were more of a landing area for loading flat files from various sources than anything. Don't be too embarrassed if this describes your current enterprise warehouse – it's pretty much how the first generation of every enterprise warehouse starts.

You probably already realize the limitations of those first-generation, unplanned analytical platforms. At some point, you'll get the opportunity to start again, usually due to the poor quality and performance of the first-generation solution, or the high cost of building solutions on top of it. The structure of these first generation warehouses is rarely worth saving, but you usually need them to keep running while you build the next generation. As the next generation spins up, you'll be able to do parallel testing to test the accuracy of the new platform against the old.

At some point, you'll find the new warehouse a much better platform for all new development, and switch to it as your primary platform. However, it's actually difficult to get rid of the legacy warehouse. Given the choice between spending your budget rolling out new functionality in the new warehouse, and spending those same dollars porting functionality that's working just fine in the legacy warehouse, it doesn't make great business sense to shut the legacy warehouse down.

Instead, the approach you'll take should be very similar to the way you would roll out any architectural strategic vision in a series of tactical steps. You'll wait until you get a business-funded requirement to make a significant change to a piece of functionality still implemented in the legacy warehouse, and take that opportunity to redevelop the functionality in the new warehouse instead. Because of the high quality and integrated model of the new warehouse, the development time will actually be shorter there. After enough of this, very little functionality will remain in the legacy warehouse, and the business cost of the hardware, software and support of the legacy solution is greater than the effort of porting the remaining functionality to the new solution.

Enterprise data marts

There's a difference between an application-specific data mart and an enterprise data mart. Application-specific data marts contain data from only one application, and typically use the same schema and code sets as the application from which the data is derived.

Enterprise Data Marts (EDM), on the other hand, are small subsets of the enterprise warehouse information, a business "sandbox" if you will. They contain the data needed for a specific business purpose, modeled for ease of use and performance. The modeling technique used depends on what you'll use the sandbox for (see page 119). The data warehouse itself can be used by reporting, but since it's a normalized model (see page 119), it isn't always the easiest solution for the business to use, nor the best performance. Instead, once the data is brought into the warehouse, conformed, enhanced, and data quality enforced, then specific enterprise data marts can be *derived* from it.

Enterprise data marts may be housed in one or more dedicated schemas within the same database as the enterprise warehouse, or they *may need to be hosted on their own platforms*. Both are acceptable. The determining factor is whether the availability and performance of the enterprise warehouse infrastructure is acceptable for the data mart. If the data mart is serving your external customers via a web portal, and your internal warehouse has no failover or redundancy and has regularly scheduled, long maintenance windows where the platform is unavailable, then you'll probably need a separate platform for the data mart. You may also wish to segregate some critical data marts onto separate hardware to decouple them from the impact of the heavy-lifting batch processes occurring in the data warehouse.

There are several advantages of building enterprise data marts from the enterprise warehouse:

- Built from the same source, all the data marts will yield the same numbers. This promotes trust and increases the use of the data.

- Because each data mart is built from the enterprise data warehouse, all the heavy work of integrating and conforming is performed one time only – not once per data mart. The data marts can be spun up much more quickly.

- Since the enterprise data marts leverage the enterprise data warehouse scope and quality, improvements in data quality or broadened scope of data in the enterprise data warehouse immediately benefit all the enterprise data marts, without any data mart specific coding.

Internal architecture of a data warehouse

There are many fine books on modeling for operational systems, as well as many fine books on modeling data marts. There are even a few excellent books that connect the dots between the two. But I find that most companies' biggest single trouble spot is creating an analytical enterprise data warehouse in a way that fits into an overall plan for managing the company's information assets.

As usual, managing complexity begins with reducing it to a few simple concepts that can be managed relatively independently. The data warehouse contains all of the information zones mentioned earlier. In the enterprise data warehouse, these tiers look like:

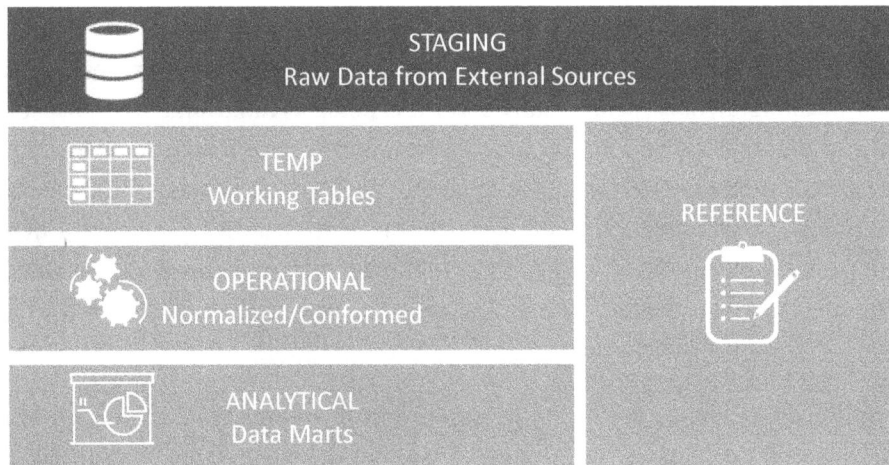

Figure 4.9 Information Tiers in an Enterprise Data Warehouse

This is similar to the convention proposed by The Data Warehouse Institute (TDWI) years ago. They didn't call out the reference data separately, and referred to the remaining four tiers as Staging, Transform, Distribution, and Access.

The seminal book on high-level enterprise data warehouse structure, *The Corporate Information Factory*, referred to an operationally modeled layer called the Operational Data Store (ODS) and a Data Mart layer. The normalized layer was labeled the ODS not because it was accessed operationally, but because it was modeled as you would an operational database, with a highly normalized design.

These days, there's a great deal riding on a company's ability to produce accurate analytics efficiently, and these days, the information domain is the weakest EAG domain at the enterprise level. Because of this, I think it's worth spending some time discussing the enterprise data warehouse analytics platform in more depth than most of the IT functions in this book.

Recommended Reading:
The Corporate Information Factory, Claudia Imhoff and Bill Inmon, 2001, Wiley.

Staging tier
The first layer of data, known as the **Staging Tier**, is the raw, untransformed data from internal and external sources, stored just as it was received, with very minimal processing. As such, it doesn't need to comply with the naming standards imposed on the conformed distribution and access tiers of the warehouse. Genealogy information about the staging tier should be stored in the metadata repository, which maps each field in the staging tier back to its source system.

If the data does not need to be accumulated or accessed directly by end users, then this staging tier is usually a schema in the data warehouse physical database. On the other hand, if the data does need to be accumulated historically, or if end users other than the data warehouse support team need to access the raw data directly, the data should be stored in a hosted data mart, typically housed on another database, with one schema per hosted application. Both the internal landing zone schema and the hosted data mart database are considered part of the staging tier of the enterprise warehouse.

Transform tier

The **Transform Tier** houses the temp tables used in the data transformation process, as surrogate keys (unique numbers meaningful only within the EDW) are being created and source-specific codes are being translated to enterprise codes. This is particularly useful if your transformations are performed in the database using SQL statements. If you're using an ETL tool that does most of the data transformation work outside the database, you may have little need for the transform tier. However, I'm one of the old school that still believes that, even if you have a high-end ETL tool, there are many types of data transformations that are going to be far faster and more efficient if performed within the database, in the transform tier.

The transform tier should not be accessible by end users and should not be accumulated historically. It is a working area, where data can appear and disappear without the business being notified. The transform tier is a bit of a mix between the source data format and the enterprise format. Don't expect this tier to map to the ELDM, or to follow naming conventions of the subsequent tiers of the warehouse. It is usually an odd mixture of the source-specific staging tier attributes and the distribution tier enterprise attributes.

Distribution tier

In almost any operational system, the data will be stored in a **Normalized Model**. Normalization rules were first set down by Edgar F Codd in 1970, and revised by Codd and Raymond F. Boyce in 1974. Normalization is used to reduce data redundancy and improve integrity.

For example, if you had a table for sales orders and a table for customer information, normalization rules would have you put only the customer key on the order table, rather than copying all the customer information onto each sales order. Putting a complete copy of all customer information on each order would not only be wasteful of space, it would lead to fewer records retrieved per I/O, resulting in poorer performance, and it would cause a great deal of overhead when customer information is changed and had to be updated on every sales order the customer ever made.

In a data warehouse, normalized data is ideally suited for verifying data quality, enforcing referential integrity, balancing transactional data to the general ledger, addressing reference data and master customer data issues, and appending contextual data and knowledge. This tier should contain all of the information assets needed for enterprise analytics in a conformed enterprise schema, using conformed enterprise reference data, with all data quality processes complete. It is the best possible version of the enterprise information assets, intended for use by the business to make the decisions that steer the company.

This highly normalized layer of the data warehouse is known as the **Distribution Tier**, because it is the source from which all enterprise information is subsequently distributed. It's also sometimes referred to as the data quality tier, the integration tier, the conformance tier, or the operational data store.

One common debate is the degree to which the distribution tier, or the ELDM upon which it is based, should reflect the source systems.

The distribution tier and ELDM should *not* attempt to reflect the model of the source systems. The operational source system data model is the way the application domain thinks about the data, but isn't necessarily how the business thinks about the data conceptually. This is especially true when the operational applications are third-party commercial products, and when there are multiple operational sources that service different segments of the same information (e.g. multiple customer or product systems, multiple claims or sales systems). In these cases, the way the business thinks about the information at the enterprise level is certainly different from the way each application models the information.

You'll occasionally find an analyst who is *very* familiar with the operational source for a system data model, to the point where they think that model represents the way the business thinks about the data. Just because the business has *had* to think about the data in this way for years doesn't mean that model reflects the actual business concept. Sometimes the person you need to talk to about the proper way to reflect the business understanding of the data concepts is someone a little less familiar with the details of the operational system models. Talk to the business experts, not the business' application experts.

The distribution tier *should*, however, attempt to retain the data values from the source systems. Yes, you need to transform source specific codes to the enterprise reference data, but you must not lose the actual source-specific codes that were used. There may be fields other than reference data that are also transformed – perhaps amount fields that different source systems interpret differently. Perhaps one source system includes sales tax, fees, withholds, discounts, or coupons in a paid amount field, where another source system does not. In these cases, you may need fields to house the original source system values *and* enterprise calculated fields. Retention of the source-specific values facilitates balancing back to the source systems, rebuilding the enterprise calculated fields if necessary, and facilitates research.

Conforming all of the disparate sources into a single enterprise model with consistent enterprise codes and consistent calculations is by far the hardest part of building an Enterprise Data Warehouse, but the distribution tier of your data warehouse can make or break how effectively it will meet the enterprise-wide analytical needs of the business. This function is far more important now than it has ever been before. Make sure you don't rush through this! Get it right!

Access tier

There's no reason to prevent an end user from accessing the normalized model in the distribution tier if they can use it efficiently. However, a normalized model isn't optimized for analytic queries. A normalized model results in the creation of lots of keys, and data spread across many tables. Data quality is much easier if the customer name and address exist on one record in one table, where it can be easily updated. Some analytical processes, such as drill-through detail reports, don't involve summarization and can be written to use the distribution tier efficiently. However, most analytical processes aggregate huge numbers of records, and perform poorly on a fully normalized model.

Many analytical processes would perform much better if the information were modeled using other techniques. They might prefer the customer name and address be duplicated on every customer transaction. Those techniques are perfectly acceptable, provided they are *not used in the distribution tier,* where data quality and contextual enhancement are occurring. The purpose of a normalized model in the distribution tier is to facilitate these quality functions. Throwing in other modeling techniques would make data quality processes much more difficult, and the overall quality of the warehouse would suffer.

Instead, you should distribute the normalized data to downstream data marts with end-user optimized models in a layer of your repository known as the **Access Tier**. The access tier contains many data marts built entirely with data from the distribution tier of the enterprise data warehouse, hence the name

Enterprise Data Marts (EDM). Each EDM is a *sandbox* for a specific business need, modeled for performance and ease of use for a specific type of access. The data has been vetted for that purpose, and, so far as possible, has been arranged in a manner so that the data cannot be misused in ways that might have occurred if an end user had attempted to use the larger, more complicated distribution tier directly.

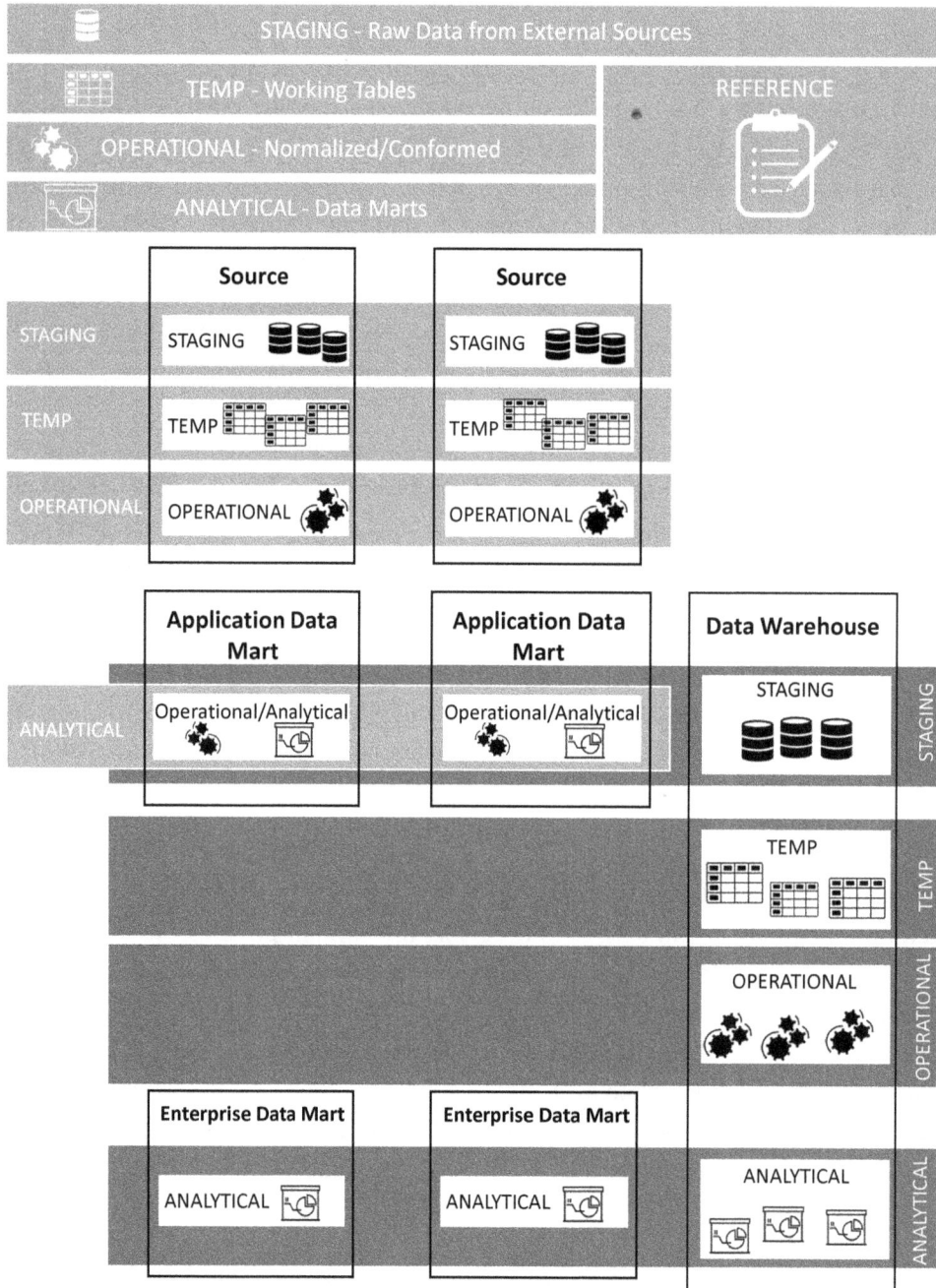

Figure 4.10 The Analytical Tier of the Source Systems can be the Staging Tier of the Enterprise Warehouse

This practice of creating specific data marts may seem a violation of the enterprise goal of not creating *redundant implementations* of the same data. Here we've taken the operational source data, replicated it in an applications specific data mart, and again in the distribution tier of the enterprise data warehouse, and now we are intentionally distributing that data to a number of enterprise data marts. That's at least four copies of the same data, probably more.

Always attempt to eliminate redundant physical representation whenever possible. In these cases, though, the business value must outweigh the risks. With the current state of technology, a single repository simply can't serve as the operational source and as the analytical source at both the application-level and enterprise-level for every kind of analytical process.

From the business perspective, these enterprise data marts provide the real value. To them, these data marts *are* the enterprise analytical platform, and the distribution tier simply an IT-centric staging area. Ralph Kimball was the father of dimensional modeling (page 120), one of the most popular business-friendly modeling techniques used in these enterprise data marts. Kimball has often been quoted as insisting the entire warehouse be dimensionally modeled. However, if you read his books, you will find that he does recommend a preparatory area where data is conformed, the quality is enhanced, and contextual data appended. He isn't recommending that prep area be a dimensional model. Instead, he's simply rebranding the dimensionally modeled data mart as *the data warehouse* because that is where most users are finally exposed to the analytical information. He isn't suggesting a difference in *architecture*; he's suggesting a difference in *nomenclature*.

Modeling techniques

There are many different ways to model information. Each technique serves a different purpose. The following sections contain a brief description of a few of the most common modeling techniques. It isn't my intention to teach modeling techniques in this book. Instead, the goal here is to show you how to use various modeling techniques to bring order to the chaos and manage your IT complexity on behalf of the business.

Relational models

Relational modeling is the type of modeling described earlier, a normalizing technique originally developed by Boyce and Codd to eliminate redundancy. It's a technique that's very useful for the IT organization because it makes the data quality so much easier to maintain. If you're bringing data from disparate sources together or maintaining it on a transactional basis, a normalized relational model is definitely the technique you want to use for business information.

I personally don't often normalize reference tables. They're small and don't change rapidly, so the disk saved by normalizing reference tables, and the cost of potentially having to update the same information on multiple rows of non-normalized reference tables is outweighed, in my opinion, by the convenience of having all the reference attributes together in a single table. Not everyone agrees with me on this.

Normalized models are extremely useful in operational systems. If a developer works on operational systems only, they may never use any other modeling technique.

That said, many operational systems in the past deliberately chose to violate normalization rules, creating data structures that are difficult to use today. There was a time when one could argue that this compromise was justified due to factors such as disk storage costs, but that time is far behind us. No new functionality should be developed using the priorities of a quarter century ago.

Perhaps one day a new modeling technique will prove even more powerful, and we will be stuck maintaining all these normalized models we've created. The data architect must always be looking out for new technologies and techniques. They must always be willing to adapt data strategies in support of the business as the industry continues to develop. But for now, the normalized relational model is the preferred technique for business information stored in operational repositories.

Recommended Reading:
Data Modeling Made Simple 2nd Edition, Steve Hoberman, 2009, Technics Publications.

Dimensional models

For slicing and dicing, drilling into and out of different views of the data, the best modeling technique to use is generally a dimensional model. Dimensional modeling is a complex technique that takes a few paragraphs to explain but years to master.

Dimensional models are still relational and can be implemented in any relational database, but the data in these tables is not normalized. The dimensional model is a relational model with a few simple restrictions.

One of the problems with most report authoring tools in the past was that they required a lot of database knowledge on the part of the end user. Specifically, the user needed to know two key pieces of information: the physical table and field names, and how to join those tables together properly.

Dimensional modeling began as an attempt to solve those two problems so that end users only had to know business names, and need not understand the underlying physical database at all.

In response to the first problem, a knowledgeable administrator worked with the business to create a cross-reference table that mapped a concept name that the business understood to an actual table and field name. This isn't a case of "dumbing down" the database for the sake of the business; it's a case of bringing the arcane complexity of the database back to the real-world concepts of the business it's supposed to serve.

The second challenge was harder to solve because, in a normalized database, there are relationships all over the place. It's difficult to tell how the user may want to join tables together. The way the challenge was solved was to impose upon the reporting tables a rule that there could be only one way to join any two given tables together. A table with all the business information was placed in the center, and joined to surrounding reference tables. This structure is now known as a **Star Schema**. The administrator then only had to define the keys that joined each of the reference tables (known as **Dimension Tables**) to the central business table (known as a **Fact Table**).

The dimensions tables were de-normalized so they could contain many levels of hierarchy fields in each row without requiring additional parent or child reference tables. The central business tables consisted purely of the keys to the dimension tables and the business **Measures** – the counts and amounts that were being reported.

After this is implemented, the business user simply picks from a list of familiar business terms they want reported. Underneath the covers, the software translates those business terms to table and field names, and adds the necessary joins to connect the tables used by the data. Simple!

Actually, it's quite complex, and takes years to master, but you get the idea. The point being that this technique gained popularity over other analytical modeling techniques because it was easier to build reporting tools over this model than the others. Because of the proliferation of tools based on this model, the database vendors added optimizations in the microcode to increase the performance of this special subset of relational modeling rules, making the technique even more powerful and more popular. At this point, it looks like the dimensional model is here to stay.

Some proponents of dimensional modeling claim that this technique is the silver bullet for analytical reporting. Some even claim that it's these fact and dimension tables alone that deserve the title of enterprise data warehouse. Dimensional modeling is an extremely powerful tool for creating analytical BI reports, but there are other analytical processes that are better served by other modeling techniques.

Recommended Reading:
The Data Warehouse Toolkit, Ralph Kimball and Margy Ross, 2013, Wiley.

Statistical models
One case where dimensional modeling doesn't work well is statistical analysis. This is the process of analyzing statistical relationships between different data elements, such as the relationship between the use of certain prescription drugs and liver damage. When performing statistical analysis, highly educated, highly compensated statisticians often spend 80 percent or more of their time just *preparing* the data for analysis, and less than 20 percent actually *performing* the analysis. This is not an effective way for IT to support the business.

Statistical modeling software isn't optimized for highly normalized models or dimensional models. The software typically works best with wide, flat data sets. This is more than just joining the tables together into one big query returning all the fields. Consider a gender code, for example. A typical wide, flat representation would pull the gender code from the business table and the gender description from a reference table. Since they are based on mathematical algorithms, statistical modeling software isn't interested in the text descriptions, and would have difficulty with alpha codes.

A typical code domain for gender might be 'M', 'F', and 'U'. Because statistical analysis involves mathematical modeling that works much better with numerical data than codes, these gender codes might be better translated, for statistical analysis purposes, to 0 (unknown), 1 (male), and 2 (female). However, if these values were all placed in a single gender field, the statistical model would tend to treat them as ordinal. Assigning the female gender a value twice the male value is probably going to throw off your statistical analysis. Therefore, a statistical model will prefer to roll those genders out into multiple discrete fields such as IS_MALE (0/1), IS_FEMALE (0/1), and perhaps IS_UNKNOWN (0/1).

Creating an automated process to prepare these statistical data sets ahead of time and refresh them regularly will go a *very* long way toward reducing the amount of time those highly compensated statisticians spend doing manual data preparation, and increase the amount of time they spend actually using their advanced degrees to analyze the results.

In today's competitive environment, corporations need to be analyzing their data deeply, mining it for insights that can be used to increase revenue, reduce expenses, and grow the business. If the competitiveness of your company rests on data mining, then IT needs to provide a solid platform for creating and testing models, for making the results operational, and for monitoring the effectiveness of those results. Forrester research recently reported that the data engineers who build this data infrastructure have become even more important than the statisticians who do the analysis.[20]

Recommended Reading:

Discrete Multivariate Analysis: Theory and Practice, Yvonne M. Bishop and Stephen E. Fienberg, 2007, Springer.

Annualized models

There are a number of other techniques for modeling presentation layers, including graph models and object oriented models. There's no wrong answer as long as the model is derived from your normalized operational model and meets the performance and ease of use requirements of the business.

One last model we will mention is the annualized model, most commonly used with profitability calculation. Profitability is, as you might imagine, very important to the business. Since you can't manage what you aren't measuring, you need to be calculating your profitability over time by whatever dimensions your business uses, such as product, region, customer segment, and channel.

There are many ways to calculate profitability, and many third party applications to help with those calculations. The simplest approach is **Allocated Costing**, in which the costs that can't be attributed to a single transaction are allocated across a larger group of transactions. If you're a bank and have a network of ATMs you service, you may want to spread the cost of the ATMs evenly across the people who use each of the ATMs when calculating your customer profitability. Customers on the west side of town share the support costs of the ATMs in their area, and so forth.

Another approach to profitability is **Activity-Based Costing**. In the previous example, if you have one ATM in a remote or inconvenient location that only a handful of customers use, do you really want to allocate the entire cost of the ATM to those customers, showing them to be very unprofitable? In activity based costing, you only allocate to the customer a percentage of the ATM cost based on their activity time, and show all the idle time as unused bandwidth. Bandwidth that has a cost to you, certainly, but is not allocated to your customers.

Regardless of the costing approach you use, most of the third party software products that perform these calculations for you prefer the data in annualized form. Every count and amount is represented 12 times on each record. Examples include JAN_ATM_COST, FEB_ATM_COST, and MAR_ATM_COST. This isn't a normalized model, nor is it a dimensional model or a statistical model. It is the model that provides the most efficient platform from which to calculate annualized profitability.

And that's the point, really. There is no one modeling technique you should use in your analytical data marts. Instead, you need to provide the models that result in the easiest to use, highest performance platform to support the business need. As there are many different business needs, you will probably have many different data marts, each of which may use different modeling techniques. Just don't try to compromise and mix multiple modeling techniques in a single data mart in order to serve multiple end users. This will result in a confusing, poorly performing data mart that does not serve the business well. Instead, dedicate separate data marts with different modeling techniques to different business needs.

---

[20] Data Engineers have become more important than data scientists: Invest in engineers to close the gaps in your system of insight, Forrester Research, Nov 9, 2017. http://bit.ly/2DRaCuy.

Enterprise modeling guidelines

By this time, you should be well aware that a good deal of the work of architecture and governance is breaking large problems down into smaller, simpler, logically distinct problems. We do this with coding, and we do it with data models. It's difficult to manage a data model of over 50 or so tables if there's no implicit information organization structure, no taxonomy, no data classification system. If you have a plotter-generated ERD diagram showing the tables and relationships, you expect the tables to be grouped into several related subject areas of interrelated business information such as product tables, customer account tables, and sales tables. This doesn't need to be a physical separation in terms of separate schemas or table spaces. The distinction can be purely logical, though I *would* recommend tracking the subject area in your data model metadata.

IBM has developed a series of industry specific logical models. In these models, they have broken the data out into nine common, cross-industry **subject areas**. All the information about people is grouped into one subject area. All the information about products is in another subject area, geographic locations in another, network information in another, and customer account information in another. The concept of subject areas didn't originate with IBM, but they developed and championed the idea that there are universal subject areas that apply to all industries.

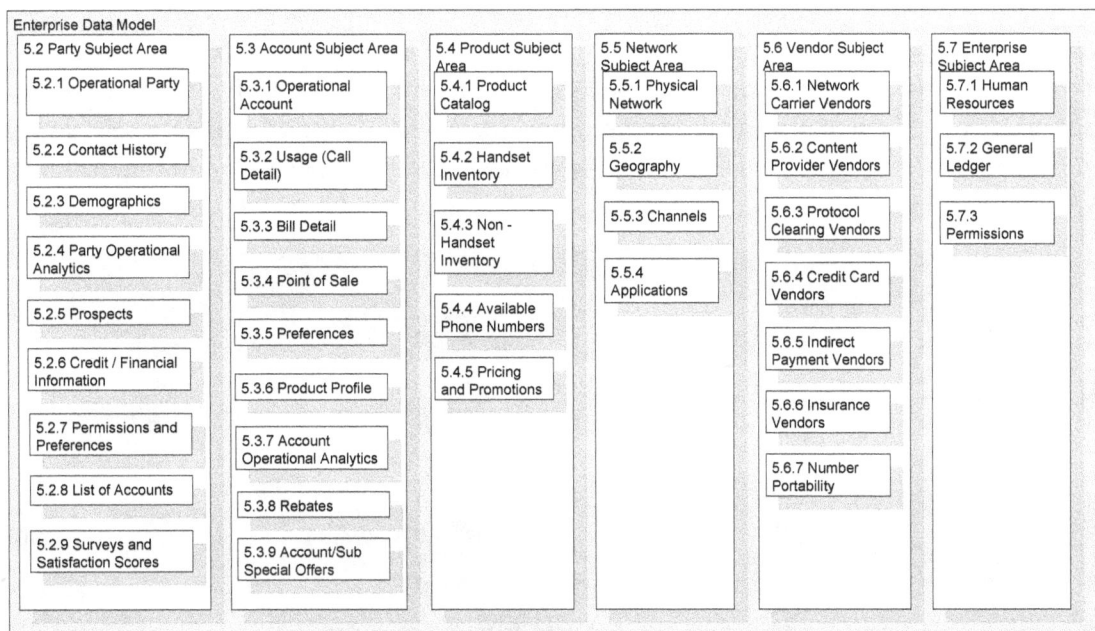

Enterprise Data Model					
5.2 Party Subject Area	**5.3 Account Subject Area**	**5.4 Product Subject Area**	**5.5 Network Subject Area**	**5.6 Vendor Subject Area**	**5.7 Enterprise Subject Area**
5.2.1 Operational Party	5.3.1 Operational Account	5.4.1 Product Catalog	5.5.1 Physical Network	5.6.1 Network Carrier Vendors	5.7.1 Human Resources
5.2.2 Contact History	5.3.2 Usage (Call Detail)	5.4.2 Handset Inventory	5.5.2 Geography	5.6.2 Content Provider Vendors	5.7.2 General Ledger
5.2.3 Demographics	5.3.3 Bill Detail	5.4.3 Non - Handset Inventory	5.5.3 Channels	5.6.3 Protocol Clearing Vendors	5.7.3 Permissions
5.2.4 Party Operational Analytics	5.3.4 Point of Sale	5.4.4 Available Phone Numbers	5.5.4 Applications	5.6.4 Credit Card Vendors	
5.2.5 Prospects	5.3.5 Preferences	5.4.5 Pricing and Promotions		5.6.5 Indirect Payment Vendors	
5.2.6 Credit / Financial Information	5.3.6 Product Profile			5.6.6 Insurance Vendors	
5.2.7 Permissions and Preferences	5.3.7 Account Operational Analytics			5.6.7 Number Portability	
5.2.8 List of Accounts	5.3.8 Rebates				
5.2.9 Surveys and Satisfaction Scores	5.3.9 Account/Sub Special Offers				

Figure 4.11 Telecom Enterprise Data Warehouse Subject Areas

Subject areas are a great technique for taming the chaos of large data models. A large application can easily have hundreds of tables. Treating them as one massive, undifferentiated list is overwhelming. Dividing the tables into subject areas has many advantages:

- It's far easier for developers and end users to conceptualize the model and find their way around if it's broken down into a manageably small number of logical groups. When ERD diagrams are printed, these subject areas are usually called out by color – by either placing tables on a colored background, or actually coloring the tables in each subject area. If a user is looking for information, they should be able to walk toward the ERD diagram hung on the wall, and from thirty feet away already begin narrowing their focus to a fraction of the whole based on the subject area groupings. In order to keep things simple, I'll typically show all the relationship lines within a subject area, but will not show the ones that span multiple subject areas. Cross-subject area relationships tend to refer only to the most important tables in each subject area, and are easy to imply without the lines.

- Subject areas often correspond to data ownership or stewardship. It is much easier to draw the lines around who owns what when the data is already grouped into well-defined areas.

- Input batch files and transactions will typically focus on one subject area. This makes it easy to assign developers, analysts, and testers consistently, allowing them to grow their expertise in one area of the model.

- Subject areas can be treated as loosely coupled, while the tables within a subject area are much more tightly coupled. Developers can use common APIs to insulate one subject area from changes to another. For example, a single API can be used to consistently load party subject area tables with names and addresses and return party key assignments. Changes can be made within one subject area without requiring major retesting of the entire system, so long as the APIs are maintained.

This last advantage is true even in a data warehouse where data is loaded by ETL tools. There will be a point at which one subject area needs to populate its business tables with keys from another table using some sort of lookup. If you implement this as a separate, reusable API, then all the processes that need to populate keys in this manner can reuse it. In fact, if you keep a flag indicating whether the API returned valid keys, you can implement a regularly scheduled process to re-attempt the API call.

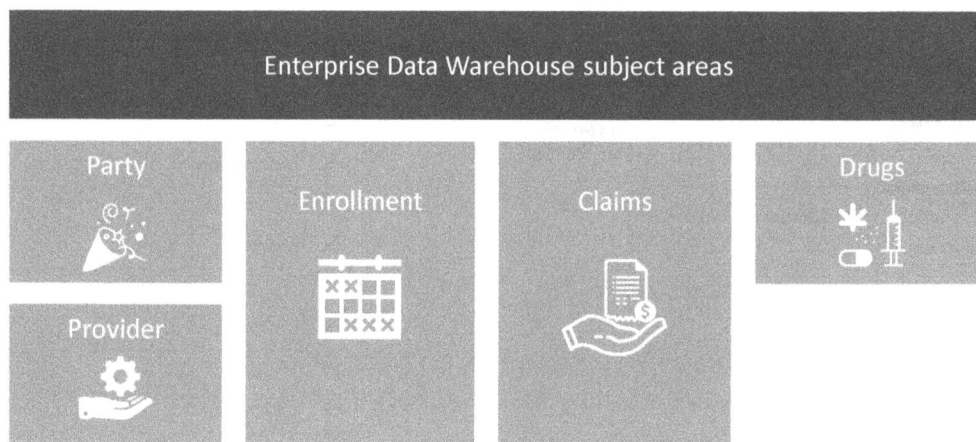

Figure 4.12 Health Insurance Industry Data Warehouse Subject Areas

Using the health insurance subject areas in Figure 4.12, you should see that a developer loading medical claims into the claims subject area would need to look up the data warehouse keys for the enrollment information from the enrollment subject area, and the provider keys from the provider subject area. The enrollment information may be missing or incomplete, and may later be retroactively added or terminated. If enrollment subject area and provider subject area lookup API services exist, they can be used to consistently look up the keys across subject areas. This enforces consistency, decouples the code for one subject area from the code for another, and allows the key lookup to be treated as a service.

Perhaps you only get updates for national providers once a month, and may not yet have a provider key to assign when a claim is initially received. I would suggest implementing a flag on the calling subject area records. The flag would indicate whether the cross subject area lookup was successful, so that it could be automatically repeated until the keys are found. I usually implement these flags as date fields, initially set to null, then setting them to the date when the API service was called successfully. This way, the scheduled process needs only look for nulls. Any downstream processes that are affected by these enrollment key changes can simply check for the records with the most recent dates. If you used a Y/N flag, the downstream processes would not know which records had been changed, and would have to implement their own flags or codes, requiring additional updates to the business tables.

If you discover an error in any subject area, the resulting changes can be localized to that one subject area; simply refresh other subject areas by setting their API successful dates back to NULL, forcing the lookup to repopulate the keys across subject areas.

If an enhancement within one subject area results in significant changes to the data model, there would be no impact on any code in other subject areas, provided they all used an API, and the API service call and response interfaces were unaffected by the underlying data model changes.

One final reason to decouple your model into subject areas and use API service calls to insulate them from one another is that this makes it possible, down the road, to completely cut out a subject area and replace it with another implementation. For example, you may initially develop your own embedded name and address information, but later have a need to replace it with a third party master data management product. That project will be far simpler if the application was already accessing the name and address information via API calls.

There are many other advantages to using subject areas in both operational and analytical information systems. This is just another example of the larger theme of the functional framework. Grouping IT management detail into areas of similarity that can be managed as a unit is critical to making things simpler, more consistent, more intuitive, and more flexible. This same thinking applies to nearly every IT management function. For EAG program architects, this concept is the closest thing to a hammer that can be used to treat every problem like a nail. Architects should live and breathe the practice of grouping similar things together. They should sort pencils on their desks and group food on their plates. This simple practice has profound effects on how you manage the world around you. I believe that the functional framework is such a powerful tool primarily for just this ability to take a thousand complex tasks and group them into a much smaller number of functions that are similar enough to be managed as a unit.

Data modeling is a great example of the large problem. If I reverse engineer the data repository of a large information system, the modeling tool I use will also attempt to create an ERD diagram. No matter how good a job the tool does of arranging the tables to minimize the crossover of relationship lines, the result will look like someone dropped a plate of spaghetti. The resulting ERD diagram is far too complex to simply and intuitively convey any usable information about the model organization. However, after I spend a few hours separating tables into tiers, and into subject areas within each tier, the complexity is reduced to a handful of concepts that are far easier to understand and manage. That process of simplification by grouping, extended to all of IT, is one of the primary jobs of the architect role.

I recently went through this exercise with data from a third-party commercial application within our corporate infrastructure. My purpose was simply to understand the data model within that operational application, so I could properly extract data from it into the enterprise data warehouse for analysis. However, when I showed the source system application developers my results to confirm my understanding, they just about wet their pants. These developers, who had worked on that application for more than a decade, wanted copies of the organized ERD diagram to post throughout their offices. I don't pretend to understand the complexity of the business logic within that product, but I do know that you'll never really understand the business logic until you first truly understand the information on which the logic operates.

The more decisions you can make at a high level:

- The fewer modeling decisions you will need to make project by project

- The more consistent your models will be across the enterprise

- The faster new repositories and enhancements to existing repositories can be spun up

- The more similar your repositories and exchange structures will be across the enterprise

We've talked about "zones" of data (internal, operational, analytical, reference data, etc.). We've talked about "tiers of data" within a zone (i.e. the staging, transform, distribution, and access tiers in a warehouse). Now let's extend our process of grouping similar things to the description of "types" within a tier.

Business tables in the distribution tier, for example, might include the following types:

- **Transactional business tables** that are inserted once, possibly with update segments that are updated from a default value to a transactional value only one time

- **Transactional golden copy business tables** which pick the best transaction (usually the latest one) to represent the current state of a business entity

- **Merged golden copy business tables** which merge data from many different records into one representation of the business entity

- **Snapshot business tables** showing the state of a business entity at multiple points in time; not ranges in time, but as of actual calendar dates

Reference tables might break down into several distinct types as well:

- **Global reference tables**, where there is a single code set that every application uses

- **Translate reference tables**, where application specific values must be translated to one or more enterprise-wide code sets

- Ralph Kimball was famous for grouping reference tables based on how the data in them changed over time (Type 1, 2 and 3 slowly changing dimensions)

You'll always need room for exceptions, but as far as possible, you should have guidelines for every "type" of table you have. These should not be decisions a modeler has to make with every model change.

There are many other common types of business and reference tables, and you no doubt have some unique table types of your own. These are *types* of tables – classes of tables that can and should be managed similarly. Define the types at a high level, and create policies and standards for each type of data for things like:

- How the tables are modeled including table and field naming standards for each table type

- How the tables are audited including how and where are changes tracked

- How sensitive data in the tables is secured

- How the tables are backed up and recovered, and how data is archived and aged out of the repository

- How standards for data quality apply to each table, including referential integrity and tracking of raw input before cleansing

- How is the data tested in lower environments

Creating and enforcing standards for groups of similar data is the key to simplifying information lifecycle functions.

Data modeling is the first function in the information lifecycle. To be an effective part of a framework of IT functions, the data model must include integration points with other functions. Some examples include:

- The data model must reflect **data security function** requirements. These might require you, for instance, to log every action that adds, changes, or deletes data. These requirements often require the addition of user ids or batch numbers, time stamps, and a history of changes over time. They will require you to identify sensitive data, which will be far easier if you have an enterprise logical data model mapped to well-documented application models.

- The data model must reflect the **data quality function** requirements, such as enforcing referential integrity and retaining the original source system value for transformed data.

- The data model must reflect the information **end-of-life function** requirements. The proper data elements must exist to be able to identify when data has outlived its value and should be deleted. It should also identify and *not* delete any information that is a part of ongoing litigation.

You can't perform data modeling at the enterprise level just by winging it. You need a system. You need an enterprise-level vision for modeling information assets that is reduced to the essential components. You need a process that ensures all the integration points with other IT functions are taken into account. A functional framework can help you put all that together, and manage information assets effectively for the business.

Consuming information

As Bob Dylan was known to say, "The times, they are a-changing." Visionary poet and songwriter, or visionary information architect? I wonder.

You will always need to consume data both on a transactional basis and via batch transmissions. I'm sure you are doing that well enough today or you wouldn't still be in business. In the context of this book, you need to be preparing your corporate infrastructure for a paradigm shift in the way we handle information. The way we have consumed information in the past is simply not going to suffice. Information is increasing in volume, variety, veracity, and velocity: the four V's. All four are driving information architecture toward a loosely coupled infrastructure of services.

Data volume is increasing. According to Forbes[21] (September 2015), more data has been created in the past two years than in the entire previous history of the human race, and by the year 2020, about 1.7 megabytes of new information will be created every second for every human being on the planet.

Gone are the days when you could create your own local copy of all the data you needed. Storage aside, there are some types of data you can't possibly copy to a local repository as fast as it is created. Even where it is possible, local replication usually isn't desirable (see page 108). Increasingly, both operational and analytical applications are going to have to rely on getting data as needed from external sources via services. Companies such as credit bureaus and retail demographics vendors now push clients toward services-oriented access to their data rather than batch downloads. If a health insurance company needs to know information about a provider requesting to join their network, they can now easily access that provider's specialty certifications, licenses, malpractice information, and more, all with a simple service call, without bothering to download huge databases, manage them locally, and try to keep them current. Information is an asset that companies buy, sell, and trade via services.

Amazon Web Services and the Google API are the shape of the future. Nearly every major information vendor offers access to their information as a transactional service these days. You will need to consider a future where you participate in this kind of distributed infrastructure. It might include accessing data services exposed by other companies, and it might include exposing your own data as a service in return. There are certainly serious security and privacy concerns, intellectual property concerns, performance and availability concerns, auditing concerns, and concerns about how the revenue model of buying and selling data on a transactional basis would work. Nevertheless, the day is coming where your operational information system software is accessing data via services, some of which are hosted by external vendors. Your company's EAG program should be planning for that future vision, and perhaps experimenting with a low-risk pilot now to work through these concerns. You might consider starting with the US Postal Service API for address cleansing at the point of data entry, or a credit bureau API for making more informed loan origination decisions.

Distributed analytical processing is a bit farther way. Security and other concerns aside, we have the technology today to access remote services one transaction at a time. What we don't have is a generally accepted solution for performing analytics over large, globally distributed data sources via services.

I believe one of the big hurdles modern business faces before they can implement a truly distributed infrastructure is the development of a robust, distributed analytical query tool. There are certainly

---

[21] http://bit.ly/2FZu6hw.

federated query tools, but most of them work by first collecting all the distributed data into one local repository. Imagine a day when different companies offer up various proprietary "tables" to the web. If you develop an application to run on your hosted app server, that application can join large numbers of records in your local customer data with address information hosted by the USPS and Census Bureau, with retail demographics hosted by Acxiom, or with inventory data hosted by your supplier – all in a single SQL query without transporting entire data sets across the network to a central location for processing.

This service would need to be able to create a distributed query plan that performs as much of the work locally on each hosted data source as possible, resulting in an absolute minimum of interim results transferred from host to host. There would have to be a way for each site to expose its metadata in a consistent way in order to build the query plan. The same set of distributed analytic services would have to be supported by each host. There would need to be a way to manage distributed security, both to prevent access to unauthorized data, and to prevent unauthorized monitoring of confidential queries. There would have to be some agreed-upon means of keeping track of resource usage, buying and selling all this processing and information. Those are a lot of gaps to fill.

But don't you believe that day is coming? Do you really think it's more than a decade away? Imagine how that will transform the way we build IT infrastructure. Imagine how this will separate those businesses that are prepared from those who aren't. This is going to be like an asteroid destroying the dinosaurs who aren't equipped to compete with those quick little warm-blooded primates.

You and I probably aren't going to be the ones to develop that application. However, we can start questioning the degree to which the infrastructure we are building is based on a scalable, service-oriented, loosely coupled, cloud-friendly architecture. That vision has to span every IT function in your functional framework.

Data variety is also going to be a challenge. Cisco reported[22] that in 2012, there were 8.7 billion objects connected to the web, consisting of about 0.6% of the *things* in the world. By 2013, driven by the falling cost of technology, this number exceeded 10 billion devices. Cisco predicts that the number of connected devices will reach 50 billion by 2020, meaning that 2.7% of the things in the world will be connected to the web.

As the network edge continues to disappear (see page 214), your back-end servers and applications will go into the cloud, your front-end input and display devices will go mobile, and many of your event sources will be devices out in the web. Wearable medical monitoring devices, internet enabled utilities and appliances – every single aspect of your life will be filled with sensors collecting all manner of data. You're going to need to be able to stream these disparate data sources into your environment as the data is created, in real time, via services.

Working in the health insurance industry now, I see a large number of home health connected devices on the market. Talking about this with our medical informatics experts, I was surprised to find that one of the most valuable connected home health devices is a simple bathroom scale. One of the single highest predictors of a dangerous complication following heart surgery is rapid weight gain accompanied by swelling and pressure. This can happen when water is retained in the tissues surrounding the heart. If this can be detected early, the critical care team can intervene and very likely save a life.

---

[22] http://bit.ly/2cC1Umm.

I mentioned earlier that 34 states now provide guidelines for telemedicine, where a doctor visit consists of the doctor in his office, and you in your home, connected by streaming video and various home health sensors. Manufacturers of mobile phones are rushing to partner with devices and apps that will enable these interactions.

This is happening in every industry. My car can provide streaming diagnostics that compare to airline black boxes from the not too distant past. My car keys have a sensor to help me locate them if lost. Refrigerators have built in sensors to assist with shopping. Retail stores can track my location in real time and message me special offers. If I order a product shipped to me, I can track its progress online. I can even order food from my favorite restaurant online, pay for it with a transaction from my financial institution, have it delivered by a third service, and track the delivery vehicle all the way to my door through GPS-enabled streaming data.

But in order for your company to participate in this interconnected future, your corporate infrastructure is going to need to be able to accept all of those different kinds of streaming data and integrate them into your business processes. Your data model and your processes are going to have to be flexible enough to accommodate data from many different sources in many different formats.

This distributed internet of things leads to **data veracity**. How are you going to authenticate the sources of all this distributed information? While this is a significant concern, it's more appropriate for the hardware domain.

Data velocity clearly accompanies these streaming data services. If the volume of data is growing rapidly, and the sources are outside of your private network and are streaming data via small transactional services, you're going to need an infrastructure designed to scale to very large service transaction volumes.

If you want to design an information infrastructure that's going to serve your company in the years to come, you need a strategy that includes a robust, scalable infrastructure for data services. You may not pass data as services much today, but that's going to change rapidly. How are you going to model those services? Where are you going to expose the catalog of available services? How are you going to create and communicate your enterprise standards for data services? How are you going to integrate and translate services from different sources, using different protocols, to enterprise standards compatible with your ELDM?

This can't be done project by project. It's going to have to be an enterprise-level architectural initiative. Do your homework. Come up with a strategic vision and roadmap. Watch business-sponsored projects for opportunities to take steps toward your target architecture while providing real business value. You need to get ahead of this!

Enhancing information

You'll have noticed by now that this book is quite data-centric. There are several reasons for that.

My first vehicle was my grandfather's 64 Chevy truck. Manual transmission, manual choke, no seatbelts, no rear-view mirror, no AC, it had an AM radio, but no FM. The bed was made of wood. When you popped the hood, half the front of the truck swung up, revealing… about six moving parts. It wasn't that hard to learn about cars in those days – there wasn't much to them. To work on the engine, you literally climbed up in the engine compartment and sat inside. These days you can hardly reach your hand down in an engine for all the maze of hoses and wires. It's no wonder that kids don't grow up working on their cars the way my generation did.

I graduated from Duke University in 1986 with a degree in computer science. Back then, if you were the *computer guy*, you did everything. You ran the network cables through the ceiling; you installed and configured commercial software; you set up the printers and configured the workstations to use them; and you were the developer for any kind of software that was needed. I've built several machines from parts and soldered together my own boards to go in them. We used to develop software in assembly language, with very little between the developer and the internal workings of the CPU. We would burn code on EPROM chips that we installed directly on the motherboards so that we could pull the hard disk, floppy disk, and the keyboard and monitor to make a black box appliance. I'm not bragging at all. This wasn't unusual at all back in 80's. It was possible, even expected, that you knew *everything* about computers. However, like my old '64 Chevy, somewhere along the line, things got complicated.

These days, kids joining the ranks of IT professionals must pick a specialty. It's just not possible to understand everything any more. There's too much, and it changes too fast. Along the way, some of us stuck with technology. Some became software administrators. Some of us became software developers. I stuck with data. I've always been a data person, and this book will reflect that bias without apology.

However, this data focus also reflects the state of the IT industry today. Informatica recently coined the term "Data 3.0" to reflect the fact that data has now moved to the center of the enterprise, ahead of the hardware and software focus of recent years.[23] Data isn't something buried within an application (Data 1.0) or in an enterprise analytical repository slung somewhere beneath the operational applications (Data 2.0). No, information has taken center stage. We have, over the years, developed solid best practices for managing enterprise hardware and software, but managing enterprise data as an asset independent of hardware and software is a relatively new thing, and a thing most of us aren't doing all that well. The increasing importance of data to your enterprise, combined with the relative lack of guidance regarding how to manage this asset has resulted in IT organizations across the world failing to manage the IT complexity of information assets on behalf of the business.

In a pure operational system, all the information is raw data. Contextual data and knowledge are technically analytical in nature, not operational. That said, most of the systems we think of as operational, the ones that run our core business processes, typically have a good bit of analytics built in.

Adding contextual data
In the information pyramid discussed earlier (Figure 4.4, page 97), the base of the pyramid is the raw operational data. This is the data created and maintained by your operational systems to run the core processes. The next layer of information is the contextual data we gather to append to the raw data. We often, for example, purchase contextual data from companies that specialize in retail demographics: what magazines people subscribe to, their education level, and what kind of cars they drive. This is increasingly valuable information for your business. Why?

23 *The Power of Data to Transform Business is Here with Data 3.0*, by Anil Chakravarthy, May 31, 2016 http://infa.media/2BgXuMu.

Consider this. It's relatively easy to determine how profitable each customer is. You already know how much they cost you, both directly and in allocated expenses, and you know how much money you made on them. What you *don't* know is how profitable the next person to walk through your doors is going to be.

You don't have transactional, operational history on your prospects. However, you can purchase their demographic data. If you can find correlations between your profitable customers and some data that is available for people who are not your customers, then you can *predict* prospect profitability.

Say you purchase some demographic information on your customer base and turn it over to your statisticians. After doing some analysis, they determine that for product A, your most profitable customers live on the west side of town, own their own homes, drive SUVs, and have two incomes. Closely behind that in profitability are resident college students who attend schools in your sales area but come from homes out of state. In these cases, they often incur lots of fees, but their parents keep them paid off. The statisticians found these correlations using one set of your data and used it to successfully predict profitability on a control group of your customers who weren't part of the original analysis.

You can then use this information to go back to your retail demographics company and ask to purchase the names and addresses of people in your sales area who live on the west side of town, own their own homes, drive SUV's and have two incomes. And you can purchase contact information for resident students in your area with out-of-state home addresses. You can now invest targeted marketing dollars for product A pursuing prospects that you're sure will look very much like your most profitable customers. You'll probably find that different product lines have very different profitability models. You'll find that some customers who are currently unprofitable on the product they have look like they would be very profitable on another product. You don't necessarily want to get rid of unprofitable customers – you may just need to steer them toward a different product offering.

The reason why this kind of contextual information is so valuable is because it's closely associated with customer lifestyle. It is often called behavioral data. You would be astounded at the breadth of behavioral data available for purchase. Does your grocery store give away those barcode fobs that can be scanned at checkout for significant discounts? The reason they can afford to do that is that they use that information for predictive modeling, and they sell it to companies that aggregate and resell demographic data. That's how a bank can purchase information about what kind of cereal you eat for breakfast, if they think it will be predictive.

You may have heard about Target, the retail giant who made national headlines for one of their predictive models. It seems that two of Target's most profitable product lines are diapers and baby formula. Unfortunately for Target, most new mothers tend to stick with the brand they first use. It's very difficult to get these women to switch to the Target brand once the child has arrived.

Therefore, the statisticians at Target used their own sales data to predict pregnancy. Yes, you read that correctly. They were able to look back through sales history, tracking people's purchases, especially those who eventually started buying diapers and baby formula. Using this data, they developed a model that very accurately predicted third trimester pregnancy, based purely on product purchases. They've been pretty closed-mouthed about the actual model, but rumor has it the model included variables for bulk wet-wipes and paper towels. Apparently, there's something to this *nesting instinct* thing. Target would then focus their advertising efforts, with high-value coupons and free samples, to encourage these women to be considering Target's brand well before their delivery and first actual purchase!

That prediction is impressive enough, but not the reason they made national headlines. Apparently, one day a gentleman entered his local Target and asked to speak to the store manager. He proceeded to ask the manager to please stop encouraging his teenage daughter to have a child. He was very concerned about all the mail the young girl was receiving depicting how wonderful her life would be with a little baby to care for. He considered this irresponsible on Target's part and asked to have the girl removed from their marketing lists, which they promptly did.

A month or so later, the father came back to the store to apologize. Apparently, Target had predicted his daughter's pregnancy long before her father was told.

You can see the value of contextual data to the business, and to fathers. There are many kinds of contextual data such as behavioral demographics, psychographic data, and genetic data. All of it provides additional context to your raw operational data. This combination of your raw operational data and the contextual data helps you understand what's going on in the real world, allowing you to predict what will happen in the future.

From an IT standpoint, how do you manage this contextual data on behalf of the business?

1. First, you need to get your raw data in shape. Since you want the data from all across the enterprise pulled together and conformed, and since the statistical analysis is an analytical process, this process will typically take place in your enterprise data warehouse. You will need to invest in the infrastructure and processes to set up this data, as discussed earlier in the information modeling function (page 114).

2. Next, you'll have to decide on some business goals. Increase profitability? Grow subscribership? Get into a new market? These aren't IT decisions, and should instead come from the highest levels of the business. Typically, the corporate executives will set a handful of corporate goals for each year – the things they want the company to focus on in the next year. The departmental business VPs will decide the specific details of how their area of responsibility will support the corporate goals.

3. Then decide which data elements are likely to be predictive. This deserves careful thought. I once worked with a bank in Chicago who purchased information on every one of their customers regarding whether they owned their own home and whether it had a fence. That seemed like an odd thing for a bank to be interested in, but they combined this with a few other raw and contextual data elements to generate a marketing campaign for pre-approved low-interest swimming pool loans. You see, in their area, by law, if you have a swimming pool, you must have a fence around it to prevent neighborhood children from wandering in and coming to harm. The cost of a pool was much more attractive to consumers if it didn't include the overhead of installing a fence. Marketing swimming pool loans only to people who owned homes with fences produced a much higher acceptance rate for the bank's marketing dollar.

4. Purchase and import the contextual data into your analytical repository. Be careful to model this data in a way that it is identifiable, usually in separate tables. Most of the vendors of this

information license the data for a limited time, and for a limited scope. You will not, for example, typically be able to pass the data on to your customers. They would have to license the data independently. When your contract expires, you will need to be able to easily remove the data from your repository. These contractual constraints will require careful consideration in your data model.

5. Once the data is brought into the distribution tier of your enterprise warehouse, you'll need to generate a statistically modeled data mart as a sandbox for your statisticians (see page 121).

Adding knowledge

Knowledge is distinguished from contextual data in that it isn't simply the acquisition of additional data. Instead, it is a layer of information *derived from* your raw and contextual data.

To be clear, knowledge is information, not statistical analysis. Statistical analysis, discussed later, is the process of building, testing, and refining the models, decision trees, and business logic necessary to create knowledge. Knowledge is the operational result of that analytics. The expression "data-rich but information-poor" refers to organizations that have not established the critical components needed to transform their data into actionable insights.

A few examples of this kind of actionable knowledge are listed below. There are many others, including master data management (page 168) and customer segmentation (page 143).

Predictive analytics generate business logic. This analysis will take raw data, contextual data, and other knowledge, and produce a score representing the likelihood of a future event. Predictive models may score customers on likelihood to churn (leave your company). They may score transactions on likelihood of being fraudulent activity. They may score the likelihood of a certain customer to purchase a certain product. They may score the risk of an insured member to develop a given health condition.

The actual production of the predictive modeling business logic is the analytics function, which IT must support on behalf of the business. But once a predictive model is accepted as valid, IT will likely be asked to "operationalize" that business logic and store the resulting scores. These scores are the knowledge; producing the predictive model is the analytics.

The software used to create the model is seldom the same as the software used to operationalize it. A data scientist may use statistical analysis software in a lengthy, complex process using massive amounts of computational resources before arriving at a model that seems to work. The model, in the end, may be a simple calculation based solely on one or two predictive variable. The *likelihood-of-fraud score* on a credit card transaction might be as simple as "three times the transaction amount squared plus one third the distance in miles from the last transaction." Totally made that up, but regression models produce exactly that sort of formula.

Regression models like this result in a formula where you simply plug in the variables. Though hard to create, they are very easy to implement, turning your raw and contextual data into knowledge. Other types of models are much harder to operationalize. Neural nets, for example, are notorious for being almost as difficult to score each night as the model was to create in the first place. We try to avoid techniques like this, if possible, due to the problems of operationalizing them.

However, sometimes the best model is one of these difficult-to-implement techniques. If the business value outweighs the cost of implementation, then you implement it. IT exists to support the business.

Fortunately, neural nets are considered risky even by data scientists, because they're black boxes. With other techniques, you can examine the resulting formula and see how it might make sense, but with neural nets, the inner workings are non-intuitive. There's a story of a neural net model that was trained by the military to score the likelihood of artillery being present on a satellite photo. They showed the engine many photos of an area with no artillery present. The next day they rolled a bunch of tanks into the area and took another set of pictures. The neural net began to produce extremely accurate scores regarding whether each photo it was shown contained a tank or not. Fortunately, the analysts did some more testing, which the algorithm completely failed. It turns out that the first day (without tanks) was quite sunny, and the second day (with tanks) was overcast. Unbeknownst to the analysts, what they had modeled was an algorithm to predict the presence of cloud cover in a satellite photo, not the presence of artillery. This turned out not to be nearly as useful.

Another class of knowledge isn't a prediction of the future, but rather an analysis of the most effective thing you can do today to change that future prediction. You may want to lower the predicted risk of future churn, or you might want to raise the predicted score of the likelihood of a future product purchase.

Predictive models predict what will happen. Treatment effectiveness scores predict the most effective thing to do about it.

This is actually much more complicated than you might think. Different customers may churn for different reasons, in which case the best prevention treatment will likely be different for each. The most effective thing you can do to provide product sales lift will differ by customer and by product.

These treatment effectiveness models are useful in every industry, but are of particular interest in the healthcare industry, where they're known as evidence-based practices. Imagine the value of an analytical model that scored the most effective cancer treatment for a given individual!

Analyzing information

In Dustin Hoffman's breakthrough movie, *The Graduate*, a self-righteous Los Angeles businessman takes aside the baby-faced Benjamin Braddock, played by Hoffman, and declares, "I just want to say one word to you – just one word – 'plastics.'" That movie came out in 1967. In 2009, the New York Times printed an article titled, *For Today's Graduate, Just One Word: Statistics*.

Analyzing information is critical to the business. This book isn't a treatise on how to analyze data. Rather, we want to discuss how IT can best support the business function of analyzing data as part of an enterprise-level information management program.

Supporting data analytics mostly involves IT functions discussed elsewhere. You have to collect the raw operational data from across the enterprise, make sure it conforms to format and quality standards, append relevant contextual data, and create a statistical model. From the IT side, that'll cover most of what you need to do.

One thing that must be added, however, is hardened process.

The term **DevOps** was introduced in 2008 to describe the operational nature of software development; how it flows through several states which differ from one methodology to another, but all include a cycle of continual feedback and improvement. The term **DataOps** was introduced in 2015 to describe *the application of DevOps and continuous delivery principles to improve the data quality and reduce the cycle time of data analytics.*[24] It includes the statistical process control common to lean manufacturing techniques, meaning that it is automated and monitored for measurable data quality and business value that drives continual process improvement.

Supporting the analytics functions of the business *doesn't* mean that IT takes over all the analysis. It means that IT is providing a solid platform to support the analytics done by the business. IT may well use analytics internally to improve IT processes like data quality, but analytics is a primarily business function that IT supports.

Granted, the results of business analytics (which can include fraud models, churn risk scores, profitability scores, next-product-to-buy predictions, and customer segmentation) are almost always given to IT to support as the knowledge generation portion of the data enhancement functions mentioned earlier. But those knowledge-creating processes aren't business analytics; they are the *results* of analytics. True analysis is the discovery, validation, and improvement of the models used to generate all that knowledge. That discovery, validation, and continual improvement all require information, information IT must make available to the business in the manner the analytical tools need.

Information analytics is critical to your business. If your IT department isn't supporting this business function, you are not doing a good job of supporting your business. Make sure there is an analytics function on the information lifecycle of your functional framework, where it will receive the visibility necessary to generate the long term strategies, roadmaps, policies, standards, processes and roles that it deserves.

Delivering information

So far in our information lifecycle, we've been talking mostly about the IT functions and information infrastructure necessary to bring information into a repository and enhance it. These are functions IT needs to perform for the business, but the end goal isn't to simply *collect* and *store* information. The end goal is to *deliver* information where it can be used – the right information to the right place at the right time. This is the information delivery function, and it's a much more complex function to manage than you might imagine. Think of your IT infrastructure as a restaurant, with a *front-of-the-house* and a *back-of-the-house*. You can't run a restaurant without the kitchen, but that isn't the part your customers interact with. The part you see, the whole point of a restaurant, is the front of the house where your customers consume the food created in the kitchen.

A pure operational application exists only to *maintain data*. The only data presentation it includes is to display a record for potential maintenance. However, very few applications are purely operational. Most applications include some sort of data reporting functionality. Analytical applications such as data marts and data warehouses are very focused on *data delivery*.

[24] *From DevOps to DataOps*, Andy Palmer, May 7, 2015. http://bit.ly/2hedham.

Data delivery covers quite a broad array of functionality. As with everything else, this complexity is easier to manage if you combine the details into similar groups. I like to break down information delivery into business intelligence and decision support.

- Business Intelligence (BI) is delivering information so that the recipient can make decisions, and includes:

  o Executive dashboards
  o Middle management data discovery and mining
  o Front line operational reports
  o Power user ad-hoc query
  o Application interfaces, such as extract files and data web services

- Decision support is delivering already-made decisions to the recipient, and includes:

  o Campaign management
  o Real time decisions

So you see, at the highest level, I have grouped the data delivery functions into those that deliver information, and those that deliver decisions. You can divide your data delivery functions however you see fit, but this is what works for me.

This outline may appear to be a listing of applications, but here, in the data domain, our primary intention is to discuss the information that supports the applications. We'll only wander over into discussion of the applications themselves to the extent necessary to understand the information we are delivering. Evaluating, purchasing, configuring, and maintaining these software products will fall under the application domain.

Business intelligence solutions (delivering data)

Business intelligence (BI) solutions deliver information. The information can take many forms, and the recipient can use the information in many different ways. Decisions will be made using the data, but the data itself is not a decision.

Executive dashboards

Executive dashboards, including balanced scorecards and key performance indicators, are graphical user interfaces that display key business metrics at a glance. The use of the word *dashboard* is intentional; this is a place where that the driver (of the company, as it were) can glance down, see all the important information, and then return their eyes to the road. These tools aren't mean to contain grids full of data that the executives pore over for hours.

The biggest factor to consider when spinning up executive dashboards will be whether to use a best of breed data visualization product, or whether to purchase an integrated suite of products. Both make sense under different conditions, but I find that the decision between these two is often made for the wrong reason.

The advantage of a best-of-breed solution is that it is faster and easier to implement and has the best visualization options. However, that comes at a cost of being a niche solution. If the executive ever wants to click on part of the dashboard and drill down and down into more and more detail, the solution may not deliver or be pushed to its limits. Drilling down into fine detail is possible, but it isn't fast or easy to develop, and it's not what the tool was designed for. Typically, these drill paths are not reusable, and are not high performance.

An integrated suite of business intelligence tools won't have all the bells and whistles of the best of breed, and the initial dashboard development may take a quite a bit more time and expertise. Regardless, these suites of products are all based on the same underlying metadata platform, so that drilling from a dashboard to an operational report is seamless and leverages reusable components.

Said another way, best-of-breed solutions provide value quickly, but as scope increases and more functionality is demanded, there is more and more custom development and the return on investment decreases. The integrated suite solution requires a lot of investment up front, making it very slow to provide initial value, but that value accelerates over time as the infrastructure tying the various products in the suite together is completed, so the return on investment increases over time.

Either approach may be correct under different circumstances. Ideally, the executives shouldn't be drilling through to detail. They should be glancing at the dashboard for a second and returning their eyes to the road. If you have executives who can avoid the temptation to mine the data, a best-of-breed solution is far faster and cheaper to implement and yields prettier results. If you're offering the dashboards to a captive audience in a business intelligence solution that you can control, best-of-breed makes sense. However, if your target audience has the curiosity and power to demand drill-through into detail, you're probably better off going with an integrated suite of BI tools.

Unfortunately, that's seldom how we actually make the choice between these two approaches. Typically, if the business is in charge of making the decision or is frustrated with the service they are getting from IT and decide to build out their own solution, they will go with the best-of-breed. It's fast, simple, cheap, and pretty. The business typically isn't focused on the long-term strategy for the software infrastructure. They just want a business solution.

On the other hand, if IT is in charge, they will typically choose the suite of products, due to the ease of integration and support. While the integrated suites take more time and IT expertise to initially set up, that's usually not the problem. The problem, more often than not, is that IT sets up these suites without involving the business. The solution becomes an internal IT science project rather than a business solution. In my experience, the reason for the poor track record of the integrated reporting solution approach has nothing to do with the tool itself, and everything to do with the way the project was managed.

Best-of-breed solutions succeed because they are designed by the business to meet the business needs. Integrated suite solutions often fail because they're designed by IT and do not meet the business need. Using a best-of-breed approach carries the risk that you'll be asked to grow the solution in ways that the infrastructure does not support. Using an integrated suite approach carries the risk that you'll spend a lot of time and a lot of money and end up with something that doesn't meet the business need because the business wasn't integrated into the project from the beginning.

Middle management data discovery and mining

This is the kind of reporting where we use data discovery. Executives don't have the time or the job role to be playing with the data all day long. Front line managers need to run their operational reports and get back to their assigned jobs. It's the middle managers whose job role it is to have their finger on the heartbeat of the data, looking for trends and anomalies, mining the information to discover things we don't already know.

Typically, the toolset used for this uses a hierarchical, slice-and-dice, pivot-table reporting technique called **cube viewing**. These are typically built over dimensional models, with the ability to swap different dimensions in and out, drill up and down dimensional hierarchies, and look at different measures all on the fly, all without writing new reports. These tools are generally referred to as **ROLAP** if they store their data in relational database tables, and **MOLAP** if they build an external, proprietary file called a micro-cube (R for relational, M for micro-cube; ROLAP and MOLAP). There are other forms of data discover tools, but these MOLAP and ROLAP cube-viewing tools are by far the most widespread.

Whatever your reporting solution is, *at least 80 percent of new report development requests should be self-serve*[25]. If every new report has to go through IT for development, then IT will *always* be a bottleneck to the business. The point of this book is to manage IT complexity on behalf of the business. The business needs a self-serve solution. A self-service solution still requires support – it is not self-sufficient. But that support is decoupled from the end user. Most of the effort is supporting the solution, and very little effort is needed to support the actual business user.

One of the easiest ways to provide self-serve is to create one or more vetted ROLAP or MOLAP cubes where the business can slice and dice all the most common measures on all the common grouping attributes such as customer, location, product, and time. Then create a handful of general-purpose detail reports for middle managers, allowing them to drill through from anywhere in the cube. Using a cube helps ensure correct assembly of data. Using a handful of detailed drill-through reports on top of this is a great substitution for writing hundreds of separate reports. If you think about it, most business reports are either aggregate counts and amounts against various combinations of filters and groupings, or are detailed rows that meet certain filtering conditions. With the cube, you can pre-create all the allowable filters and hierarchies as dimensions and show the aggregate sums and counts (measures) at any level and combination. Then, using this result as a filter, allow a drill through to pull the associated customer detail, product detail, and sales detail. Typically, the cube is in the access tier, and the detail reports run against the distribution tier. A good initial list of detailed drill-through reports is a one-line-per-item and a one-page-per-item report for the major concept in each subject area.

This is where the value of having an integrated suite of products really shines. In an integrated suite of tools, you don't have to put all the detail in your cube-viewing solution. That would make extremely large, poor performing cubes that contain a great deal of information unrelated to slicing and dicing. Are you really ever going to slice and dice on a person's middle initial? Likewise, using this approach, if you need to add more detail, you have to redesign and rebuild your entire reporting solution. The cube should only include the measures you're aggregating and the dimensional attributes you're using to sort and filter. Everything else is poor architecture, slowing down your performance.

An integrated solution will allow you to dynamically slice and dice your counts and amounts in the cube using any combination of filters and hierarchies you have built into the solution, until you discover something interesting, then, without writing all the filters down, signing out of that tool, and signing on to an operational reporting tool, you can just right click, select one of any number of detail operational reports, and "drill through" to that report, carrying all the current filtering with you automatically. The

---

[25] https://bit.ly/2uxmeBQ.

detail report runs with the same filter that you were using at the point you left the cube. Both the cube viewing tool and the operational reporting tool all use the same metadata infrastructure, and drill seamlessly back and forth. Even the dashboarding tool runs on this same infrastructure, and can drill through to operational reports or cubes.

Consider this example: An executive glances at their dashboard of KPIs, and notices that the sales metric is now in yellow, frowny-face status. They right-click on the graphic, and *drill through* to a cube view that shows, perhaps, sales by date and channel. This view clearly shows lower than expected numbers for this month for the direct sales channel. The executive *drills down* (expands) the direct sales channel and finds that the problem is in the corporate agent channel, and another drill down reveals that the particular problem lies with Bob Smith. The executive can then right click on this month's numbers for Bob, and select to *drill through* to a detail listing report showing detail information about Bob's sales for this month. On that screen, the executive sees a massive return of products originally sold to ACME corp. The integrated suite of tools allows you to connect the dots between many applications, seamlessly integrating them into one business solution.

Not all enterprise reporting tool suites have this level of integration. Virtually every vendor in this space has built part of their portfolio through acquisitions; the application integration may not be smooth. You'll need to check carefully whether the vendors you're looking at support drill through. Not drill up and down a hierarchy, but actually drill through to another report, passing the filters along automatically.

One of the nice features of the cube-viewing products is that you don't actually have to start at the top of the cube every time you enter. If you slice and dice and drill down to, say, a location in the cube showing some rolling year-over-year product sales by region and state on the left, and product line across the top, with color coding for significant gains and losses, you can save that combination as an entry-point, giving it a "report" name. Next month, instead of starting at the top of the cube and performing that slice and dice again, you can just "enter" the cube at the position you saved, viewing the same information with updated data.

This is a very powerful technique that can be used to provide self-service reporting to middle management, who are typically the largest segment of new report requests. You don't expect an executive to be writing reports or dashboards. The front-line managers would love to play with the data, but you want to prevent that and keep them focused on their assigned task, giving them just the information they need to perform their job. Power users only need a reporting tool – they'll write their own reports without your help. Those internal and external middle managers are the users who most need a self-serve reporting solution. If you want to serve your business well, don't design an infrastructure where IT is going to be a bottleneck. Your strategic vision for information delivery should include self-serve reporting solutions.

Front line operational reporting

The front-line resources would love to have pretty dashboards, and would spend all day playing with reporting cubes, but you don't want them doing that. You want to provide them the information they need to do their jobs; a list of loans to process, a list of high-risk patients to call, a list of sales targets they need to meet. Give them exactly what they need in a canned report to keep them focused on their daily assignment, without providing overhead or distractions. Analysis doesn't fall to these front-line managers; they perform the detailed tasks that keep the company running.

Most front line operational reports don't differ too much from the fan-fold green-bar printouts of my early years. These reports tend to contain detailed, rather than summary information. The data is quite often served from operational systems, or an operationally-modeled distribution tier of an analytical system, rather than from analytically-modeled data. Audit and compliance reports are often generated as detailed, row-oriented reports.

It's very important, of course, that the different business intelligence solutions, the dashboards, cubes, and operational reports, are all based on the same underlying data, giving the same answers, no matter which tool is used. This is especially important for calculated fields such as net sales. Does that include rentals? Does it include replacements for damaged equipment? By building your entire reporting suite over one consistent infrastructure level, you can ensure that everyone is interpreting business requests consistently throughout the enterprise.

Power user ad-hoc query

In every company, you're going to have those special few power users who just need to get in, get their hands on the raw data, and do what needs to be done. You want to provide a solution that removes any impediment to them doing their work. These information assets belong to the business, not to IT; don't put up unnecessary walls between the business and their information.

I once installed a data warehouse product at a company whose internal departments were set up on a cost center model, where each business unit charged for its services and was required to demonstrate profitability. The enterprise data warehouse department, in an effort to remain profitable, required all other departments to submit report requests to them, rather than access the data directly. While the technological solution was very impressive, the business model made the unit very ineffective at meeting business needs, especially the needs of the power users who needed direct access to the data.

For these power users, the work will be unpredictable; different every day. Some days they'll be doing research for legal, other days they'll be working on a special project for the VP, and other times they will be researching a data anomaly. If their work is the same every day, they aren't a power user; they are a front line operational resource.

These power users typically have very broad security access and know the data better than anyone else in the company, including you. You know who these people are, and you know that if the workforce were ever cut drastically, these would be the last people standing. They are that valuable to the business. Make sure that your data delivery functions include the tools these special people need to do their jobs. Remember how valuable they are to the business. If one of you has to go, it's not going to be them!

Application extracts

Make sure your data delivery strategy contains the infrastructure necessary to deliver file extracts to both internal and external destinations. The data model, service level agreements, and security concerns are just as important for these extracts as for traditional reports, even though applications rather than people will probably consume these files.

Typically, extracts are at a detail level, not summary information. Usually, detail information is best served by an operational or normalized model rather than an analytical one. However, there are reasons why you might want to create a data mart for application extracts anyway:

- The extracts may need to be point in time, periodic data, such as monthly snapshots after each month's books are closed. Unless you can guarantee all your extracts will run before the first transaction in the next period occurs, you may want to create a static area from which to extract data.

- You may wish to stage your extracts into tables that reflect the extract format in your repository, so that you have them readily available for query and analysis. If there is a problem with a file you generate, you don't have to load it; you already have it in a table.

- Ideally, you will be able to mandate "standard" extracts rather than dozens of similar, but different extracts. If you can manage this, then you may want to dump the data into a generic extract area first, so that you can reuse it many times, pulling the subset of records needed for each specific extract. This way, you really only manage one set of extract logic. Corrections and enhancements are much less complicated with this infrastructure.

The approach just described uses a modeling technique of simply building the data for each extract in table form for retention, reuse, and extract analysis. You may be asked to build some more general tables that are not extracts themselves, but sources from which extracts can be taken. This is normally a poor idea, because extracts are at a detail level and are best served by an operational model. It doesn't make much sense to take data from one operational model and put it in another operational model just for the extracts. That second model may be a small subset at first, but it will inevitably grow over time, and become essentially a copy of the first operational model. End users will begin using it for purposes other than extracting data, and will begin asking for modifications and enhancements to suit their needs. Just say no.

If you do create a data mart specifically for file extracts, you should limit it to file extract functions. Other kinds of data delivery are better served with different modeling techniques.

Data as a Service (DaaS)

One objective of the information domain is to define a *system of record* for every data element, and to access that source whenever possible. You do *not* serve the business well by making multiple copies of the data and sending them all over the company. This practice:

- Ties up the network bandwidth
- Consumes Direct-Access Storage Device (DASD) and other resources
- Makes it inevitable that different copies will be out of sync and yield different results to the same questions
- Requires many different developers in many different departments to write many different access interfaces, inevitably with different logic
- Exposes dramatically increased risk of security breaches

Instead, your data delivery solution needs to include the capability to expose its Data as a Service (DaaS). This eliminates the need for permanent copies of the data instantiated throughout the company, with all the issues described above. We previously discussed DaaS services as part of the enterprise service bus in the exchange layer of your corporate information model (page 108).

Each repository should only expose the data for which it is the system of record. When taken as a whole, there is only one system of record for each data element, though they may be spread out across the company infrastructure. In some cases, there will be multiple applications containing similar, but unique information, two different loan systems at a financial institution, or three different billing systems at an insurance company. In this case, the same service may actually be instantiated more than once, but for different subsets of the enterprise data. For any detail data value the business may need, there should be only one, well-defined system of record where you will go to look it up.

Even analytical systems can be the system of record for certain kinds of data. An analytical system might be where the master customer index is created, uniquely identifying a customer across all your systems. It might be the system of record for profitability scores, risk scores, or propensity scores. It might be the system of record for customer segmentation. Any of these might be exposed to the infrastructure as a service from an analytical repository.

That said, any component that exposes services is operational, and will inevitably require much higher availability than is currently architected into most analytical systems, complete with failover and redundancy. As the wall between analytical and operational systems continues to fall, this distinction may one day disappear. For now, you will probably need to build a downstream, high-availability DaaS data mart under your analytical repository. It's here where the information necessary to support the DaaS services is housed. A separate physical machine should host that data mart, if possible. This analytical information DaaS data mart isn't the system of record, but it is the system of access. This is still a much better solution than bulk copying the analytical data all over the company infrastructure. If you *must* have a separate system of access than the system of record, then have *only one* system of access. In effect, the DaaS server is an operational data store (ODS) for your analytical repository.

Decision support (delivering decisions)

Collecting, cleansing, and delivering data and knowledge in the form of business intelligence solutions is the low hanging fruit of the information delivery function. With BI tools, it's still up to the end user to interpret the knowledge and decide on an action. However, there's a growing class of products that automate the decision-making process, thereby delivering actionable information directly to the business. Recent advancements in artificial intelligence make this an especially exciting area to be working in these days.

Of course, you have to have valuable information to make good decisions. The data needs to be complete, accurate, timely, and accessible. You can't jump very far into decision support until you've done a good deal of grunt work to build quality data.

However, once you have good data and good context, the possibilities are endless! If you aren't involved in delivering decisions, you've built a Cadillac to drive to the mailbox. You need to get that machine out on the road and open her up.

Today, almost all decision support is model-based. Mathematical modeling has been around long before computers, but the number-crunching capability of the computer has certainly made widespread decisions support possible.

There are basically three types of models: descriptive, predictive, and prescriptive.

Descriptive models

Descriptive models don't assign predictive scores, but instead summarize what has happened in the past. They are useful for summarizing and categorizing complex data in order to make it understandable by human beings.

There is an endless array of descriptive analytics available. One example is a process known as segmentation. Customer segmentation separates your customer base into groups that have exhibited similar behaviors, since they can generally be treated similarly. It's easy to talk about a *segment of one* (i.e. customized treatment for every customer, not groups of customers), but most business processes are still designed around groups of people. In a sense, segmentation is also predictive, because you are segmenting things based on your assumption that they will behave similarly to the rest of their assigned segment in the future. Although the end purpose is predictive, the analysis itself only looks at what has already happened in the past.

I once worked for a large company during a major customer segmentation initiative. After the segmentation was complete, everyone on the team eagerly looked up their own records to see how we'd been bucketed. Of all the people on the team, I was the only one to be bucketed in the *Active Gray* segment. I was in my early 30's at the time, but age wasn't actually part of the model – only behavior. According to this model, I exhibited behaviors that put me in a marketing segment with healthy retired people who were technology-adverse but traveled around a lot. I guess my entertainment preference of reading, combined with my hobbies of blacksmithing and woodworking makes me a throwback from another era.

A descriptive model is contextual knowledge, not a decision. In theory, someone still has to use that knowledge to make a decision. In my example above, my segmentation resulted in me automatically receiving many product offers designed for *my* active gray customer segment.

Predictive models

Predictive models assign a rank or score to data based on the likelihood of some future event. Predictive models are just scores, not decisions, but they are very effective tools for driving decisions. A marketing department might use predictive models to assign a "likelihood to buy" score to each customer for each product, which can be used to automate marketing decisions.

A heath management organization may use predictive models to generate disease risk scores or compliance risk scores in order to automate treatment and outreach decisions. I was once discussing predictive modeling with a peer at another health insurance company. He told me that they had found in their market that there was a strong negative correlation between boat ownership and dental insurance purchases. In his marketing area, people who fish don't buy dental insurance. I'm not sure how to explain that, but that's exactly the power of predictive models. They wouldn't be terribly useful if all they predicted was the obvious, common sense stuff. It's the non-intuitive predictions that are really valuable.

Years ago, a statistical analysis software vendor advertised their product with a picture of a grown man in a grocery store, wearing nothing but a large diaper, carrying a case of beer. Apparently, they had found that beer was much more of an impulse purchase to someone entering the store to buy diapers. That's why they always put the milk in the back of the store, because you "have" to buy milk, and putting it in the back forces you to walk past display after display of likely impulse purchases. Anyway, they found that placing beer and diapers close together dramatically increased the purchase of beer. I checked this week in my local grocery store, and yes, the diapers are one row over from the beer. The power of predictive modeling.[26]

Prescriptive models

Prescriptive models take the next step and generate decisions. This is a bit misleading, because most "decision" models are really just one or more predictive models with another layer added to convert the score to a decision.

A predictive model for customer churn (i.e. a rate of leaving the company) may be automatically fed into a discount or upgrade offer, converting the prediction into a decision. Modern decision models will start with the prediction, plus a large number of known operational data, contextual data and derived knowledge information attributes, and model the effectiveness of many different potential actions. Some customers might react more favorably to a bill discount, while other customers might be much more inclined to stay if offered a free upgrade.

A likelihood-to-buy *predictive model* may give a customer scores for many products, but the most likely product to buy may have a far lower profit than the second most likely product. The *prescriptive model* must balance the *likelihood to buy* scores with factors like product profitability, and then recommend which score to act upon.

Decision models help predict which action on the company's part will give the desired reaction. Regardless of model type, every new model must first be created and validated. Once that is achieved, they can be made operational.

The initial development of a model is a very resource intensive operation. With rare exceptions,[27] models are not developed on the fly during the operational process. The data scientists who work with these statistical tools are very valuable, highly-compensated resources, often with advanced degrees. You don't want them spending large amounts of time extracting and massaging data before they even begin analyzing it. Provide an area where data is pre-built for these resources, in a model appropriate for the work they need to perform. See *Statistical models* on page 121 for more information about modeling for statistical analysis.

The operationalizing of the models, or scoring, typically takes place in your operational model and doesn't usually require the statistical analysis tool to execute. It takes very powerful statistical analysis software to come up with a linear regression model, but once the formula is produced, almost any software can be used to calculate the model output (see page 119). A few modeling techniques such as neural networks require more specialized tools, but for that very reason, neural networks are seldom the first choice if other modeling techniques can be found to give similar results.

---

[26] There are many different versions of this story, but it does appear to be based in fact. Thomas Blischok was a leading a team of data analysts working for NCR/Teradata on contract to Osco Drug in the 1990's. The team found that the two were often purchased together between 5:00 and 7:00 PM. NCR later used the story in trade journal advertising as a vivid image of the power of analytics. http://bit.ly/2mUmkMU.

[27] Google actually creates and validates models in production. New response ranking and advertisement selection algorithms are put into production immediately, and tested on a select user segment. At any one point in time, Google may be testing many different algorithms at once, each on different population segments. Those algorithms that provide better results are retained. Most of us though, create and validate models in a test environment, not in production.

Campaign management

Campaign management is a classic form of delivering decisions. This has been around forever. I imagine accountants in Dickens' day using quill pens to add up numbers in ledger books to generate campaign lists. Sales force automation is a form of campaign management, generating lists of likely candidate leads for a specific action.

Campaign management is a complex practice, involving segmentation, predictive modeling, control groups, and some way of tying back the campaign response into the model for revision. One of the hardest parts of campaign management, believe it or not, is tracking the response to an offer, and getting that response, positive or negative, back into the campaign model as feedback to adjust future models.

All the deep statistical stuff is hard, but there are really smart people and really good statistical software packages that handle that part. If you can't get the responses back to the campaign, though, you're cutting those smart people and their software off at the knees. You're asking them to fly blind.

To some degree, you can assume responses, but that isn't very accurate. You can generate an email campaign for a product purchase, and assume that if anyone on the campaign list buys the product, it was because of your wonderful email – but they may have never opened it. After all, the campaign list was probably people who were very likely to buy the product anyway. However, if you give some kind of tracking number in your offer (for instance, "enter discount code CAMPAIGN123 at checkout for free shipping"), then you can be much more certain about the effectiveness of your campaign.

It's up to your information architects, working with the business and application architects, to design an infrastructure that will allow campaign responses to be tracked and fed back to the campaign management statisticians and software. Closing the loop on campaign management function requires an enterprise effort across all architectural domains.

I once read an inspiring little book called *212° the Extra Degree,*[28] which talked about the difference between water at 211 degrees (Fahrenheit) and water at 212. At 211, it's just hot water, but at 212 it boils, producing power than can drive a locomotive across the country. One degree extra makes all the difference. Putting the architecture in place to track and return campaign responses to the campaign management system is that one extra degree that makes all the difference.

Real time decisions

Real time decisions are essentially a very fast campaign cycle, combining real-time information with information you already knew to generate on-the-fly decisions. Earlier (page 92), I gave an example of a real-time decision proof of concept developed by a single developer in less than two weeks that saved the company 6 million dollars in expenses in its first two months of operations. That's powerful stuff! That's IT supporting the business in a powerful way.

The hard part about managing the data for real-time decisioning is that analytical data hasn't traditionally been integrated back into the operational world. In fact, that separation has been, in the past, considered best practice. Very high walls existed to keep the analytical processes from impacting the operational world. You never wanted your operational processes to be dependent on intermediate analytical steps.

But the world is changing. The wall between operational and analytical is falling (page 92). One of the first breaches is real-time decisions.

28 212° the Extra Degree, Sam Parker, May 1 2005, the Walk the Talk Company, Dallas, TX.

In order to provide the IT infrastructure to support this function, the analytical data has to rise to the availability (failover and redundancy) and performance necessary to integrate with the operational world. There are techniques to bring your entire analytical infrastructure up to this standard. Companies like Amazon, eBay, and Google are delivering operational analytics on a mind-numbing scale.

Most of us aren't quite prepared for that. Even if we had the expertise, our business models wouldn't support the accompanying expense. Setting up a real-time analytics platform on the scale of Amazon would be a fantastic project, but you most likely don't work for Amazon.

For most of us, the best answer is a hybrid environment. You have very traditional operational applications designed for high performance and high availability transactions, and you have very traditional analytical applications designed for batch processing. You can build a downstream enterprise data mart as an operational platform to expose analytically derived knowledge as operational services. With this platform in place, you can implement real-time models that combine real-time operational information with batch-generated analytical information, scoring them using a pre-generated model, and make a decision.

There are commercial software packages that will host this real-time scoring for you, and even adjust the model dynamically over time based on responses. You can also choose, as we did, to dip your toes in the water with a POC and some hard-coded rules until the value of this functionality is more widely recognized. From an information standpoint, you'll need to be able to support transactional access to all the necessary data, even if the system of record is an analytical system. You don't want to send extracts of all your analytical data to be loaded locally by these systems. You always want to access the data at the system of record if possible, rather than proliferating copies of data all over the place in order to give the necessary performance.

Ensuring the quality of information

The next IT function in the information lifecycle is data quality. Data quality should be an enterprise initiative, not a departmental one. The business case for cleansing data could be negligible within the scope of the application that initially collects data. But the value of the data is the value to the enterprise, not the value to one application. The application owner will not have insight or incentive to care much about the downstream consumers of the data they create. This is why it's so important to have an influential executive sponsor who will support the functional framework at the enterprise level.

Dimensions of data quality
The *dimensions* of data quality are all the different functions necessary to ensure the quality of your data. I use the term *data* rather than *information* because the quality of your information pyramid is largely dependent on the quality of the raw and contextual data information tiers. Knowledge is derived from raw and contextual data. Decisions are built on all three.

If you run an internet search on the phrase "dimensions of data quality," odds are that on the first page of results, you'll get at least four or five different lists, each with a different number of data quality dimensions. I've seen lists as small as three, and as large as twenty-three. I think this is due both to the level of detail the lists go into, and to differences of opinion regarding whether functions like performance and security are data quality dimensions. Clearly, there's no universally accepted definitive list of data quality dimensions.

The base premise of this book is that you have to organize your functions into something that's conceptually simple to grasp. If you can't visualize the concept, you can't manage it. In keeping with that line of thought, you're going to need to create order out of the chaos of these data quality functions.

You can do this any way that works for you, provided it is easily manageable. I certainly can't fit 23 top-level data quality dimensions in my head at once. You can't manage that many peer functions without imposing some higher-level organization to reduce the number of items on the top-level list. I don't believe it's useful to have more than five data quality functions under the data quality functional area. You can break those down into as many sublevels as you want, but I would try to group them into no more than five top-level functions

When I look at the various lists out there, some of the data quality dimensions in them are ambiguous and overlapping, and some aren't what I would consider data quality functions at all. In an enterprise-level functional framework, I don't think it's wise to bury functions like security underneath the data quality heading. Honestly, many of the lists appear to be arbitrary. Other lists are championed by vendors, and are based on the tools they are trying to sell. The proliferation of different lists doesn't make me confident that I've got all the bases covered. I need some kind of intuitive organization that makes the gaps obvious.

I think most of those data quality functions are useful, but I prefer to impose the following organization structure to them:

- **Collection Quality**. All the things we do to make sure we captured the data accurately and completely from the source.

- **Validation Quality**. All the things we do to make sure that the data is reasonable for what it is supposed to represent in the real world.

- **Verification Quality**. All the things we do to make sure that the data is correct for what it is actually represents in the real world.

- **Integration Quality**. All the things we do to make sure we integrate the data into our repository in a way that is meaningful.

- **Delivery Quality**. All the things we do to make sure the data is accessible by the right people at the right time.

This structure makes sense to me *because it represents the flow of the data: we collect it, clean it up, integrate it, and deliver it.* This is, if you will, a data quality lifecycle. All the detail data quality functions on all those lists seem to me to belong under one of these headings, or they don't belong under data quality at all. This organization makes it easy to grasp and manage data quality at a high level without being bogged down in details. If I have a new data quality function I want to add, it should be pretty clear which of these top-level data quality functions it will fall under.

This organization applies to both operational and analytical repositories. One may collect data from a user interface or service call, and the other from a batch file, but data quality is data quality. Some data quality functions, such as latency, aren't as relevant to operational apps, but even that is changing as our user interfaces spread out into a distributed internet of things.

Here's an attempt to file many of the common data quality dimensions under this organization structure:

- Collection

    o Integrity/Accuracy/Fidelity. The data values we brought in, right or wrong, match the source.
    o Completeness. The data we brought in represents all the data on the source.

- Validation. The data is valid for the field, mostly done at the field or row level.

    o Data type validation. Does a date field contain alpha characters?
    o Pattern matching. US individual social security numbers follow the pattern "NNN-NN-NNNN" and cannot begin with "000" or "666".

- Verification. Is the data correct? This isn't about whether the captured email address is formatted correctly (i.e. with one "@" sign and no spaces), but whether it is actually the correct and still valid email address for the correct person in the real world today. This is much more difficult than validation and often requires specialized tools.

- Integration. Mostly done across multiple rows or tables.

    o Consistency. Is there a way to identify all the information for one customer, account, and product across all tables and rows for consistent reporting?
    o Conformed. Are all source-specific values conformed/transformed into a common set of codes?
    o Balancing. Do the sales numbers received from the customer account system match the numbers posted to the general ledger?
    o Uniqueness. Do two different people share the same SSN?
    o Referential Integrity. All codes used on the business tables must exist in the reference tables. All business child table rows (i.e. order lines) must have business parent table rows (i.e. order headers). Years ago, we enforced referential integrity only in development environments due to performance impact, but now it's common practice to do so in production as well. The overhead of referential integrity in most major databases is quite small.
    o Cardinality. Every purchase order header record must have one or more purchase order line records. Very few lists contain cardinality, because it is often considered the other half of referential integrity, saying, for example, that a parent row must have one or more child rows; that an order header must have at least one order line.

- Delivery

    o Latency/Timeliness. Is the information available to the end users when they need it, before it becomes too old to be relevant?

o   Accessibility/Ease-of-use. Can the end user get to the data easily, or are there walls between the information and the business that needs it?

o   Availability. Is the data actually available when the user needs it, or are there large windows of unavailability?

Undoubtedly, you'll find that some of your sacred data quality functions are missing from this list. Perhaps you're right. Quality is, to a large degree, in the eye of the beholder. Data quality doesn't mean *perfect* data, it means data that is *fit for use*. That definition will vary from business to business and from data element to data element within your data model. That said, I intentionally omitted a few functions that appear on many lists:

- **Relevance and Utility**. Everything IT does should provide business value. That's true of data, but is just as true of software and hardware. I absolutely agree that data should be useful, but I don't consider that primarily a data quality issue. I consider it instead to be the core purpose of IT – to support the business. You should identify irrelevant data elements during the business requirements function of the software development lifecycle. They should never make it into the model in order to become a data quality issue. If a data element becomes irrelevant over time, then that data element is ready for the information end-of-life function, not a data quality function.

- **Compliance**. Like relevance, I consider compliance critically important, but I don't consider it to belong under data quality. Information compliance mandates are usually covered by information security functions and information retention/end-of-life functions.

- **Time Stamped**. If the business would be best supported by including a time stamp, that's a business requirements and modeling issue – not a data quality issue.

- **Fit for use**. Data quality is relative. There's no such thing, on any large scale, as "perfect" data. For every single one of your data quality functions, you will need to develop a way to measure the quality. You can't manage what you don't measure. Your measurement must define what's acceptable and what isn't. *Fitness* isn't a separate data quality function; it's part of the definition and measurement of *every* data quality function, and something that's subject to change over time as various pieces of information become more or less critical to the business. It shouldn't be necessary to say that the acceptable level of data quality in any of the data quality functions is determined by the business, not by IT. *Any effort IT spends doing more than is useful to the business detracts from the value IT is providing*. This is a business, not a science project!

You're free to disagree with me. Judging by that internet search mentioned earlier, I think everyone disagrees with everyone else about data quality functions, so I won't be offended. The point of a functional framework is that it's a framework upon which to hang *your* functions. It is not a mandated list of functions to which you must rigidly adhere. You should consider the ideas proposed here, but you should also consider your unique environment and adapt the functional framework as necessary to help you effectively manage *your* IT on behalf of *your* business.

Profiling/discovery

Data profiling is most often thought of in terms of a data quality tool, but an enterprise data profiling solution should serve many purposes:

- **Data Quality**. Data profiling can be an enormously helpful aid to data quality. There are commercial tools available what will analyze any given data set for patterns, outlier values, and value min and max range. This is especially useful when bringing in new data, to determine the types of quality issues the data contains. With the current state of technology, this deep scan is typically done when the data is initially introduced, and only periodically thereafter. Other edits and processing checks are usually developed based on the findings to execute on an ongoing basis whenever this data is modified or appended. Like predictive models, data quality tools are resource-intensive tools that can suggest an algorithm you may want to consider implementing. Of course, if you want to make that algorithm operational, you'll probably have to look outside the tool despite the vendor's claims.

- **Data Modeling**. Profiling tools should build a data model and data dictionary for the new source that can feed the data modeling function (page 98). Does the data contain nulls? What is the longest value? What is the precision and scale of a currency amount or percentage? What is the complete list of code values? This information can then be mapped to the enterprise logical data model, so that the data and its relationship to other information within the enterprise can be documented, tracked, and researched.

- **Data Security**. Profiling tools should identify the presence of sensitive data that can feed the information security function (page 155). The data security function will have identified labels and categories of sensitive data and decided how that information needs to be protected. Of course, the information cannot be protected unless it is first recognized. A tool that scans existing files and repositories should be able to identify "special" data. A profiling tool can, for example, figure out that the data in a field labeled CLIENT_ID actually looks suspiciously like social security numbers.

Choose a data profiling solution at the enterprise level. It should be able to scan all data sources and physical repositories from different database vendors, as well as flat files and social media feeds. The solution should analyze both structured and unstructured data, and should produce output that can be consumed by all the information lifecycle functions listed above.

Metadata

Ask any data architect what metadata is, and you will almost certainly hear the definition *data about data*. Maybe it's just me, but I don't find that to be a very helpful definition. I'm going to briefly discuss four types of metadata, certainly not an exhaustive list, to try to give some sense of its importance in an increasingly information-centric business.

- Reference tables
- Data glossary
- Data dictionary
- Genealogy

Reference tables

Reference tables are tables containing lists of valid values for codes and keys used in business data, often listed as name/value pairs. A business table might contain a state code populated with the two-character state abbreviations (e.g. AL, AK, AZ). A state reference table would contain a row for each of those two-character codes, with additional information such as the full state name and the FIPS code. Not everyone agrees that reference tables are technically metadata, but those that do justify that stance by saying that the reference tables are data about the codes and keys used in the business table data.

These tables are useful for several purposes.

- **Enforcing referential integrity**. From a data quality standpoint, the references tables allow the data modeler to create referential integrity constraints. In the state code example above, the modeler can create a constraint on the business table specifying that no value can be inserted into the state abbreviation field on the business table unless that value exists on the reference table. With this constraint defined and enabled, the database will reject bad data with a referential integrity constraint violation error. You don't have to depend on the source to send only valid values, or for the user interface application developer to cleanse the data. This is a great way to ensure data quality. Years ago, the practice would be to enforce referential integrity in the development and test environments, but not the production environment. In the last decade, the major database vendors have made great improvements in their products, and referential integrity performance is seldom an issue for most business processes.

- **Improving query accuracy and performance**. If the database did not enforce referential integrity from the business tables to the reference tables, it would be possible for rows in the business table to contain state abbreviations that did not exist in the reference table. If you wrote a query to join the business table with the reference table, perhaps to provide the full state name for reporting, you would have to write the query using the more complicated *outer join* in order to prevent business table rows that have no corresponding reference table value from dropping out of the result set, giving misleading results. Not only are you taking a risk that the end user will remember to use an outer join, but in many databases an outer join performs much more poorly than an *inner join*. If referential integrity is enforced, and you can guarantee that every business table row only contains codes that exist in the reference table, then you avoid the risk of improperly written queries and improve query performance. This improves the data quality, performance, and delivery functions.

- **Internal documentation**. Reference tables serve as internal documentation of the codes and keys used on business tables. In most production information system repositories, there are hundreds or thousands of different business codes and keys. If there were no reference tables, a business user would have difficulty remembering what all the codes meant. The reference tables serve as documentation to your internal users who are exploring the database directly.

- **Configure business logic.** The reference tables often contain much more than name-value pairs. They may contain processing indicators, such as "this subscriber type can make payments but can't change contract information," or "this diagnosis is PHI sensitive." These flags help business analysts better understand the business information. The application business logic can be coded to use these flags, rather than hardcoded values, allowing business users with the correct authorization to configure the data and alter the way the application logic processes information.

- **End user reporting.** In end user reporting, the reference tables allow the codes on the business tables to be expanded into human-readable names and descriptions.

These tables are usually maintained internally by a QA team. Even if reference table values are received from an external source (i.e. a USPS zip code list), the reference tables themselves are usually managed by the data quality resources. If the governance processes and roles document this operational responsibility, then the approving role for the reference data maintenance function is, by definition, the data steward of the reference table data (see page 58).

You should try to create standards at as high an organization level as possible, to ensure consistency and minimize the effort of creating rules for each information system. Reference tables aren't new. You aren't the first company to ever use them. There are well-defined best practices for a number of common reference table needs:

- Ralph Kimball's *The Data Warehouse Toolkit* is the source for the best practice approaches to handling reference data that changes over time, known as **slowly changing dimensions**.

- There are also recognized best practice for data that is always received in the enterprise-standard code set (**global reference tables**) and data that is received from various sources with source-specific codes that must be translated to an enterprise standard (**translate reference tables**).

- There are classic approaches to gracefully handling data that can come in with invalid or unknown values that are not in the reference table and would violate referential integrity.

And so forth. There is nothing new under the sun, so they say. You aren't the first person to encounter these problems. Use industry accepted best practices, document them as enterprise standards, and model them in your Enterprise Logical Data Model (ELDM).

Reference data that is managed at the enterprise level can be classified as a simple form of master data management (see page 168). Ideally, any reference tables which are used by multiple applications are managed at the enterprise level, not as duplicated effort within each application area.

Data glossary

It's important that the business terms are consistent across the enterprise. I once worked for a company that invested a significant amount of time, money, and resources implementing a data warehouse for the first time, not because they saw a particular need for enterprise analytics, but because they suspected internal fraud. The sales numbers from each manager didn't add up to the accounting system's total numbers. We spun up a data warehouse primarily so that the executives could see which divisional managers were embezzling from the company.

Fortunately, we found that no one was stealing money. It turned out that the entire misunderstanding was due to inconsistencies in how different managers interpreted various business terms. What was included in net sales? Were leased units counted as units sold? If a product was sold now for future delivery, when would the units be counted? Once we had all the divisional managers reporting out of a single source with consistent business logic, all of the numbers magically added up just fine, and the executives were able to make much better decisions.

I've witnessed mind-boggling loss of productivity and insight due to an insurance company having eleven different definitions of "large group" versus "small group." I've wasted many hours because nearly every department uses key terms such as "line of business" to mean something completely different. These are the problems that a glossary tool is designed to resolve.

I once had a sales rep for a very large software company keep hounding me about purchasing their glossary product. It didn't matter what business need you described, the answer was "glossary." Want to end world hunger? "You need the glossary!" Unfortunately, I developed a very adverse reaction to all products in that space. To this day, I can't hear the word "glossary" without looking for a way to escape the room. But I have to admit, having well documented, consistent business definitions is an extremely important, often overlooked service that IT needs to provide the business – one that can make or break your information management solution.

A business glossary isn't just a nice little thing to provide for the education of your end users. Like many IT functions, a business glossary is part of a complicated network of interwoven IT functional dependencies across the enterprise. Consistent terminology can impact integration efforts, can impact your data modeling, data delivery, and data quality. Security regulations often include very specific business term definitions that must be mapped to internal data concepts. Ideally, the enterprise definition would be tied to the ELDM, which is mapped to physical instantiations throughout the enterprise.

Data dictionary

Building a complete and accurate **data dictionary** is an important part of managing data assets. Both the business and IT need to be able to agree on what's being discussed. Ideally, this would be an enterprise effort.

If you build and maintain an enterprise logical data model with all your physical data repositories and services mapped to it, then you can capture the data dictionary in a single place. Implementation-specific information need only document the deviations from the enterprise definition or code set.

Genealogy

Data genealogy describes how data flows from table to table, from information system to information system, including transformations that happen along the way.

Data genealogy is built into some development tools but is seldom an enterprise-wide concept. Ideally, from an enterprise information management standpoint, you should be able to trace all of your information assets using a single data genealogy tool or repository. This capability is important to support the need to analyze the impact of potential changes, to retrace data back to its source for root cause analysis, and for meeting regulatory requirements for things like analyzing the scope of security breaches. Protecting sensitive data assets involves protecting them throughout the chain of custody. If you protect ninety-nine links in the chain, but leave one link exposed, the data is not protected.

In May of 2017, the *WannaCry* ransomware attack was activated on over 300,000 computers spanning 150 countries across the world. In a ransomware attack, the data is not stolen but encrypted; any user access is met with a request for payment. The National Health Service (NHS) in the UK was one of many institutions affected. Many non-urgent appointments were cancelled, and some systems had to be shut down entirely. Not all of those systems were actually impacted, but the NHS did not have any enterprise-level genealogy information to tell them how their own data flowed through their systems. Therefore, they did not know which systems depended on which other systems and had to shut them all down to avoid failures and further spread of the ransomware.

An ELDM maps all the various data instantiations, both repositories and services, to a single data model. Ideally, this repository will also show how data flows from one instantiation to another.

Some regulatory bodies have explicit requirements to document data genealogy. Drug trials, for example, are only valid if analysts can maintain the chain of custody of the information, and can prove that the blind study remained blind. In other cases, regulatory bodies contain privacy and security requirements that carry an implicit requirement for data genealogy in order to prove compliance to the standard during an audit.

Securing information

Information security becomes more critical every year, primarily because data becomes more valuable and more powerful every year. This information lifecycle function is often the driving justification for initially spinning up an EAG program at many institutions.

When Social Security Numbers (SSN) were first introduced in 1935 as part of the New Deal, there was no thought to making them private. It was only the social security program that would use the number, so it was of little use to anyone but the cardholder. However, over the years it has become convenient to use the SSN as a de facto national ID number. Today it's difficult to conduct legitimate business without one. The SSN is used in bank accounts, employment contracts, medical records, and utility contracts. I can remember when my state assigned driver's license numbers using the driver's SSN! But as the SSN data became more widely used, its value increased, both to the cardholder and to criminals. This trend isn't limited to SSNs; many of your corporate information assets are becoming more valuable, and hence more sensitive, over time.

These days, information security impacts nearly every IT function in your enterprise framework. Data should be secure by design and by default. I have to admit to lengthy arguments regarding whether security should be a vertical *function* column in the functional framework, or whether it should be a horizontal row within architecture or governance. Security specialists within IT tend to think of security as a pervasive part of every function we perform.

I can see their argument, but I'm going to insist that security is indeed a function – an IT job we perform on behalf of the business. Security isn't a governance-task like policies, standards, processes, and roles; security is something we *do* – a function that *has* policies, standards, processes, and roles. It has a strategic vision and a tactical roadmap.

You should select, at the corporate level, which of the many different security compliance programs you will pursue, and design your functional framework to comply with those practices across every aspect of the business.

I don't recommend trying to develop your own security program. Pick one of the national standards: NIST, HITRUST, ISO/IE 27001, or GDPR. Odds are that your industry is already mandating your compliance with one or more of these standards. That compliance often comes with a rigid deadline, and noncompliance is penalized by large fines and even jail time. More often than not, security regulations are the driver behind the initial adoption of an enterprise-wide architecture and governance initiative.

Unfortunately, many companies see security as a technology domain initiative, not an initiative that crosses all domains of IT. Even at the highest level of abstraction, I prefer to break security down into lifecycle-specific functions within each of the information, hardware, and software domains. A functional framework that crosses all domains is a great way to set up and manage your security initiative across the enterprise in the most efficient manner.

Regardless of which regulatory standard you choose, they all lay out requirements that fall naturally to the different domains. Here are a few of the more common security requirements.

Information domain security

This information domain is mainly concerned with *the security-related attributes* in the information itself, not the processes or platforms supporting that information.

- **Security Labels.** These are the various types of sensitive data, such as Personally Identifying Information (PII) or Payment Card Industry (PCI) information. Security labels apply to individual data elements and are the foundation upon which all security is built. How can you build a security program without understanding what information is being secured? It's information, after all, that you're securing, not hardware or software. These labels and the data they apply to are usually documented in the ELDM as part of the data modeling and data dictionary processes. Most security labels are associated with *columns* of data. Some particular columns, such as social security numbers, are quite sensitive. Never expose these without business justification. Alternatively, some sensitivity labels are associated with *rows* of data. Those rows could be masked but are usually just hidden. More on this in a minute.

- **Audit Trail.** When production data is changed, most security regulations require that you have an audit trail of who changed it, and when. Not only must you have security policies, standards, and processes documented, but normally you are also required to have an audit log to prove that the processes were followed. This includes regular transactions, batch updates, and emergency patches.

- **Genealogy or chain of custody.** Many security regulations now require you to document how data flows through your information systems, both the data at rest in repositories and the data in motion in web services and flat files.

Application domain security

The application domain is mainly concerned with security *processes*.

- **Security Classifications.** It's sometimes hard to explain the difference between security labels and security classifications. The best way to explain it is to think of paper-based information at a military intelligence installation before the days of computers. In a filing cabinet full of folders, some folders will contain PUBLIC information anyone will be allowed to see, provided they have some business reason. Other folders will be *classified*, clearly stamped on the front with the appropriate security class, perhaps SECRET or even TOP SECRET. The file clerk has a process they must follow for each of those classifications of data. Secret information should only be accessed in a special room; after using, it should be returned to the file clerk. Top secret may require a security observer to be present at all times. There are different types of top-secret information: advanced weapons research, troop deployments, foreign intelligence, and so forth. Different folders will be *labeled* with the identification appropriate to the data. When the file clerk receives a request, they must compare the security label of the data with the security clearance of the person requesting access. If that matches, then access is granted. The same process is followed for all the labels that are top-secret. The *security label* identifies what kind of data is appropriate for different roles to access, the *security classification* identifies what processes must be followed when that data is accessed. Many labels can fall under the same classification. Every security regulation will require you to define your security classifications. Many of them actually define the classification system you are required to use. You will have to put processes in place for each classification, document those processes thoroughly, and audit them to make sure they are followed. While data labeling is typically an information domain function, data classifications are an application domain function because they are the processes which must be followed for secure data access, including authentication, authorization, logging, etc.

- **Security provisioning and de-provisioning**. The processes involved in granting and removing security access to people. Typically, security roles will be aligned with the information domain security labels. Consider how you add people to security roles, and regularly verify with their supervisors that access is still needed. Also consider how you might de-provision access when the person leaves or transfers.

Technology domain security
This technology domain is responsible for the security *of physical assets*.

- **Physical Security.** Mainly providing physical security of physical assets, including computers, network, and the building site itself.

- **Appliance Solutions.** With today's technology, many hardware platforms come with embedded software (i.e. network routers). While technically an application, the technology domain usually assumes responsibility for the software that runs on appliance solutions.

In short, security is complicated. You knew that already. Security is one of those functions that really can't be performed department by department, or project by project. You need a comprehensive enterprise initiative involving coordinated functions that span all EAG domains.

In keeping with the purpose of this book, I want to talk a little bit about some of the more challenging areas of such a coordinated enterprise-level security initiative; the areas where many companies seem to struggle.

Like all other IT functions, the security functions should *begin* with data, but instead is often managed by technology domain resources. Those resources seldom have much experience with information management principles, and struggle with things like security labels and classifications.

Data security labels
It's critical that you create consistent, enterprise-level definitions of all your security labels. Your labels are generally determined based on two factors:

- What regulatory mandated labels are you required to support? Some security frameworks such as HITRUST give you a good deal of leeway in the definition of your security labels, but are quite rigid on the subject of security classifications. Other security standards such as HIPAA are much more rigid on the definitions of your security labels (i.e. PHI) than your security classifications. When defining your security labels, there may be some labels you are required by law to support.

- Other security labels may be created internally based on blocks of data for which you wish to enable and disable access as a unit. You probably have a corporate policy that you hide employee accounts from most users. In this case, in addition to PII and PCI, you may also want an EMP label.

Information security should not be vertical silos of data elements, where each new project results in a project-specific security role. Security roles should relate to data security labels, not projects. Project-oriented security is easier on the developer in the short term, but much harder to manage in the long run.

Instead, you should think of your data in terms of which elements are "base," no risk elements, and which are sensitive. There are several universally accepted forms of data sensitivity, such as personally identifying information or personal health information, which may or may not apply to your particular industry. When you classify data as sensitive, you will be using the specific sensitivity types that apply to your business. These are your security labels.

When you use these data sensitivity labels rather than project scope to set up security roles, the result will be a general-use base access that includes all the fields that are not sensitive, to which can be added supplemental roles for allowing access to each sensitivity label. Users with the base role only are usually set up to be able to see sensitive fields, but the data in those fields will be hidden, masked, de-identified, or encrypted. For example, they will see a column called SSN, but all the data in that column will be masked in some way. Users with business justification can be granted the additional "add-on" supplementary roles for each of the sensitivity labels they require. A PII label security role can be granted to view unmasked personally identifying information, and a PHI label security role can be granted to view unmasked personal health information.

Every user will be able to run the same SQL queries and reports, but, depending on the set of security roles each user has been granted, different users will see different variations of masked and unmasked data.

The following sections describe common implementations of security data sensitivity labels. These descriptions should not be considered compliant with every company's interpretation of every industry's regulations. Rather, they are merely examples of how you might define your own choice of sensitivity labels.

Personally Identifying Information (PII)

Personally Identifying Information (PII) is any information that might be used to identify an individual in the real world. There are dozens of regulations and guidelines that require a business to take every reasonable precaution to reduce the risk of data being used to identify real people. The trouble is, those regulations are not very helpful when it comes to defining actual implementation rules. They don't define a list of elements, or how to treat them. They don't define what is "reasonable" and what level of "risk" is acceptable. They don't define these things for the same reason that I'm not: there are always exceptions and weighing work effort and business impact versus risk is a judgment call that will be different at every company.

Several factors contribute to making PII labeling more complicated than you might assume. It's straightforward to decide on a field-by-field basis which information uniquely identifies a single person.

THE INFORMATION DOMAIN • 159

A social security number, of course, is a unique identifier. That's a rather simple exercise, taken one field at a time.

However, data isn't dispensed one field at a time; it's dispensed in combinations. Several fields that cannot be used individually to uniquely identify a person might be able to identify a person when used in combination. One study recently found that zip code combined with date of birth and gender could uniquely identify 87% of the people in the United States.[29] How do you decide which fields can be used in what combinations? Even if you do somehow figure that out, how do you enforce that during information delivery?

Typically, you simply can't. Instead, the approach taken by most companies is to recognize that some fields limit the candidate population more than others do. For American domestic businesses, a field containing country of residence doesn't narrow down the candidate population much. State information still isn't personally identifying. However, when you get down to county or zip code, there are some values that represent a small population.

County	Population
Kalawao County, Hawaii	88
Loving County, Texas	113
King County, Texas	289
Kenedy County, Texas	404

Table 4- Smallest US Counties, by Population

ZipCode	City	Population
05141	Cambridgeport VT	1
98222	Blakely Island WA	1
99790	Fairbanks AK	1
67843	Fort Dodge KS	1

Table 5 - Smallest US Zip Codes, by Population

At most companies, the legal department will mandate that the acceptable threshold of risk for any single field is a specific number – say 5000 individuals – and that proven need is required above this threshold. For instance, you can't expose a field that can be used to narrow down the list of people to fewer than 5000. In theory, by not revealing the fields that seriously narrow down the population, you dramatically limit your risk of uniquely identifying a single person even using combinations of fields. This isn't perfect, but is considered due diligence by many companies.

Using this threshold of 5000, *state* information would not be PII, but *county* and *zip code*, would. Table 4 and Table 5 show that some counties and zip codes are quite small indeed.

People with the special PII label security role will see the raw data for fields identified as PII sensitive, and people without the PII role will see only masked data. For PII data elements, if a field could contain PII, all values in the field are masked. There may be many zip codes with more than 5000 people, but if even one zip code contains less than 5000 people, then all values for the zip code field are considered sensitive. You don't typically mask just the tiny zip codes – you mask all of them.

---

[29] Uniqueness of Simple Demographics in the U.S. Population LIDAP-WP4 Carnegie Mellon University, Laboratory for International Data Privacy, Pittsburgh, PA: 2000 (1000) by Latanya Sweeney.

Typically, you can't be held accountable for special knowledge that people have in their heads, especially your internal employees who know the data very well. "If I see a bank account with a balance of $100 million dollars, I know who that account belongs to, even if the accountholder name is masked."

You have to make sure that you don't expose data which explicitly connects the dots, certainly, but how far beyond that does your obligation go? Most companies decide that if information is widely available from public sources, then you have to assume that everyone knows it. However, you really can't be held accountable for obscure information that some external user might know. Perhaps your de-identified medical records include blood type. Some blood types are quite rare. Are you responsible for masking the blood type field because of a handful of end users who might have unusual and specific information about the people who have rare blood types in your customer area? If you believe so, then you need to treat the blood type field as you treat county and zip code, masking all values if *any* value could narrow the population below your risk threshold. Most companies would not go that far. As long as the data that you provide does not contain the information to connect all the dots and uniquely identify an individual, most companies take the position that you are not responsible for what other information people can add to yours.

The scope of your due diligence is usually considered to end at what information you are actually exposing that, in itself, can be used to connect the dots and identify people within your acceptable level of risk.

PII sensitive data must be de-identified in a way that cannot reasonably be expected to tie the information to a unique person in the real world. Some of the possible techniques for "de-identification" include:

- **Hiding**. When used to de-identify fields, this technique simply replaces the data with a constant. Usually blanks, but quite possibly hard coded values like "NOT REPORTABLE."

- **Encrypting**. Encryption doesn't necessarily have to involve special cryptographic algorithms. It can be as simple as replacing the actual ID that is seen by the end user with the surrogate key that's used in the database. That surrogate key is meaningless outside the database, and cannot be used in the real world the way a social security number could. The difference between encrypting and other de-identification techniques is that the sender should be able to use the encrypted value to restore the missing information.

- **Obfuscating**. This is the practice of generating values that may look real, but are not. It includes practices like looking up values in a list and swapping values between rows.

- **Masking**. Masking is the practice of revealing part of the data, but not all of it. A common example would be revealing only the last four digits of the social security number. Another good case for masking is replacing the month and day of the date of birth with 01-01. This allows age-related processes to perform reasonably, without revealing as much personal information.

Most major database vendors allow implementation of any of these techniques at the database level, driven by security roles.

Users should first request access to the BASE role, which does not have sensitive information, then request to have PII added to it. The higher levels of access require increasing scrutiny of the underlying business justification for exposing the data. Users who don't have access to the PII role will still see the fields, but all values in the fields will be de-identified in an appropriate matter.

Personal Health Information (PHI)

Not every company stores Personal Health Information (PHI), but if you do, it is extremely sensitive. According to Reuters,[30] medical information is now worth ten times as much to hackers as credit card information.

Technically, the definition of PHI includes PII. That said, I find that most businesses who deal in both have business needs to be able to manage them independently. A user in human resources may need to see employee PII name and address information, but would have no business need to view the employee's health-related PHI information. A user in actuarial may need the PHI health information for all customers in order to calculate group insurance rates, but would have no business need to see the individual PII name and address information. Therefore, access to the PII and PHI information needs to be able to be granted and revoked independently. For that reason, I usually implement them as two separate security labels.

Some elements of personal health information, such as a diagnosis of a broken arm or a prescription for Tylenol, are not sensitive. They are PHI, but not sensitive PHI. This distinction is made in several regulatory documents, and is, therefore, subject to interpretation by your legal team. Sometimes the regulations themselves give you some guidelines in this area. HITRUST says that, "Care shall be given to ensure patient *information subject to special handling*, e.g. HIV test results and mental health and substance abuse related records, is identified and appropriate labeling and handling requirements are expressly defined"[31] (emphasis mine). According to HITRUST, any information that could indicate one of the following is *sensitive PHI*, with a higher standard of custody than normal PHI:

- Substance abuse treatment records
- HIV/AIDS status, testing, diagnosis
- Mental health status, counseling, or treatment

One could find this kind of information in many different databases. HITRUST lists those as examples only, not as an exhaustive list. Your legal department will need to examine all the relevant regulatory policy verbiage, as well as state law, court decisions, and case studies related to compliance. This is *not* a decision for the IT security team.

Your legal team may also want to consider:

- Abortion services
- Rape or sexual abuse treatment, counseling, or services
- Sexually-transmitted diseases treatment, counseling, or services
- Pregnancy testing or results
- Gender transition treatment, counseling, or services

You need to protect both regular PHI information (e.g. broken arm) and sensitive PHI information (e.g. mental health), but the standard for needing access to sensitive PHI is much higher.

---

[30] http://reut.rs/2DTChLz.
[31] *HITRUST Common Security Framework*, version 6.0, section 07.e. http://bit.ly/2BeCYfj. The HITRUST Alliance charges for later versions, but as of version 9.0, this warning regarding sensitive PHI remains unchanged.

As with PII, the scope of your due diligence only includes the information held within your corporate repositories. If an end user happens to know that Dr. X is a psychiatrist or that the clinic with address Y only performs abortions, they are bringing in knowledge from outside your repositories to their query. Most companies consider their responsibility to be met if they do not provide the information necessary to connect all the dots for the end user, and do not consider possible knowledge that end user may bring. But again, that will be a decision that your legal team needs to make.

Like PII, users should first need to get BASE access to the fields that are not subject to any sensitive security label, and then add the PHI and sensitive PHI security label roles to that base, provided they can show business justification. Unlike PII, which de-identifies all values if a column is considered to contain sensitive information, the sensitive PHI usually only de-identifies the values that are actually sensitive. For PII, only a few counties may contain fewer than 5000 people, but since at least one does, you de-identify all county names. For PHI, only a few diagnoses indicate one of the sensitive conditions, and only those sensitive values are de-identified, usually by returning something like "NOT REPORTABLE" instead. The rest of the regular, not sensitive PHI fields are available to people who have access to the regular PHI information, but not access to sensitive PHI.

This usually required the maintenance of a PHI sensitive indicator on a reference table. If the reference table is an industry standard, such as ICD10 Diagnosis Codes, then the code itself, as well as the description, must be de-identified. This means that the reference table must be assigned a surrogate key, so that the natural key (the ICD10 code) won't be propagated to the business tables where there is no PHI sensitive indicator available for the database to de-identify it without forcing a join to the reference table. You must implement the processes and roles to maintain these sensitivity flags. You must also decide the default value for these flags when receiving new data. Should new values be considered sensitive by default, or not sensitive by default until they are reviewed? Again, this is a decision for the business and legal, not for IT.

All of these decisions should be made at the corporate level and documented in your EAG artifacts, including the ELDM. You don't want to have inconsistent implementations across the enterprise, nor do you want project resources spending time trying to figure this out on their own. Make it clear; make it easy.

Payment Card Industry Information (PCI)

Payment Card Industry (PCI) information includes card numbers, expiration dates, and card verification numbers (CVN). Companies that process credit card payments are subject to a number of regulatory requirements surrounding this information. Non-compliance can result in expensive fines and loss of customer trust.

Because PCI deals with the account identification information rather than account balances, many companies elect to subject banking routing and transit and account numbers to the same security requirements, placing them under the same security label. This isn't required by PCI regulations, but isn't a bad approach. After all, if people have no need to see your credit card account numbers, why would they need to see your checking account numbers? With EFT, a routing and checking account number have much the same fraud risk as a credit card number.

THE INFORMATION DOMAIN • 163

Like PHI and PII, access to PCI data is a role that is added on top of BASE access. Without PCI access, the contents of the fields are de-identified to the end user, typically by hiding the data and returning blanks instead.

Other security labels

There are many other potential security labels:

- **Financial**. The PCI label only covers financial account numbers. This label would cover salaries, family income, sales commissions, and other wealth-related information.

- **Employee**. At most companies, there are many people who have a business reason to see customer records. However, there is usually a caveat that stipulates that only a few highly trusted employees can view the customer records of employees.

- **VIP.** At many companies, some records will relate to VIP customers: prominent politicians, sports figures, and celebrities. To reduce the temptation to view these records, they may be given a special security label, and require special justification to access.

- **Personal harm.** In cases of real or potential domestic abuse, you may be required to provide extra protection for the information related to person in danger, especially place of residence.

Data security classifications

Once you have your data sensitivity labels precisely defined, you will also need to define classifications of data treatment. Each classification is based on the risk to the company if the data is exposed. Typical data sensitivity classifications might include:

- **Publically available information**. You may not intend for the data to be exposed, but there is no risk to the company if this data is exposed, because it is generally available elsewhere. For example, information about the company's publically traded stock price or the publically available financial statement.

- **Internal information**. Data which isn't publically available, but which has no real risk to the company if exposed. For example, a log of the times you ran an internal job.

- **Restricted information**. Information that is sensitive in nature, and can adversely affect the company if exposed, but is often shared as part of regular business operations with well-defined access control structures in place. This might include PII, PHI, and PCI information.

- **Confidential information**. Information that could seriously affect the company, and is never exposed in the normal course of business, such as strategic marketing plans, planned mergers and acquisitions, and new product development.

Another way of looking at this is:

	Not sensitive	Sensitive
Not shared outside the company as part of regular business	INTERNAL	RESTRICTED
Shared as part of regular business	PUBLIC	CONFIDENTIAL

Table 6 – Non-sensitive and sensitive information

These are, of course, just examples of classifications. Your own data classifications will be much more formal, or mandated by the regulatory body you are using for compliance. HITRUST, for example, has specific verbiage that you must use for your data classifications as well as specific disclosures and handling treatments for each.

Once you've defined these classifications, you need to map your data labels to your classifications, showing how each type of sensitive data is treated. Many labels will share the same classification.

An approach to data security compliance

We've discussed briefly how security is integrated into many different IT functions, such as data modeling, a business glossary, data lineage, data profiling, data quality, data masking, and archiving. It's worth taking a moment to discuss the order in which each of those functions must be implemented when initially spinning up an information security compliance program:

1. **Data label and classification definition**. Before you can go looking for data and implementing security roles, you first need to study the regulatory requirements, making sure you document all the relevant terminology and business rules. Many of the regulatory bodies are more than a little vague. You'll need to work with your business and legal areas to clarify any gray areas. These definitions should be incorporated into your corporate glossary and EAG artifacts.

2. **Data discovery**. Once you understand what you're looking for, you have to…, well…, go look for it. You need to find all the locations where sensitive information is physically stored, including relational databases, flat files on shared drives, and unstructured data sources. This discovery needs to be an ongoing and recurring automated process which updates a central repository. The discovery process needs to have a documented owner responsible for its operation. The data discovery process needs to document:

   a. What label or labels the data falls under
   b. Where you found it (the repository location, and the location within the repository)
   c. What processes create, read, update or delete the data
   d. Who is responsible for the data, the data steward who owns it
   e. The access controls that are in place for the data

3. **Data dictionary**. It's unlikely that every data element in every physical repository in your organization will be mapped to your enterprise logical data model (ELDM). However, you should definitely map the sensitive subsets of those repositories. At this point, your concerned more with security labels than with classifications.

4. **Data lineage/genealogy.** It is unlikely that every sensitive data element was created within the repository where you found it. Like most of your operational data, sensitive information flows from one location to another throughout your integrated suite of applications. Once you have identified all the sensitive data, you should document how this data flows from repository to repository. Likely this will lead to the discovery of even more locations where the sensitive data resides. This is the chain of custody of the sensitive information. The entire lifecycle of sensitive data, from creation to its end-of-life must be documented and secured.

5. **Implement and enforce**. Put the data access controls in place, the technical details and the EAG policies, standards, processes and roles. This includes working with the other IT domains to

ensure the information security function integrates smoothly with application and technology security functions. This is the point where the classifications become important, as different controls will be defined for the different security classifications.

6. **Monitoring and control**. Like any IT function, you can't manage what you don't measure. Refer back to the section on page 59 for more information about how measurements are required part of any a mature process. If you're audited, you must provide evidence that you have consistently adhered to your security function governance policies and processes over time. Even if you consistently followed your policies and processes to the letter, if you can't easily provide that evidence, you will fail the audit and be subject to penalties. The audit requirements should be built into your policies and processes, so that they are well-defined requirements, known throughout the enterprise. Audit by design and by default.

7. **Reporting and event notification**. Although this might be considered a natural part of monitoring, I'm calling it out for specific attention. Audit data is irrelevant and a waste of time unless there is some way to communicate it and some role assigned the responsibility of looking at it. If serious events occur, the information should automatically be pushed to a data steward for security compliance review and to any others who might need to know. Ideally, this reporting mechanism is the means by which you will provide the evidence of your compliance to the auditors, and the feedback with allows you to improve your processes over time. These audit logs can also be mined analytically, identifying risky behaviors such as a valid ID accessing from a remote IP address, and outliers such as off-hour access by resources who normally don't work those shifts.

Aging and archiving information

The last function in the information management lifecycle of the framework is aging and archiving – data end-of-life. You can perform end-of-life functions for data either alongside software end-of life functions (migrating or simply terminating and application) or as a standalone process. The two key data end-of-life functions are archiving and aging.

- **Archiving** involves making a copy of some portion of the repository's data somewhere else. This is not the same as regular data backups for disaster recovery purposes. Those have nothing to do with end-of-life. Nor has it anything to do with tiered storage, which relegates lesser-used data to lower cost storage, while still keeping it actively available to the source application. Archiving is not an IT-centric application continuity function. It's a business-centric retention of data that may be needed later for business purposes. The archive target is usually some less-expensive platform, possibly even offsite storage, though that is less common with archives than with backups.

- **Aging** involves deleting data from a repository. This can be either an operational or an analytical repository, and is *usually* preceded by first archiving the data to be deleted.

From an enterprise perspective, it's important to have an information end-of-life solution in place. A recent storage assessment survey conducted by NTP Software[32] revealed that 61.6% of file data stored

---

[32] http://bit.ly/2BhFEZB.

on primary storage systems had not been accessed in more than six months, 49% had not been accessed in over a year, and 19.1% of physical storage is consumed by duplicate files. Gartner estimates that the average annual growth for physical data storage is 30% to 60%,[33] and that a well-designed archiving strategy can prevent 67% of that annual growth. Those cost savings, they claim, include the full operating cost, not just the cost of archiving.

Clearly, while aging and archiving functions don't have the flash and sizzle of something like predictive modeling, there's real business value in an enterprise aging and archiving solution. Eliminating unused data from operational and analytical information systems makes the resulting repositories smaller and faster, and makes the backups take less time and less storage. Ideally, you'll leverage one corporate data archiving solution to serve many different application repositories. Such an enterprise solution, however, requires vision, planning, and effective oversight. It takes a holistic enterprise architecture and governance program. A functional framework ensures that this valuable function isn't overlooked.

Don't consider the archive a permanent retention. You will eventually want to age data out of the archiving solution when it has outlived its usefulness. This suggestion isn't universally popular with all business users, but it's a very good idea to have policies to that effect in place at the corporate level. An aging solution is critical to reduce overall litigation risk. It is perfectly acceptable to reply to a legal inquiry with words to the effect that "our regular retention policies, documented here, deleted that information over a year ago…" Once the data is requested, if that data still exists somewhere, even on one data-hoarding senior business analyst's local workstation drive, you are legally obligated to turn the information over and retain it indefinitely until the legal hold is released. Yes, there *is* value to old data, but there's also risk, and the acceptable risk-reward balance needs to be determined and policies created at a corporate level. Retention risk isn't a department-by-department decision. You need an enterprise aging and archiving policy.

How long should you retain data, then? There is no way I'm going to give you an answer to that. Many agencies compare the declining utility of old data to the continuing risk of retaining it, and incorporate this into regulatory requirements. Patient health information must be retained by healthcare providers for the life of the patient plus ten years. Financial industry transaction history must be retained for seven years. You need to have a conversation that involves your business users, your security compliance office, and your legal department. Between the three of those groups, a consensus must be reached. The resulting enterprise policy is sometimes known as a **Records Retention Schedule (RRS)**. Retention periods are not an IT decision.

Also, keep in mind that there are many different types of data. There is customer information, product information, and network information. There is transaction "flow" data, and point-in-time "state" data. There is core operationally modeled tables and copies of the information stored in other repositories. Your legal retention requirements don't necessarily include all of this information. You may need sales history including product name and sales price, but not need the history of the product pricing changes over time. You may need daily account balances for one year, monthly back to three years, and only year-end balanced back to seven years. Make sure and work out with the subject matter experts mentioned earlier the details of the retention requirements, and document and enforce that decision at the enterprise level. Your corporate record retention policy should specify what data is retained, what kind of access is required, and what encryption, if any, is necessary.

---

[33] Gartner Symposium, "Ten Critical Tech Trends for the next five years," October 2012.

There are many commercial data archiving solutions, with many different approaches and feature/function. One way of grouping them is by dividing them into two broad categories:

- Those that offload data into less-expensive application-specific archive repositories while retaining the same data structures and values. Unfortunately, few business analysts will be comfortable accessing raw application data without going through the application screens, and you'll need some level of operational staff to administrate this platform and the regular archiving process. Even if the archiving software is managed at the corporate level, the repository and feeds are application-specific. Still, as noted above, you can easily make a business case for this approach. This is especially true if the archive implementation is an offline solution such as tape backups. A Clipper group study found that the total cost of ownership of a disk-based solution was 26 times that of a tape-based solution.[34]

- Those that integrate the application data into an enterprise analytical repository like a data warehouse. Don't forget about your enterprise data warehouse when considering application archives. They often contain most of the key business information already integrated with other data from applications across the enterprise, in a centrally managed, active repository with reporting and analytical tools already in place, and a body of analysts already trained in accessing it. Moreover, the data feeds to this "archive" repository are probably already in place. It may be much less expensive overall to add the few extra fields you need archived to the warehouse than to stand up an independent application-specific archiving solution.

Traditionally a data warehouse isn't the system of record for operational data, but in many cases, where the legal retention requirements are being held in the warehouse rather than the source applications, the warehouse can actually be designated as the system of record for legal inquiries that span the enterprise or exceed the retention of the operational applications.

More and more archiving solutions use big data repositories as the archiving target, which has a lower initial cost than integrating into a formally managed schema such as a warehouse. However, dropping the source system data structures and values into these repositories still produces application-specific archive repositories. This is an inexpensive single-application archiving solution, but any cross-application mining will require each end user to perform the types of integration that would have been necessary to put the data in a warehouse.

Don't confuse backup/recovery functionality with archiving/retrieval. According to one survey, 57% of respondents say they use their regular backup solution to provide archiving functionality.[35] Backup solutions provide short-term operational recovery functionality, not long-term retention and retrieval functionality. Backups don't integrate history across time, are typically not immediately accessible, require more overall storage to store the same amount of retention, and cannot be used for cross-application analysis.

Note that the process of archiving irrelevant production information is often leveraged as part of a practice of reducing the amount of data in lower environments (development and test). If your production retention is five years, you might use the same basic logic to produce two-year retention in your

---

[34] http://bit.ly/2mTjNTm.
[35] http://bit.ly/UNH0H5 p.2.

development environment, and perhaps three-year retention in your test environment. This will reduce the data storage costs and job execution time in development and test.

Information services functions

You may have a specific need to add information services as a standalone functional area outside of the information lifecycle functional area. It's generally a bad idea to complicate your functional framework by spelling out individual services unless there is something so unique about them that they cannot be said to fall under the same architecture and governance as other information. Is the security for this service significantly different? Is the aging and archiving different? Don't create an information services functional area just because you have information services. Only create one if you really must manage those functions differently than other information.

Master Data Management (MDM)

One of the few areas that might be a candidate for consideration as its own function in your framework is **Master Data Management**, or **MDM**. Consider master data management the practice of managing the master version of data that is used across the enterprise in many applications. This can include many different types of information, but the two most common are customer information and reference tables.

Typically, your operational systems will treat your customers as account relationships, not as globally unique individuals. Since the globally unique individual identifier needs to span all your operational systems, the process needs to happen outside of those systems. At the enterprise level, you need a way to identify a single person across all account relationships.

In the early days of this technology, the term "customer" caused some confusion. What is a customer? These software applications left some ambiguity regarding the line between the people and their account relationships. The term *party* was coined to address this problem. A "party" is a person, not an account. The party concept includes both biological and legal entities (buildings and belly-buttons). A corporation, after all, is a legal person. If you own your own business as a sole proprietorship and someone sues you and wins, they can lay claim to your "company truck," but they can also take your comic book collection and game console. When you incorporate, you are creating a new legal entity. If someone sues the company and wins, they can lay claim to assets that belong to the company, but your comic books and game console are safe. You are just an employee of the company. Both you and the corporation have names, addresses, phone numbers, and tax ID numbers. You are both "parties." The downside of incorporating is that both parties, the biological party and the corporate party, pay taxes.

In healthcare, a provider can be a physician or a hospital. Your supplier may be a person or a manufacturer. You may sell telephone service to a homeowner or to a business. A legal entity and a biological person are interchangeable in so many aspects of our business operations that customer data hubs generally work with both kinds of data. There are two overlapping technologies in this space:

- **Customer Data Integration (CDI)** is the process of managing the shared customer information across the enterprise. It includes the customer's name and address, but can also include the customer's account information and products.

- **Master Data Management (MDM)** is broader in scope, including managing the master customer information, but also including all the other data assets that need to be managed and shared at the corporate level such as product inventory, network information, and supplier information.

Customer data integration products can act as an analytical hub, collecting information from operational source systems in a one-way flow of information, or they can work bi-directionally and push the "golden copy" information back into the source systems as updates, or, in the most advanced implementations, can actually replace the customer component of the source systems.

The master customer number, also called the **master customer index** or the **party key**, can transform a business. It gives you the ability to tell that two different customer accounts are really the same person. It can tell you which vendors are also customers. It can stitch together information for the same person across multiple source systems that use different customer identification numbers. It can allow your internal data to be supplemented with external contextual data such as retail demographics. It can let you easily track the customer lifecycle as prospects are converted to members. Your call center applications can use the customer data hub to look up customer accounts by name and address across all applications. Your billing systems can use the customer data hub to make sure address changes in one system are propagated to all relevant applications or to perform consolidated billing.

At the health insurance company where I currently work, both the providers and the insured members were assigned party keys. One side effect of this assignment was that it allowed us to easily tell when a provider was filing a claim for treating themselves, or writing prescriptions to themselves. It actually isn't illegal for a doctor to prescribe medicine to themselves, but it is illegal to file a claim and ask an insurance company to pay for it. This information is being fed to our fraud department. Oddly enough, the most commonly self-prescribed drugs weren't the narcotics or mood altering drugs you might expect. They were anabolic steroids, by quite a large margin.

In the age of competing with information, you must know your customer base. This is a vital function that IT must provide to the business. There are several different levels of complexity available in the implementations of these solutions. Typically, a company will start with the simplest implementation, and gradually evolve into the more mature technologies.

A batch solution for analytics is usually the first kind of customer data integration (CDI) that a company takes on. The operational systems continue doing what they do, and the enterprise data warehouse will implement a solution on the analytics side to scrub, match, and merge names and addresses. In the beginning, this data is only produced via batch processes, and only used by analytical processes. The assignment logic will keep a reference "pointer" to all the source system variations that were assigned to each golden copy key, but that is only for reference purposes.

Over time the operational systems will inevitably recognize the value of a master party key. They'll want this analytical information made operational. They'll want it on a high-availability server, exposed via services to the operational world. The data may be assigned in batch processes, but can be read on a transactional basis. Those reference pointers will become very important, as they are the entry points from the source systems.

The operational systems will eventually come to rely on this information so heavily that they require the ability to assign, not just read, party keys in real time. The assignment logic must be made operational. As the processes are hardened and the information becomes increasingly trusted, the source systems will want the data integration to become bi-directional, so that, when an address is changed in the CDI/MDM tool, it is automatically updated on the source systems as well, using those reference pointers. Finally, the CDI/MDM will take over responsibility as the system of record for the information it integrates. The source systems will no longer update local copies of information, but will look directly to the CDI/MDM solution for the data in real time throughout its processing.

I don't know of any company that goes through all of these stages of CDI/MDM solutions evolution, but most progress through at least two or three. You will probably need to start with a simpler solution, but keep in mind what your long-term strategy will eventually look like, minimizing the need for redesign as you evolve. Earlier, in the modeling function, we discussed the use of APIs to isolate one subject area from another in analytical systems. Later in the data delivery function, we discussed separating data from business logic in operational systems using Data as a Service (DaaS). Both of these techniques have many advantages, one of which is that it decouples the data implementation from the rest of your systems, allowing you to snap in a new solution with far less effort. It is possible to design a home-grown solution in such a way that it can easily be unplugged and replaced with a commercial product at a later date. This strategic design is the responsibility of the EAG architects.

The other common implementation of master data management is the management of the master version of reference data. Many global and internal code/descriptions are used throughout the enterprise. These code sets change over time and must be maintained. Master data management tools detect when unknown values appear in various local repositories, and include tools to research and cleanse the data, maintaining a single version of the truth for master data.

Managing reference data is a large chunk of the work performed by a typical QA team. The MDM tools help manage this data in a single location using automated workflow management tools.

Mastered customer and reference information is an extremely valuable corporate asset, critically integral to so many data repositories, applications, and business processes. It's possible that you'll want to develop a specific strategy plan and roadmap, specific policies, standards, processes, and roles at the enterprise level in order to manage customer information effectively on behalf of the business. The functional framework gives you the tools to do this.

CHAPTER 5

The Application Domain

As we begin the discussion of a new domain of architecture and governance, I want to refocus the goal of this book, which is to create a framework for managing the complexity of IT functions by creating an organization structure that reduces those thousands of individual IT functions into a simple conceptual napkin drawing, the functional framework.

At the top level, we first divided the functions into four architectural domains: business, information, application, and technology. The business drives everything. They tell *what* the company will do. If the IT department is serving the business well and has built trust, then the business will trust IT to say *how*. Within IT, the first priority is to determine the information needed to support the business. Once the information needs are understood, then consideration is given to the business logic needed to maintain, transform and analyze the information. Only then can you begin to consider the technology necessary to support the information and application domains.

At this point we've discussed the business domain and the information domain, and are now ready to discuss the application domain.

Most companies today are better served building infrastructure comprised more of purchased third party solutions than of in-house developed solutions. In the information domain, the information lifecycle functions are somewhat indifferent concerning whether the application hosting the data is built in-house or purchased from a third party. Both create, maintain, deliver, and destroy data. However, in the lifecycles of the application domain, that *build-or-buy* distinction makes all the difference.

In the application domain, many differences exist between the IT functions that support the development of new applications and those that support applications in production. So many, in fact, that we divide the functions into two separate lifecycles.

- The **Software Infrastructure Lifecycle** functional area includes all the functions related to software *ownership*: acquisition, implementation and configuration, release management, license compliance, security, and end-of life. Even in-house developed software may be managed through the software infrastructure lifecycle once it reaches production.

- The **Software Development Lifecycle** functional area includes all the functions related to software *development*: project initiation, tracking, requirements, design, development, change management, testing, and implementation.

There's sometimes a third lifecycle for software services, which we'll discuss later.

Notice that the application domain functions aren't the information systems themselves. There isn't a billing application function and a separate sales application function. Billing and sales are business functions. In the application domain, both the billing and the sales applications are supported by the same software infrastructure lifecycle functions. The information domain supports the data needed by billing and sales, the application domain supports the software used to support the billing and sales information, and the technology domain supports the technology required to host the billing and sales software. The billing and the sales business functions may be quite different, but the governance needed to manage them is the same at the framework level. If there are any significant IT functional differences, they can be spelled out in individual information system-specific documents within the same framework function. There's no need to create a separate IT function (column) in the framework for each information system. The software infrastructure lifecycle covers all the IT functions necessary to support production application software on behalf of the business.

Not all software infrastructure functions will apply to every information system. In-house developed software may not require any acquisition, contract management, and licensing functions. Cloud-based software may be managed in such a way that the configuration, release management, and operations functions are taken care of by a third party transparently to you.

The purpose here isn't to give detailed information about the internals of each of these functions, but rather to discuss how these functions integrate at a higher level into an enterprise architecture and governance program. None of these application domain IT functions can be effectively managed in isolation of the larger context. There are many integration points that must be built in order to reduce the overall IT complexity and simplify effective management of IT functions.

For the most part, software management is a mature concept, with decades of well-defined best practices, solid vendor toolsets, experienced professional services, and a large body of practical advice and training available from industry experts. All of that is critically important, but well beyond the scope of this book. In keeping with our goal of taming IT complexity at the *enterprise* level, I'm going to focus on how all these various IT functions integrate together in the larger context of an enterprise functional framework, with particular emphasis on some of the common cross-functional gaps. I'm going to assume each of these processes are pretty mature in your organization within the scope of any individual information system, and focus on the complexity of managing all of these functions at the enterprise level across all systems in some sort of unified, cohesive manner.

Two kinds of people – structured learners versus researchers

There are two types of people in this world: those who learn better when turned loose to explore material on their own path, and those who learn better in a structured community setting. My wife and I are good examples of both extremes. Both of us decided to pursue additional degrees online long after graduating from college. My wife did much better in a classroom setting where there was a lot of structure and a lot of interaction with other students, all learning from each other. She's much more of a people-person than I am, and appears to be wired to learn best in a social setting.

I, on the other hand, did much better in classes where they gave me the book and told me when the test would be. When I was in a more structured class, I often felt that my time was being wasted while the class progressed at the pace of the slowest student. More often than I care to admit, I *was* the slowest student. I was feeling rushed and pressured to move on without really understanding. I don't want to learn just enough to pass the test, I want to really *understand*. I prefer to study when it's convenient for me, where my wife likes the accountability of regular class hours. I don't want people trying to talk to me when I'm trying to study. Most of all, I like to use the textbook as a guide and do my own research, finding and reading the experts on each individual topic. My kids constantly make fun of how often I respond to their questions with, "Well, I did a little research, and…"

Some roles within your functional framework are well suited to formal training. You aren't breaking new ground every day. You aren't the first person to ever face this challenge. There are other roles where you really are doing something that's never been done before, and it's up to you alone to figure it out. You need information and there's no handy textbook to teach you what you need to know.

I recall my very first day on the job working for a major telco where I was hired to lead an effort to convert part of their infrastructure from a mainframe platform to client-server architecture. I showed up early, eager to get to work. As it happens, everybody was busy with a production issue that morning, and no one had time for me. An important new retail store was opening that morning, and the network hardware in the store wasn't working. While everything had worked well in the test lab, out in the field they couldn't get the store to come online.

Everyone was rushing around trying to fix the issues at this store opening, which had been heavily advertised. I had no idea what was going on, and no one really had time to bring me up to speed. I finally gathered they were having problems with a special two-channel modem. It was unsettling to listen to the baffled IT staff as they faced this challenge. "This was supposed to work…" "It worked in the lab…" "Have you tried powering it off and on? Try it again." "This was supposed to work." "It worked in the lab…"

I should say that these were extremely talented, technical people, very good at what they did. However, the mainframe platform they worked on changed very little over time. Once you learn COBOL, everything you do after that is just more of the same. Ok, that's not fair, but it's true that the environment they worked on was much more stable than the world I came from, where everything you knew at dinnertime is obsolete by breakfast.

I don't pretend to know anything about that particular device, but these people were getting nowhere! Thankfully, this wasn't the first time I've been in well over my head, in desperate need of information and no idea where to find it. You learn out how to figure things out.

I found the manufacturer of the modem by looking at the box in the lab, and started through my list of contacts making calls. The first few numbers I called either didn't work anymore, or wanted to charge for consulting, but I eventually found a hardware tech at the manufacturer who said he could help. I got the attention of the people in the room, and put the phone on speaker. Best first day ever! I was a hero, just for being able to find information without access to a structured learning environment.

Architecture involves a lot of cutting-edge concepts and technology. A great architect one year can be a dinosaur the next if they don't keep current. No one can teach you everything you need to know. An architect is going to have to be someone who can go hunt down the stuff they don't know, and then share that knowledge around.

Do you have someone you're considering making an architect? Ask them a question about some new topic they can't possibly be prepared to answer. Do they get upset and flustered? Angry or defensive? Do they try to bluff their way through, pretending they know more than they do? On the other hand, do they admit what they don't know, and come back tomorrow, or even this afternoon, with a good handle on the basics? Guess which one is going to work out as an architect?

Software infrastructure lifecycle functions

Outside of third-world countries, it's hard to imagine a company in this century surviving without any software. I do blacksmithing as a hobby, and have found that even the artist-craftsmen and women specializing in ancient trades as a full-time career use accounting software to run their business, pay taxes, interact with their peers, and market their product.

Most companies own a *lot* of software, integrated and supported in unimaginable complexity. As with everything else in the IT industry, supporting software infrastructure is a whole lot more complicated than you think it would have to be.

Software has to be acquired, installed, configured, and kept current with updates. You have to worry about license compliance, security, and what to do at the end of its life. Without IT managing all of these software infrastructure support functions in an efficient, coordinated manner, the business would quickly suffer. A well-executed business plan, supported by solidly architected and governed information can be brought to its knees within months by poorly executed software infrastructure support functions.

These application infrastructure lifecycle functions are necessary for *all* your software, whether developed in-house or purchased from a third party. These functions are even needed when your software is outsourced in a third-party managed hosting solution, though the roles change.

The key is to bring some kind of organization, reducing the complexity. The result should be easily understandable, and flexible enough to adapt as needed, yet reflect the whole subject area in a way that instills confidence in the framework.

For production software support, the best way to conceptualize the functions is to think of them as supporting the lifecycle of an application. The application is conceived and placed into the environment. You watch over it through the years, keeping it out of legal trouble, keeping it safe from those with bad intentions, patching it up when needed, until the time comes to lay it to rest with dignity, leaving a solid legacy for the next generation. It's no accident that managing the software infrastructure life cycle sounds a lot like parenting. And, like parenting, most of us are just winging it.

Software acquisition

The software infrastructure lifecycle functional area begins with the functions involved in initially acquiring software. Once the software is paid for, you're going to have to live with it no matter how poorly it fits into your long-term strategic vision for your software infrastructure. The software acquisition function, therefore, is critical to the task of building that vision.

There are a number of sub-functions to the software acquisition function, including:

- Business need prioritization
- Business requirements
- Architectural review
- Build versus buy
- Total cost of ownership
- Budgeting cycles
- Proof of concept
- Request for information/proposal
- Vendor selection
- Contract management

Depending on your industry and the size of your company, your software acquisition process may be more or less complex. Most of these software acquisition functions are related to performing the due diligence necessary to make sure that the business' money is being spent wisely. Really, most of these are common sense. As my father says, "It's just work." It's a great deal of very hard work, but it's not black magic. Just make sure these processes are integrated, documented, communicated, and monitored for compliance and you'll be fine.

You're probably already doing most of these functions at the enterprise level, sending all software purchasing requests through a central process. However, it can be tricky to integrate these software acquisition functions into the framework of an enterprise architecture and governance program. We'll discuss a few key points in the following section.

Architectural review

One of the more important software acquisition functions when it comes to managing IT complexity is **architectural review**. The EAG program team should review any proposed software acquisition. The software architects may lead this discussion, but the final decision must be endorsed by all EAG domains.

That architectural review needs to include discussion of each of the following elements.

Alignment with the strategic vision

Hopefully, your strategic vision for the relevant functional area is complete and the tactical roadmap up-to-date. If not, you may need to move quickly and flesh it out now. It's hard sometimes trying to stay ahead of the business. Things move fast, and you don't always see change coming.

Examine your strategic vision to make sure that the software aligns with your vision of the future. It doesn't have to be a full-blown implementation of every aspect of your long-term strategy, but it should take you as far as can be justified given the budget, time, and resources available for this project. Also, the strategic vision doesn't have to be a utopian ideal. You can't impose an architectural burden on a project that will kill the business case that was being used to justify the project in the first place. This is still a business, not a science project.

By "strategic vision," we mean both the strategic vision for the IT infrastructure, such as a services oriented architecture, and the strategic vision for the business function. If you are investing in new business software, you need to make sure that the software is going to meet the business process needs, deliver the desired functionality, and integrate smoothly with the rest of the business. This may require the EAG business architect to flesh out the strategy for the business function in question.

Compliance with corporate policies

There are likely quite a few corporate policies that will apply to the software once it's up and running. That's not the time to find out that the solution you just purchased isn't compliant. Do your research ahead of time. The EAG team owns those corporate policy documents. Part of your responsibility in an EAG software review is to see if the solution is compliant with the governance policies you manage.

You're going to look like a real idiot if you approve software spend, then find the software isn't compliant with the rules that *you* put in place!

Eliminating redundancy

Does the enterprise already own software that provides the desired functionality? Most companies own a number of products that provide the same basic functionality, purchased by various departments at different times. This creates needless IT complexity, the very thing we are trying to reduce! Even if there's no annual maintenance, there's still expense for operations, user training, administrative support, resource usage, and disaster recovery.

Eliminating all redundancy isn't the goal. Supporting the business efficiently is the goal. When deciding whether redundancy should be eliminated, you must weigh the risk versus reward, not weigh the architectural purity of your infrastructure. There are times when it makes sense to retain two existing applications that do the same thing if they are both already in place, have minimal total cost of ownership, and generate minimal security and data quality risk. It will be *much* rarer to be justified in purchasing new software functionality that duplicates functionality you already own.

Your application architectural strategic vision should definitely depict a software suite that has no duplications of functionality. Write that down and communicate it as a standard. However, recognize that, like any strategic vision, it will have to be rolled out over time in a series of tactical steps. Like any standard, you are going to have to have a process to grant waivers and exceptions.

Remember that a business request for software acquisition may be that chance you were looking for to hijack a business initiative to implement an aspect of your long-term vision. At the very least, you can make sure your infrastructure doesn't get even farther from the strategic vision than before.

There will be exceptions to your policy of no duplication of functionality. Just document those exceptions with waivers to the standard, and move on, still holding the standard high for everyone to follow.

Enterprise scalability

No software is purchased for just one information system. That system isn't the business. Every software solution has to be examined in the large context of all information systems. Does any other team need this functionality? Have the requirements for all those information systems been included in the evaluation process?

You are the team who is supposed to have the crystal ball that tells what your infrastructure will look like in the future. You've already compared the functionality in the software with your vision, but make sure you also consider how the software will scale as the company grows, and as your infrastructure grows with it. Will this software handle the load?

It's easy to say that the architectural team needs to review all software acquisitions, but good intentions are not always enough. Your company likely buys a *lot* of software. Your architectural team may quickly become a roadblock to the business getting things done – the last thing you want to happen.

You're going to have to decide on some objective means of determining which acquisitions are reviewed and which are not. All software that costs over $5000 must be reviewed? All software needed by strategic projects must be reviewed? Some combination? This is a policy decision, not a standard. Phrase it clearly enough so there is no room for ambiguity. Just recognize that you are probably going to have to pick your battles here. Again, remember the end goal is not architectural purity, but effective management of IT complexity in support of the business. As with any policy, this decision needs to be reviewed annually, and may change over time.

Vendor selection

Another area where it's easy for IT to lose control of IT complexity is in the selection of which vendor's solution to purchase. You can easily make shortsighted decisions that duplicate functionality, don't fit the long-term strategy or current infrastructure, and don't meet the actual business requirements.

Certainly all software purchases that go to architectural review should go through formal vendor selection, but if you have a simple, flexible process, you can create policy that *all* software acquisitions go through a formal vendor selection process, regardless of whether the architecture team is involved or not.

Likely, your purchasing or contract management process will have some input here. Many companies mandate that at least three different vendors be included in the analysis. Choosing one vendor over another is a lot harder than you would think. It's very hard not to make a subjective decision, regardless of personal integrity. It's difficult to compare products when the feature function sets aren't apples-to-apples. By the time you talk to the last vendor, it's been weeks since you talked to the first and the memory of that first product's selling points is fading. One vendor may have had a sales rep that shared extracurricular interests with you or took you to your favorite restaurant for lunch, and that pleasant experience can be reflected onto the software product without you actually realizing. Objectivity doesn't come without careful preparation. You need a system.

When you were looking through the enterprise to find if you already owned applications with the desired functionality, you probably got a lot of, "We don't have that, but we sure could use it!" responses. All of those departments are your requirements committee, not just the department that initially requested the software.

You need to gather all the business requirements and figure out how to measure and weigh each possible vendor response in terms of the value to the business. Then add in your IT requirements (information, application, and technology), thinking in terms of both the existing infrastructure and your long-term strategic vision. You may in fact need to bump heads and actually figure out what the long-term strategic vision is, if you haven't done that before. You should do all of this before you talk to a vendor. As you talk to vendors, you may learn more and modify your initial requirements, but they still need to be captured, scored, and weighed.

This doesn't have to be rocket science. I've used variations of the same spreadsheet for vendor evaluations for several companies in at least three different industries with great success:

- Collect, organization and categorization your requirements and organize them into groups.

- For each requirement, assign a weight. I use a scale of 1 to 5. This relative importance should be assigned *by the business*, not by IT:

    o   0 – no importance at all (don't even put these in your requirements document)

    o   1 – Feature not required, but would add future value

    o   2 – Feature not required, but would add significant value to initial business case

    o   3 – Feature required – significant development/integration/configuration effort on our part is acceptable

    o   4 – Feature required out of the box – minimal customization effort by the vendor or the addition of third party add-on components is acceptable

    o   5 – Feature required out of the box – must not be a customization or third party add-on

- Decide and document what the acceptable range of responses is for each requirement. For example, when evaluating enterprise report writers, you might have a requirement that the product support capability to prevent runaway queries from consuming all of the reporting platform's resources. The scoring might be

    o   0 – functionality not supported

    o   1 – Supports resource caps and execution time caps, but not configurable user-by-user and report-by-report

    o   2 – Supports both resource caps and execution time caps, configurable by both user and by report (Max score).

- Create a spreadsheet that auto-scores the responses. Consider a feature that was assigned a weight of 3 and a max possible score of 2. If a particular vendor received a score of 1 out of 2, then they got 50%, multiplied by the assigned weight of 3 yields a weighted score of 1.5 (50% of 3). The weighted score is always ((vendor's raw score for requirement / max possible score for requirement) * assigned weight for requirement).

- Total all the weighted scores for each vendor, and you'll get the cumulative score. This is the best way I have found to ensure a fair, objective vendor evaluation.

When you select a candidate pool of potential vendors,[36] you can actually send them the list of requirements and scores up front, before they bother coming around for the inevitable dog-and-pony show. It's only fair to be up front with the vendors regarding your requirements. Ask them to score themselves and provide any supporting documentation or explanation they feel is needed. I usually provide the list in a Word document, rather than providing the actual spreadsheet with weights and calculations. No need to give away all your secrets!

Your first pass might be based on the scoring by the vendor. If they admit up front they don't have the features you need, then there's no need for you to waste any further time. For those that claim near perfect scores, tell them that you want to discuss these particular features with them personally as the next step. Get all your stakeholders (representatives from all the business units that gave you requirements, and representatives from all four architectural domains) in the room with the vendor, and go through the list, asking pointed questions. Odds are pretty good you'll score the vendor lower than they scored themselves.

I recommend using a decision matrix similar to the following. It's a great way to make sure that your requirements are well documented, that your evaluation is as objective as possible, and that the relative importance of each requirement is factored into the final score.

You can add pretty much anything to this matrix: a score for number of installs of the product, a score based on an interview with a client reference. It's a pretty flexible method of objectively evaluating vendor solutions.

If two or three vendors all score well, then consider going to a **Proof of Concept (POC)** showdown, where you ask each vendor to prove their claims for your most critical requirements. Ideally, you should make the vendor POCs be as similar as possible to each other, using conditions as near as possible to your production environment. Typically, the vendor will pay for this engagement. Make sure the POC occurs in your own environment, if possible, not in the vendor's lab. And, if the vendor is doing the installation and configuration, ask to sit with them while it occurs, so you can measure how long it takes, what kinds of problems were encountered, and how they were overcome.

Contract management
We aren't going to speak in depth about every single IT function, but contract management is one of the functions that are critical in order to tame the IT chaos at the enterprise level. Contract management impacts your EAG functional framework in many non-intuitive ways. One key to managing IT complexity at the enterprise level is to run all the contract negotiation, execution, performance monitoring, modification, and termination through a single, dedicated office. This includes contracts with customers, vendors, and employees (full time and contractors). There are a great many legal aspects that require specialized management (such as non-disclosure agreements), but a surprising majority of the work involves following established processes and managing working relationships.

---

[36] I recommend looking at evaluations from both Gartner and Forrester. Both companies are well-respected industry analysts who perform unbiased reviews of products and solutions. I like to use both sources. In my experience, Gartner's reviews lean toward an IT perspective, and Forrester leans toward a business perspective, both of which are valuable.

Reporting/Dashboard Vendor Comparison Evaluation				Vendor Evaluation			Weighted Score		
Feature	Scoring	Max Score	Weight	Vendor A	Vendor B	Vendor C	Vendor A	Vendor B	Vendor C
General Functionality									
Zero footprint - no software installed on client. Solution is 100% browser based for end users, for developers, and for administrative functionality.	0 - reader requires software installation 1 - author/ admin requires software installation 2 - no software installed on any client	2	5	1	1	1	2.5 [37]	2.5	2.5
Dashboarding Capabilities									
Advanced GUI components: scatter plots, and fuel gauges	0 - no 1 - partial 2 - yes	2	5	1	2	2	2.5	5	5
Hierarchical Reporting Capabilities									
Hierarchical report executes and results displayed in real time, on demand	0 - no 1 - yes	1	4	1	1	1	4	4	4
Reports can be saved as Excel spreadsheets (pivot tables)	0 - no 1 - yes	1	5	1	1	1	5	5	5
Development Features									
Style templates available for all interface types (dashboards, hierarchical reporting, traditional reporting)	0 - no 1 - yes	1	4	1	1	1	4	4	4
Delivery Features									
Ability to create "books" which bundle together many reports into one output (typically for printing or saving as PDF or Excel)	0 - no 1 - yes	1	4	1	1	1	4	4	4
Security Capabilities									
Reader interface complies with corporate requirements for network edge applications (provided separately)	0 - no 1 - partial 2 - yes	2	4	1	2	2	2	4	4
Performance									
Provides options for future scalability	0 - no 1 - yes	1	4	1	1	1	4	4	4
TOTAL SCORE		207		42	59	56	161	207	199
							78%	100 %	96 %

Figure 5.1 Sample Vendor Evaluation Spreadsheet. As you can tell from the totals, the actual evaluation was much longer.

[37] ((vendors raw score)/(max possible score)) * (weight)

It's surprising how many companies don't have a centralized contract management organization with infrastructure designed to integrate with other IT support functions such as asset inventory, sales, and performance metrics. Whether you are the vendor or the customer in the contractual relationship, there are going to be requirements in the contract that relate to these other IT functions. If you want to ensure that your contract management activities are being managed efficiently on behalf of the business, then you need to make sure your contract management software doesn't *only* do a good job of managing the contract text, but is designed to integrate to the relevant business metrics you're collecting within other IT functions.

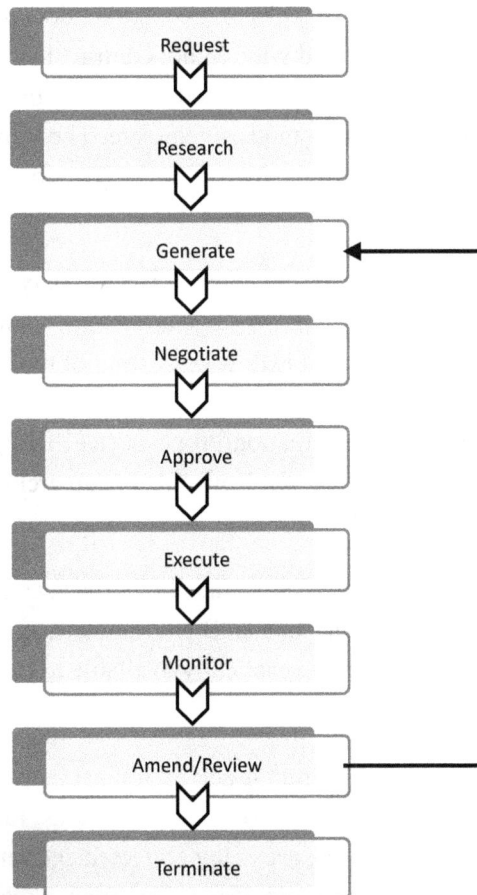

Figure 5.2 Simplified Contract Management lifecycle

The stages of contract management include:

- **Request**. An ideal enterprise contract management system will have a repository of contracts and contract type templates. There should be an online tool to allow business users to request new contracts as needed. Many of these tools have the ability to request contract templates for any contract type.

- **Research**. Existing contracts should be able to be searched online by any user with the appropriate security authorization and business need. When requesting a vendor contract, it isn't at all uncommon in a large company to find that another area of the organization already has a contract in place with the same vendor. The business users need to be able to examine and compare the terms and conditions in various similar contracts, without digging through filing cabinets full of legal documents. Forrester claims that a centralized contract repository is by far the most common use case for purchasing commercial contract management products.[38]

- **Generate**. The requestor should be able to use an online wizard that makes use of predefined contract templates with up-to-date terms and conditions pre-vetted by Legal. The legal department can then spend most of their time managing the exceptions that require additional negotiation or special terms and conditions.

- **Negotiate**. A contract management system is more than just a document repository and templates. It should be able to track changes to the contract documents and templates over time, noting who made the change, when, and why. Many contract management systems have the ability to collect a database of pluggable terms and conditions that can be added to contracts as needed, even if they are not part of the standard template. The standard template for each type of contract, in fact, can be thought of as a custom subset of the globally available terms and conditions.

- **Approve**. Contract changes and changes to contract templates typically fall under a workflow management tool to allow customized, multi-stage approvals, with automatic routing and tracking. Contract approval may be a workflow consisting of multiple documents and multiple signatures. For example, before a major new software purchase, you may require various non-disclosures, a formal Request For Information/Proposal (RFI/RFP), and a Proof of Concept, all of which involve paperwork and approvals. Your EAG team architectural review would be part of this approval workflow.

- **Execute**. Once the contract is approved, it is placed into the searchable repository, and becomes a legally binding business requirement. In a B2B environment, contractually approved sales, pricing and service levels need to be automatically available to the procurement and invoicing systems.

- **Compliance monitoring**. While a contract is active, it must be periodically reviewed to make sure all parties are complying with all the terms and conditions. Ideally the contractual metrics, such as user licenses and service levels, are being collected and retained automatically, so that compliance monitoring is quick and simple. If non-compliance results in automatic penalties (paid or received), your contract management process should include the necessary monitoring and alerts. *This integration piece is the main thing that needs to be addressed in order to lift the contract management function from an isolated silo of expertise to an integrated component within an enterprise wide EAG program.* The relevant sales, license, and performance metrics that are under contract need to be collected across the enterprise into a central repository, and tied automatically to contractual requirements. Compliance monitoring is not an afterthought, and should be automated and continuous, with alerts when compliance is at risk. The EAG templates for policy, process, and role governance artifacts need a section that requires that these metrics be included in every project.

- **Amend/review**. The original contract had a business justification such as revenue generation, expense reduction, and risk reduction. This justification should be periodically reviewed to ensure that the contract is still meeting the original business need. Included in the analysis of the

---

[38] http://bit.ly/2FZ866i.

business need should be the growing or shrinking demand for the number of licenses, units, or performance levels under contract. In some cases, the contract may need to be amended over time in order to best meet the changing needs of the business. This periodic review should be an automated workflow, and should be able to accommodate changes in staffing and ownership over time. The affected staff should be periodically interviewed to see if the nature of the contractual relationship has change, or needs to change. Many contracts have built in termination dates, which should automatically trigger a review.

- **Terminate**. At some point, every contract will come to the end of its useful life, and will need to be terminated. The termination process should have been spelled out in the contract, and the workflow and approvals processes created. Terminated contracts should be retained in the contract repository for future research.

This is not a treatise on contract management, and I am *not* a legal expert. There are many complexities and some major differences in contracts depending on whether you are the vendor or the customer, or whether the contract is for products or services. None of that detail is covered here. Rather, the goal here is to show how your contract management function fits into your enterprise architecture and governance program, primarily in the area of compliance monitoring. It should have an architectural vision that is an integral part of your overall high-level software infrastructure lifecycle management program (functional area), and it should have a tactical roadmap to implement that vision over time. This vision and roadmap should be reviewed at least annually prior to budgeting the next year's infrastructure spend. There should be documented policies, standards, processes, and roles that are all retained with the rest of the company's architecture and governance documents.

Any contractual metrics should be part of the requirements and standards for the relevant IT infrastructure components. If the contract guarantees certain service levels, the contractual requirement should generate an automatic requirement that the actual service level be monitored and collected automatically to facilitate periodic compliance review, and alerts generated proactively and automatically when the terms and conditions of the contract are not being met.

These contractual requirements are integral to your IT infrastructure, not just words on paper in a file cabinet in the legal offices. Managing IT complexity on behalf of the business requires that the contract management process be as central to IT development and operations as any other business requirement.

The cost of failure to provide an integral contract management process includes business delays due to contract creation inefficiencies, legal penalties for non-compliance, damaged customer relationships, bad publicity, and loss of revenue. With an integrated contract management process, your sales cycles will be faster, your lead conversion rates higher, your highly paid lawyers will be focusing on complicated exceptions rather than mundane paperwork, processes will be streamlined and automated, contracts will be consolidated and consistent, and contracts will be automatically monitored for compliance and continuing relevance.

Recommended reading:
- Enterprise Contract Lifecycle Management: Mastering Integration. By Gerard Blokdyk
- Forrester Wave: Contract Life-Cycle Management. Forrester Research, 2016 Q3

Software implementation and configuration

When you stand up new software, some work must be done to make sure that it is configured correctly and consistently. This is easily confused with Software Configuration Management (SCM). SCM is that part of the software development lifecycle concerned with managing various releases as they are assembled and propagated through the development, test, and production environments. We'll discuss that later, under the software development lifecycle functional area.

In the context of the Software Infrastructure Lifecycle, software configuration plays an important part in your ability to support IT functionality on behalf of the business. It's important for disaster recovery, for software upgrades, and important when re-implementing software due to a hardware replacement (upgrade or recovery). Most companies I've worked at regularly replace hardware such as servers, workstations, and network equipment on a three-to-five year rotation. Rather than looking forward to a newer, more powerful desktop, most people tend to dread the inevitable three weeks loss of productivity that occurs after their workstation is replaced, when they have to slowly identify and re-configure all the stuff that's no longer working. This occurs both when the machine is upgraded, and when the hardware has a failure and needs to be replaced. It's even worse if it's a server that is being upgraded.

There are many approaches to this problem, from archived images that can be laid down quickly, to cloud-based software that can be provisioned pre-configured. The point being that you can't support the software infrastructure lifecycle IT functions for the business if you don't provide support for installing and configuring software.

Think about it. For many of us, the main contact we have with corporate IT resources outside our immediate working area is when the powers that be are coming through and messing with your workstations and servers. How pleasant and efficient has that experience been at your company?

Software release management

Software release management is very similar to implementation and configuration management. The main distinction being that release management is the entry point for "new" configurations. These configurations need to be tested thoroughly to ensure there are no interoperability or system integration issues, and that the new configuration complies with all business requirements for feature/function, and security.

Software development release management is another function altogether, and will be discussed later.

Software licensing

Most server-based software has the ability to track and report licensing. Client-based software can be tracked with network scanning tools and agents installed on each workstation. From an enterprise IT management standpoint, the important thing is that the contractual licensing requirements are known and exposed, the licenses-in-use are collected in an appropriate manner with all relevant information (i.e. software release levels, machine ID, user ID), and that alerts are automatically generated when a risk threshold is exceeded. This involves integration with contract management, network security, application

THE APPLICATION DOMAIN • 185

configuration, and software discovery agents. All of these different IT functions must work together in order to support a well-documented unified strategic vision of enterprise software license management. Policies must be set in place to ensure that each function meets the larger business needs. Standards must be defined for interoperability. Processes and roles must clearly define who is responsible for doing what, when.

Most of the licensing requirements begin with software contracts. It is imperative that you have a contract management system in place that collects licensing requirements in a central repository that can be accessed by processes that compare the contractual requirements to the actual usage.

Polices should ensure that no software should be installed within the enterprise until all three of these requirements are met:

- The contractual licensing threshold information is entered into the centralized contract management system.
- A methodology has been implemented to collect the licenses in use into a central repository.
- Alerts have been set up to notify the appropriate roles when licensing thresholds are exceeded.

Standards will define how these policies are to be implemented. There may be different standards for server-based and client-based software or different standards for mainframe versus Unix servers. You will have to consider how you are going to manage cloud-based software. All of that is fine so long as all of the permutations have defined standards, and all of those standards comply with the corporate policies.

The processes and roles in your framework need to specify who is responsible for license compliance, what process they use to determine compliance, and how often that process must be performed.

Software security

Security is at the top of everyone's priorities these days. Regulatory requirements exist in almost every industry to address the many breaches that have occurred. If you have not had a security breach, your time is coming. Alternatively, and more likely, it's already come and you just haven't realized it yet. Just this week I was sending an internal email regarding a CDI issue, and our email software auto-complete feature sent it to my wife instead. Because the email contained a Social Security Number, I had to follow our corporate processes to report this as a breach.

Software security is a discipline unto itself, one that would take a lifetime of study to master, and one that's changing every day as new technology is created to address growing threats. The information, application, and technology IT professionals who are responsible for managing the security function day-to-day are experts in their field and tend to work independently, without consulting other areas. To some degree, that's inevitable due to the level of technical expertise needed, but in other respects, that can lead to an ivory-tower, IT-built security solution that looks great on paper, but doesn't actually meet the needs of the business. For holistic security function management at the enterprise level, certain aspects of the security function have to be managed in a larger context, not in a security silo.

In the larger context of an enterprise wide IT function management framework, there are a few important considerations to add:

- **Information**. You need to carefully read and understand what it is you are actually securing. This is usually an interpretation of regulatory requirements by your legal department. Security usually begins with information. Typically, you only secure applications because they access and manipulate information, and you only secure technology because it contains or grants access to sensitive information. Security is information-centric.

- **Unified provisioning and de-provisioning**. You need a central group within the enterprise that handles provisioning requests for new access across the enterprise. Using one team dedicated to this function across the enterprise ensures:

  - Proper separation of duties
  - Consistent, well-documented governance artifacts
  - Auditing of process flow and approvals
  - Integration with contract management (contractual user count metrics)
  - Regular review of active users, to ensure they still require access
  - Integration with HR functions so that terminations and transfers automatically de-provision access
  - Integration with user authentication products, such as LDAP and Kerberos

- **Support for labels**. See page 157. The information domain will define which data elements fall under which labels, and may actually implement the label-based masking based on user authorizations in the database. In cases where this can't be achieved, the application domain must implement an equivalent solution.

- **Support for categories**. See page 163. Classifications define what data can be exposed under what conditions. These are often defined by a regulatory body. Any application that delivers information must comply with the rules for the security classification of the data it is exposing. Requirements might include authentication and authorization, logging both successful and unsuccessful logon attempts, logging who actually accessed which information, etc.

These days, security compliance is one of the most intrusive, disruptive, resented IT functions in the corporate environment. If you want to manage your overall IT infrastructure efficiently and effectively, you are going to have to find a way to address those factors. I believe that the use of a functional framework can help put security in context, ensuring that the integration points are well defined in terms of the larger business drivers. Remember, security decisions are ultimately business decisions, not IT decisions.

Software operations/support

IT operations and support functions are what keep the IT infrastructure running from moment to moment. While the rest of us sit around talking about IT complexity, the operations and support staff are frantically dealing with it all day long. Clearly, if you want to control the IT chaos, you are going to have to address IT operations, where the rubber of your architecture and governance meets the road of reality.

For the most part, your operations support polices, standards, processes, and roles are going to be specific to your organization. That said, there are many operations support best practices that you should be driving at an enterprise level.

Here again, there are several different approaches to thinking about operational support functions. During my years in the telecom industry, my own thinking was heavily influenced by the TeleManagement Forum (TM Forum) especially their eTOM Business Process Framework,[39] which was an operating model for telecom providers. I understand it has since been expanded to be more industry agnostic.

Regardless of what framework you use, your application management and operations will probably include the following functionality:

- **Job scheduling**. Running and monitoring both the core business applications and supporting jobs such as backups.

- **Production environment support**. Such as running backups and bouncing servers.

- **Production job support**. Identifying and resolving production issues. Traditional production support includes an "emergency fix" environment where production-outage fixes can be quickly tested outside the normal development pipeline, usually subject to later review by development after production functionality is restored.

- **Change management**. Implementing upgrades and new software. The operations staff often also functions as the change management team responsible for moving from development to test, which can be viewed as a dry run of the production implementation. No code or database structure changes should enter the production environments without going through production support, with full audit trail and signoffs.

- **System Integration Testing**. While user acceptance testing is largely under the control of the QA and test staff, system integration testing is a mini-production environment, something that used to be known as a *model office*. All production job schedules also run in this environment, supported by operations staff.

- **Operational requests**. Handling requests for data patches and ad-hoc job execution, usually through a request management system replete with signoffs.

Provisioning and de-provisioning application access is considered by some to be an operational function. Though it's often performed by the same resources that support operations, I would consider it a separate function under application security, not part of the application support function. This enforces a separation of duties between those who grant access and those who use that access.

The term **DevOps** was originally introduced by Andrew Shafer and Patrick Debois in 2008. As originally envisioned, Devops was simply an effort to bring the development team and the operations team closer together. It's no surprise that Shafer and Debois introduced the term at an Agile conference. The fast cycle turnaround times involved in agile development and test methodologies require corresponding frequent iterations of operations and support production updates. Likewise, many of the functions in the

---

[39] http://bit.ly/2DyH7Qs.

software development lifecycle (i.e. release management, change management) seem very operational in nature. It was inevitable that someone concluded that these two teams, development and operations, needed to work more closely together and come up with some integrated commonality of processes and tooling.

All that's well and good, but in recent years I think some DevOps proponents are taking things too far. Some suggest that the development and operations teams not just work together, but actually comprise the same team. "Who better," they say, "to install and support applications in production than the developers who built them?" I don't believe this is a good idea at all. There's a reason why most companies mandate a separation of duties between development and operations (page 45). Developers are incented to turn projects around as quickly as possible, where the operations team is incented to maintain the stability and uptime of the production environment. These are conflicting goals; the good kind of conflict that creates much-needed checks and balances. Furthermore, your development staff is usually a highly skilled, highly compensated set of resources. Why would you want development resources supporting production rather than developing new feature function? One of the prime objectives of the Scrum Master role in the agile Scrum methodology is to remove roadblocks so that developers can focus on developing. Turning a developer lose in production invites a great temptation to game the system. The developer should never be responsible for final QA testing of the code they build, nor should they be responsible for implementing and supporting it in production.

The EAG program sets the vision and the processes by which IT processes are managed. One important part of that responsibility is to ensure that the proper separation of duties exists. Without this separation of duties, you have the fox guarding the henhouse, and no amount of paper policies are going to protect your IT chickens.

As more and more of your operational systems move to the cloud, the nature of your applications operations support functions will evolve. If the vendor is managing the software as well as the hardware, then the vendor will take over much of the traditional responsibility of release management and production support. They may even handle the ad hoc requests. You may only be responsible for monitoring that the service levels comply with contractual obligations. On the other hand, your company may be hosting the software as a service for other companies. In this case, the operations support function becomes your core business, critical to your business model. In this case, you'll want very robust, well-defined, scalable processes that recognize the importance of this function to your business.

Software operation support isn't a standalone function. Like all IT functions, it's integrated with other processes across the enterprise. Operations is the heartbeat of the business where many events are generated that impact information and application security, contractual service levels, data acquisition, information quality, and hardware performance. These functions must be coordinated across the enterprise information systems and across domains. The functional framework helps create the structure which can be used to articulate and coordinate those integration points.

Software end of life

Application decommissioning is the process of identifying outdated, unsupported applications and removing or replacing them.

From a *business process* perspective, the application's functionality may still be required by the business, in which case the functionality and information may need to be migrated to a new solution.

From a *business data* perspective, if the information is still relevant to the business, the application's data may need to be archived to a repository where it can be accessed without the continued license and support costs of the application whose functionality is no longer used. In the context of an enterprise framework, keep in mind that these applications may contain information that must be retained for legal, operational, or analytical purposes after the application and the hardware it runs on are removed from the infrastructure.

From either perspective, decommissioning an application involves coordination between all three IT architectural domains. It's unwise to let any single domain make all the decommissioning decisions, any more than you would let that domain make all the decisions when the application was first spun up. Software end-of-life must be coordinated with application and technology end-of-life. It might be argues that coordinating all three simultaneously is actually easier than coordinating the decommissioning and replacement of one domain while retaining the others; perhaps completely replacing the software infrastructure while retaining the hardware and porting the information.

Once an application is retired, you don't want to be forced to continue to support the application infrastructure just to have access to the legacy information. There are many third party products that can help you archive information without continuing to support the application that created it. While each offering is unique, I think you'll find two basic approaches. Both were discussed from a data standpoint in the information lifecycle end-of-life function, but will be revisited now from an application standpoint.

One approach is to archive the data to a single archive solution that has a model capable of supporting archiving from many different applications into a unified solution similar to your ELDM. While there are products that claim to do this, it's a huge undertaking to map application data to an enterprise model. The only way I've seen this work effectively is when the majority of the data was already being loaded into such a repository already, in the form of an Enterprise Data Warehouse (EDW). In this case, though the destination model isn't the same as the source application, the data concepts themselves are retained. One advantage of this approach is that, if the operational functionality is migrated to a new application that will also be integrated into the data warehouse, then integrated analytical reporting can be performed across both sides the migration. Another advantage might be that a good bit of the data you need to retain is already being propagated to the warehouse, greatly reducing the effort of implanting the archiving application solution. Note that this is *not* the same as a backup solution, as the data in a warehouse would not be suitable for restoring to the source application.

The other approach is to archive the data into an Application-specific Data Mart (ADM), usually simply a dump of the source data, using the original data structures. This is much less expensive to implement, but, without the application interfaces, the data may be difficult to collect and interpret. In this case you are literally shutting down the application but retaining the underlying application database.

The choice regarding which route would work best in your environment really depends on how many data elements need to be retained, and of those, how many are already being retained in an enterprise model.

The ROI of decommissioning an application is calculated by comparing the cost to maintain the legacy application (in continued hardware, software, and human resources, plus the costs of any compliance or security risks) to the cost of the decommission effort itself (analytical archiving plus operational migration). The analytical archiving and operational migration costs both have a one-time cost and an ongoing support cost. Whether or not application decommissioning makes sense is a business decision that must be made in the context of these relative costs, not based on architectural IT infrastructure purity.

If you plan to be in business very long, this decision is going to come up more than once. The architecture domains should consider whether a greater business benefit would be realized by establishing a repeatable process for decommissioning legacy applications. This repeatable process can take the form of a robust commercial product, or it can simple be documented enterprise policies, standards, processes, and roles that apply to future application decommissioning decisions in your functional framework.

Two kinds of people – motivated versus unmotivated

There are two kinds of people in this world: those that will do the job enthusiastically, and those that do it reluctantly.

I once joined a product development team where all the developers wanted to work on the new features and functions, but no one wanted to address the outstanding customer-reported issues related to the older code. Several of the original development team had long since left the company, leaving large sections of complicated code undocumented and little understood. No one wanted to spend their day trying to root out the cause of these issues and fix them. An attitude had developed that working customer support issues was a task for second-string developers who could not be trusted with the new stuff. As you can imagine, the product suffered for this.

A new manager joined the team at the same time I did, and initiated a very simple, effective program that turned this attitude around in a matter of a few weeks. Without saying anything about her plan, she went to a party supply store and bought a box full of plastic alligators (I'm still wondering why a party supply store needs to stock plastic alligators in bulk). At the end of the next team meeting, she asked one of the developers to stand up, and presented him with an alligator, in recognition of his willingness to "wade into the murky waters of legacy code, find that beast, and wrestle it into submission." She explained that she had picked certain difficult problems that had been sitting on the queue for months to be *alligator issues*. At this particular company, we all worked in cubicles, and no one was allowed to put anything on the tops of the built-in bookcases where it could been seen from across the floor. This manager got a corporate exception for alligators. Imagine looking out at a sea of cubicles, and seeing nothing but one lone alligator.

The next week, this developer, who had been unlucky enough to get assigned support duty that month, found and resolved another long-outstanding issue, and was presented with another identical alligator. By the following week, developers were asking to work on those most difficult support issues. Everyone knew she was buying our attention with a dime store toy, but these alligators became badges of honor, like silhouettes painted on the side of a fighter pilot's cockpit to proclaim past victories. It was silly, but it worked. People started wearing alligator themed t-shirts, and buying alligator coffee mugs.

I think this technique wouldn't have worked everywhere, but it worked in this case because the people she was trying to motivate thrived on recognition of their coding prowess. I've thought about this a lot, and think there's something going on here that lies at the heart of team motivation.

If your job responsibility includes managing a team to accomplish some business goal, odds are pretty good that the team members don't leap out of bed each morning eager to get to work and help you make your incentives. You can crack a whip and force them to do the work, but to be really effective, you have to find a way to motivate them. The problem is that different people are motivated by different things.

Later at this same company, this manager left, and I threw my hat into the ring to be the replacement. One day I was a peer, the next day I was the boss. That's a very difficult transition to make. As a developer, I could point to a stack of code printouts at the end of each day to show what I had accomplished. As a manager, these tangible outcomes are harder to come by. My uncle, a top-level executive at Marriott, sat me down and explained that, as a manager, I was still building things, but instead of building programs, I was building a team, and that was going to take a great deal of hard work on my part but was going to result in even more satisfaction. He was absolutely right on both counts.

Thinking back to those alligators, I realized that wouldn't work for my new team. Not everybody was looking for recognition. I had one older mainframe developer whose greatest fear was that he would lose his job and not be able to find another at his age. I had a business analyst whose main reason for coming to work every day was to get out of the empty house and interact with people socially. I had another developer who only worked the minimum hours to get group health insurance – her husband had a small business and brought in most of their income, but private health insurance would have been very costly. She actually put almost 90% of her salary in 401K. And so on.

I realized that to really motivate a team you have to be able to cast a vision of your goal in terms of what really appeals to each individual team member. To those that really just wanted job stability, I had to cast a vision that showed that the new product we were developing was intended to be a competitive differentiator, very important to the company, and a key component of our long-term corporate strategy. To those that wanted social interaction, I emphasized how closely we would all be working together, and the big release party we would have when it was done. For those developers who wanted recognition, I promised that the new product would have a scrolling list in the Help/About box with the names of the team members who met their deliverables on the project.

I had one young mainframe developer right out of school who I couldn't figure out how to motivate. She seemed to feel that she was in competition with the older developer who had 30-plus years of experience. He had been doing this so long that he could drop hands to keyboard and perfect code flowed from his fingertips. No matter what you gave him, it was complete and tested by the end of the day. He was assigned quite a bit more project tasks than the younger developer, and would wind up completing all of his and helping her figure out the all the problems in her code. Really, he could have written it faster, but that was OK. We hired her out of school and expected this to be a learning period. However, she didn't see it that way. She started coming in later and later, and leaving earlier. She called in sick a lot. She didn't talk much, and, I kid you not, even began dressing in very drab clothing. It was clear she was miserable and something had to happen.

I happened to hear her talking one day about how she did a lot of volunteer work for her church because of her familiarity with the Microsoft Office product suite. She showed us some of the publications she had developed, and they were *truly* impressive. They looked very creative and professional. It was clear this young person had untapped skills. I consider myself a power user of those tools, but that doesn't mean I can make the font, color, and other choices that set a publication apart as professional. Hers were truly polished.

As it happened, we also had a task on the plan to develop a customer-facing spreadsheet that our sales teams could use to gather all the information used to calculate the properly sized technology infrastructure for our product at a client location. Seeing her work, I asked her to take that task on, even though it meant reducing some of her mainframe development workload. The result was like night and day. She started coming in earlier, staying later, and being much more outspoken in meetings. Her "health" improved, and I swear, she started dressing in bright, flashy colors. I've never seen such a dramatic turnaround. Moreover, the work she produced was brilliant. The sales team loved her, and begged for more. I still had her on programming tasks, but those tasks no longer *defined* her. This woman was motivated by respect. She needed it like she needed air to breathe. When she received real, honest respect, she flourished and the team benefited.

My uncle was right. Managing a team is hard, hard work. But it's one of the most personally gratifying things I've done. I can no longer remember all the software I've developed over the years, but I remember every one of the people I've managed. At the end of my career, I'll be much prouder and happier to remember making a difference in someone's life than in having written a particularly elegant algorithm to make widgets.

Architecture involves change. In particular, it involves changing the way people do their jobs. Coming up with the architecture and governance documents is long, hard work, but it will all be for naught if you can't motivate people to make the changes. Standing over people with a stick isn't viable in the long term. You will literally drive off all your best people, who know they can get a job somewhere else where they aren't micromanaged every day. After a while, all you'll have left is the people who either have been beaten down until they don't care anymore, or people who hate their jobs but aren't good enough to get hired somewhere else. Is that what you want?

It seems like a contradiction, but if you want a team of people who are self-motivated, you are going to have to supply them with the motivation. You're going to have to cast this vision of the future in terms that let them see how that vision will benefit them personally. How is this going to make their lives easier than the way things are done today? How is this going to be less work instead of more? How is this going to make the company more viable and their jobs more stable? Yes, it's very true that we're all adults and that, if you cash the paycheck, we should be able to expect you to come to work and do what you're told. However, you aren't the only employer in town. People aren't going to stay in a position where they believe they'll be miserable when they could easily go work for someone else. Back in August of 2015, Victor Lipman published a famous article in Forbes magazine entitled "People Leave

Managers, Not Companies."[40] In that article he attributes unmotivated employees with $450 billion in lost productivity annually in the US.

Motivation isn't just a buzzword. This is real business impact. If you want to retain the best talent, it's up to you to cast the strategic vision in attractive terms. It's part of your job. If you can't do that, you are not fulfilling the responsibilities of the architecture role.

Software development lifecycle functions

Software development seems at first to be project-centric; something that could be done in isolation without a lot of thought about the larger enterprise. You have your business requirements. As long as you meet them, what difference does it make how you got there, right?

If you've worked in the real world very long at all, though, you know this is incredibly naïve. When you're working on hundreds of projects, with hundreds more already completed and in production, things get very chaotic if you don't have some shared vision and common processes to coordinate the work and assure compliance, consistency, and smooth integration.

The accepted approach to coordinating all of these development projects is to think of the various software development functions as part of a **Software Development Lifecycle (SDLC)**. I want to step through some of the functions in this lifecycle. I don't want to discuss how to develop software, but rather how to integrate the software development process into an overall EAG program. This will simplify the integration of all the work efforts into a unified whole that efficiently manages the IT software development functions.

Initiating and tracking projects

Software development begins with a request. Depending on the methodology you use, the request process can take many forms, but in the end, all software development begins with a request. Even at that early stage, things can go horribly wrong very quickly.

The first hurdle is ensuring that all of the projects actually benefit the business and are the best use of the business's investment. The NIST model (see page 9) insisted that all project requests flow downhill. Corporate executives set the company's goals for the fiscal year. Then executives responsible for each information system (page 55) design strategic projects for how their area of responsibility will support those corporate goals. Any project that doesn't directly support the corporate goals is not in alignment with the corporate objectives.

That's certainly true for the big strategic projects, but in the real world, the owner of each information system also has the responsibility to maintain and improve the business functionality they've put in place over years past. Problems need fixing, workflow needs automating, business growth must be accommodated, and new regulatory requirements need addressing.

---

[40] https://bit.ly/2uozGZ3.

Let me describe a typical project initiation pipeline from years past. Hold on to that criticism for a minute.

All kinds of project requests will be coming in; far more than can possibly be completed. All of these project requests should already have **business requirements**, stated in business terms. There needs to be some preliminary process of weeding them down and prioritizing them, only allowing a few to proceed farther into the project pipeline. There are several terms for weeding, but I'll call this **Gate 1**, where projects are prioritized based on their value to the business. Strategic projects are the first through the gate. Then follow the departmental objectives that don't directly support the corporate goals, in the order of the value they provide. At some point, the next holding area is full, and the gate is shut. Projects that can't show any business value don't make it through gate 1. Who's the gatekeeper? Ideally it would be the EAG program, but realistically, at least until those strategic projects make it through, the Information Systems business owners will want to be very involved. But these business owners are high-placed executives, who don't need to be bogged down in evaluating all the little projects that follow.

This doesn't sound very agile, but you can't really turn a development team loose on a project backlog until those projects have been approved and prioritized. You might think of this as an agile "Sprint 0." In rare cases, you will be have a development team that receives only vetted project requests, something like a development helpdesk, where the requestors are all authorized to initiate projects, and no Gate 1 is necessary. I haven't found this to be all that common among development teams that support large, complex projects.

Typically, what happens is that the business owner will first decide what their strategic projects are for the next year, and will put those in the budget. Some of those strategic projects will be the ones that support the corporate goals. Others will be the business owner's pet projects for their area of responsibility. There will hopefully be a pool of budget dollars remaining for *keeping the lights on*, which is set aside for all the project detail that the business owner doesn't care to be involved in, so long as the strategic projects aren't at risk.

Therefore, the business owner already knows which projects are strategic and identifies them as such. I like to think of this as a field full of project *sheep*, waiting to get through the gate. The business owner goes through and paints his favorite sheep to identify them. The business owner then leaves all the work of sorting out the sheep to the EAG team shepherds, who know those painted sheep have to be at the front of the line. Once they get through the gate, more sheep are let through using some rough prioritization based on business value, until there is no room for any more.

When Gate 1 closes, the EAG team will begin designing very high-level architectural approach requirements for each project, followed by a level of effort. This level of effort is like a t-shirt size: under 80 FTE hours might be small, under 200 FTE hours might be medium, and under 1000 large. This whole process shouldn't take more than an hour per strategic process. This isn't a detailed estimate; it's just a level of effort. Based on the t-shirt size, the sheep might be reprioritized, and a few sent back to the outer pasture. This is **Gate 2**. Some projects also have hardware and software purchase costs. Usually, the EAG knows about these strategic projects ahead of time, and has good estimates for those costs. You may or may not know which vendor you will use, but you know the cost range they are going to fit in.

Once through Gate 2, each project gets the architectural requirements. Several project management methodologies call these the **functional requirements**. Architects don't need to be a bottleneck here.

The architectural requirements that apply to all projects should be documented in your standards, and don't need to be repeated in each architectural requirements document. All that is needed is to capture the relevant information about the desired architectural approach for each project that isn't in the standards document already. If you find yourself documenting the same thing repeatedly, it probably needs to be a standard. Several EAG domains might contribute domain-specific architectural requirements, all of which should be agreed upon within the whole EAG team before releasing. In many cases, the original business requirements did not contain sufficient detail, and the architects will need to work with the requester to flesh them out.

The architectural approach documents (the functional requirements) are often quite simple, and may be no more than a paragraph or two specifying which infrastructure is to be reused and which is to be developed. If the project is going to play a part in rolling out some new strategic functionality, hopefully that design was put together by the EAG team long beforehand.

For traditional project management, this is the point where the project plan would be created and the lead developer assigned. The architectural requirements are given to a lead developer or project architect, who will expand them into a detailed design, also known as **technical requirements** that could be given to a developer to code. Since the EAG architects are matrixed to the EAG team from their day jobs where they are embedded within an information system (see page 27), the person writing the technical requirements might actually be the same person who created the architectural requirements, wearing a different hat.

For large t-shirt sized projects, the lead developer may need to create a detailed estimate from the detailed design. This detailed estimate isn't a t-shirt size; it should be as close as possible to real hours. The detailed estimate may take several days to produce, which is why they are usually only performed for the large t-shirt sized projects. The detailed estimate may then go through a final **Gate 3** to get approval for the spend, now that an accurate estimate of the final cost is available. Gate 3 may not be required for small projects.

At this point, the project initiation function would be complete, and the software development function could begin.

This gating process was very typical of the way projects were initiated twenty, perhaps even fifteen years ago. However, when the Agile Manifesto[41] was signed back in 2001, many other approaches to project management were already being practiced. Agile development processes quickly became very popular, for many reasons.

I like Agile a lot, and use it myself for many types of projects. But for other projects, I find that other approaches work better.

Agile versus Waterfall – which is "better"?
One of the biggest discussions in the realm of project management for the last decade is Agile development.

Waterfall development methodology refers to the practice of first gathering all of the requirements. When all of the requirements are formally documented, the project is passed to a design team. When all of the design is finished, the project is passed to a development team. When all of the development is

[41] http://bit.ly/1fzzUi3.

completely finished, the project is passed to a test team. This methodology, when displayed on a Gantt chart, looks like a series of stages, each of which end with a drop to the next stage, similar to a waterfall dropping from level to level. Waterfall development has been practiced for many decades and has many advantages. There are many project management tools in place designed for this methodology, and it is very easy for management to tell whether the project is on track or not.

Agile development methodology isn't a single project management approach; it's any project management approach that complies with the 12 principles of the Agile Manifesto. A team of IT and business professionals must work together with the business, communicating constantly, to deliver iterative content showing incremental business value using any one of these methodologies.

Like many techniques and technologies, agile development processes work really well for some types of problems, and not so well for others. It might be more fair to say that Agile works better for some phases of projects than others.

Agile is fantastic, for example, in taking on small projects that don't build on one another – a help desk queue for new report creation, for example. Agile also works well for incremental enhancement to a mature product whose architecture is already well established.

A pure agile development approach begins to break down, in my opinion, when dealing with large projects that will be building out complex new architecture. In these cases, it's often inefficient and problematic to design the architecture incrementally, without looking ahead at all known requirements.

In a pure agile process, you tackle and deliver a small chunk of functionality before looking ahead to the next chunk. I've found that this only works well when the architecture for the current chunk is relatively unrelated to the requirements of future chunks. By "relatively," I do acknowledge that no architecture is every set in concrete. It's always subject to change. However, if you're designing a brand new system that will need to integrate information or business logic from several similar, but different information systems, you're often better off looking ahead and finding out all the related requirements before going ahead and implementing a design based solely on the first set of requirements.

For example, perhaps your company just acquired another. Both companies have more than one commercial application to manage your accounts and products, and you've been asked to create a new front-end processing system that integrates all of these products into a single interface. You can break the project down in many ways, but even if you start with some limited functionality such as an account inquiry, do you want to do a quick sprint to expose the functionality of one application, then, after moving that to production, start the next, only to find your architecture isn't going to work for the second source? So you change it, get both applications working and move that to production only to find in the next sprint that the third application is going to cause you to start over yet again?

For projects that require the design of complex new information and business logic, it's often better to spend some time focused just on design. If you can find relatively isolated areas of functionality, you can slice the business request vertically so that you design and move into production one component before beginning to design the next. This will deliver business value sooner than if you designed all components before turning anything over to development. This is part of why we recommend loosely coupled subject areas within any application (page 123). But designing even this limited functionality may take much longer than an agile sprint would allow.

You can make compromises, stretch your terminology, and pretend that you're still doing agile development, but you're just kidding yourself. Agile is a great tool, but it's not the only tool in your toolbox. Sometimes it's the right tool, and sometimes it's not.

As time goes on and your information and business logic becomes more mature and complete, you don't expect small projects to result in major design modifications. At this point, an agile process may be more feasible.

In the interim, you don't necessarily have to settle for a pure waterfall approach, either. It's mainly the architectural analysis and design that is problematic. You can and probably should consider an SDLC that takes a more traditional waterfall approach to high-level business requirements and high-level design for projects like this. Once the core architectural decisions are made, you don't necessarily have to stick with waterfall for development, testing, and implementation. The actual development may be rolled out in a very agile manner.

The choice of whether to use waterfall or agile development process, or a hybrid of the two, really depends on how many potential subsequent sprints require architectural changes so large that the initial sprints have to be re-done. This is more likely when initially building out large architectural components than when incrementally adding small changes to a mature architecture. As your architecture matures or as the business changes and forces you to build out new architecture, the type of SDLC that is most appropriate for you may change...and later change back...and then change back again, unfortunately.

More than likely, at any one point you will have both types of projects: large architectural changes, and small incremental fixes and enhancements. You should recognize this very real distinction and provide more than one project management track for projects to follow, with some guidelines to help your teams know which is most appropriate in any given case.

This goes back to the discussion of the problems with a rigid development process (page 199). No rigid development approach, including Agile, is going to meet every need. You need to provide a way to take alternate paths through the possible development steps based on the needs of the project.

You can't leave it to the individual developer to decide which methodology to use. The EAG architects are going to have to give some guidance regarding the appropriate development methodology to use for these large, complex projects. Of course, any project can ask for a waiver to the project development methodology, so you don't have to consider every remote possibility beforehand, but you'll probably define two or three different "standard" approaches. Perhaps:

1. One path for **strategic projects** that are critical to the business, and need more formal, dedicated project management to provide the necessary management insight. Because these projects are rolling out critical new infrastructure components, the initial design stages of this path would look very waterfall, but the later development and testing may look more agile, provided enough management oversight is included.

2. A second path for small projects well suited to a **pure-agile project** backlog, like non-critical bug fixes or new report requests. Every application in production use is going to have a backlog of small bug fixes and enhancements that would be well suited to an agile process.

3. Possibly a third path to fast-track **urgent projects** that are relatively small in scope, but are needed to move very quickly into production.

If the EAG team can initially tag each project by type during the gating process, and provide formal governance for each type, this still allows a lot of flexibility. This may even help reduce the EAG team effort if you can say that the pure agile projects don't really need high-level estimates, or Gate 2 decision, or Gate 3 decisions. Once the project tagged as pure agile passes Gate 1 approval, it can go straight to technical design. The point is that you have to strike a balance between trying to cram every project into the same development approach, and letting the developers do whatever they want. That balance may be different for different types of projects, and may look different in different organizations.

Agile is a more efficient approach – if it makes sense for the type of project you are managing.

Agile for the wrong reasons: communication

I've seen several organizations adopt agile development processes for what I would consider the wrong reasons.

In some cases, organizations get frustrated with a waterfall approach because they end up doing so much work in isolation, then *throwing it over the fence* to the next link in the development chain. Developers don't participate in the requirements phase of the project, and refuse to start coding until requirements are fully complete. The business may wait months before seeing the product for the first time. If the business claims the results were not as expected, the developers blame it on poor requirements. Management eventually becomes aware that there's a communication problem. They have heard that there's a lot more cross-functional communication when using agile development processes, so - out with the old waterfall methodology, and in with Agile! Now all our problems are solved!

This is a very real, very serious, and, unfortunately, very common problem. Many organizations make the decision to move to agile development purely to fix a communications problem. This is a terrible reason to move to Agile. *There may be many good reasons to adopt more agile processes at your organization, but getting people to talk to each other isn't one of them.* There's no reason in a waterfall development methodology that a developer can't talk to a business analyst, and vice versa. If your company is strict about logging all time against project tasks, as might be required when your revenue model involves billing customers for hours, then you may have to add tasks to your plan for this communication, but the exact same kind of cross team communication can occur in a waterfall project as in agile methodologies.

If your team isn't communicating, it is unlikely that moving to an agile development process alone will address the underlying problem.

There is an episode in the Star Trek, New Generations TV series titled *Hollow Pursuits*. At the beginning of this episode, an engineer named Barclay is having trouble fitting in with the elite Enterprise crew. His academy scores indicated that he had the aptitude, but on the Enterprise he constantly appeared hesitant, nervous, and intimidated. The chief engineer decided to have the young man transferred to another ship where the pressure to perform would not be so high, and frankly, Barclay appeared relieved. However, Captain Picard refused to approve the transfer. "That sort of thing might be acceptable on another ship, but on this ship, you deal with your own problems, you don't pass them on to someone else."

Ditching your current development process and moving to Agile purely to force your people to talk to each other is just passing your problems on to someone else instead of dealing with them. If your people aren't communicating, odds are good there are other issues you need to deal with.

Two kinds of people – process-oriented versus innovation-oriented

There are two types of people in this world: those who would rather follow a predefined process and those who would rather find their own path. You need both types of people on your team.

Some people are most comfortable when given well-defined rules and a process to follow. They are happiest when they can come to work each day and carefully check off each box in their process. It's ok if things go wrong, as long as there's a process for handling that. When new challenges arise for which there is no existing process they tend to get very stressed, locking up until a new process can be defined to deal with the situation.

Other people are most comfortable when every day is unique and different than the day before, presenting new challenges that must be overcome with innovation.

Some roles really need process-oriented people, including security provisioning, change management, regression testing, and production support. These are areas where there very much needs to be a well-defined process that's followed every single time.

There are other areas, like strategic planning or developing new product features, where there can't be a process. Here, thinking "outside the box" is a good and necessary thing.

The problem comes when you have a person in a job role unsuited to their temperament. If you have a creative person in charge of operations, they'll quickly tire of long, tedious checklists. They'll believe that more time would be wasted following the process than if you just addressed any issues that pop up as they happen. They will alter their environment to minimize processes and maximize creativity. Despite their best intentions, this cowboy mentality is *not* a good thing in job roles such as production support.

You've seen this before. The person who's supposed to just follow the process *doesn't*, and all hell breaks loose. "You had one job…" "All you had to do…" This cowboy actually seems happy about all the excitement, in high spirits, suggesting all manner of innovative solutions. You almost think they broke things on purpose just to have something more interesting to do than to check things off on their daily list.

Other times, you'll have a process-oriented person in a position such as software development that requires flexibility and rapid adaptation to new and changing constraints. Rather than just dealing quickly with the changing world, this person will call meeting after meeting seeking someone to create a process that can be followed. They're trying to change their environment from one that requires innovation to one that has a formal process.

You've seen this one too. The person who's responsible for addressing the issue schedules a meeting for everyone remotely connected to the problem area. The discussion just keeps rehashing the issue, what happened and why, but no progress is being made. That responsible person is beginning to look a little green and increasingly desperate. Finally, one person suggests a solution, and hope dawns once more in the eyes of the person responsible. What's the first thing they ask? "Can you write that down and send it to me?" Right? The relief is immediate and obvious, which is strange, because the problems still exists. But now there's a process to follow. The problem was never the problem; not having a process to follow was the problem.

A good architect is, by definition, a creative person. But a great architect is one that understands the value of process, and is willing to write all that creative stuff down in a way that process-oriented people can understand and follow.

Some of the biggest problems I've seen in IT have boiled down to the wrong person in a job. Most of the time, the person is a talented individual, trying to do their best, but unfortunately placed in a position that does not suit their temperament at all.

I once worked for a software development company where we calculated a project cost by estimating the time to code and test the project, then multiplying that cost by a factor of *fourteen* to account for administrative overhead! In some departments, the overhead was a factor of twenty. A project that took half a day to code and test would cost the company two and a half weeks by the time you went through all the formal processes required by our **Project Management Office (PMO)**.

I asked our PMO about this, and was told it was based on industry best practices. Finding that hard to believe, I asked to see those industry recommendations for myself. I was given several examples, one of which was a statement by *Jack Welch,* one-time CEO of General Electric (GE) between 1981 and 2001. Mr. Welch, who was named "Manager of the Century" by Fortune Magazine in 1999, had once stated that if a manager at GE made a commitment to deliver a project within a certain timeframe, within a certain budget, at a given level of quality, and failed, but was able to show that they followed all the formal processes, then "no harm, no foul." It wasn't credited against them and they were given another project. If, however, a manager made those same promises, and came in ahead of schedule, under budget, and with higher than promised quality, but failed to follow the documented process, then that manager was immediately fired with a black mark against their name, never to be re-hired at GE.

Our PMO organization used this and similar anecdotes to justify a process-centric culture. Follow the process and you're safe from blame no matter what happens, but deviate from that process at your peril.

This anecdote really surprised me. Being an IT person, I'm not a huge follower of business news, but it was hard not to have heard of Jack Welch during those years. Our company had actually done some subcontracting work for GE. But the Jack Welch I had heard of was famous for fostering innovation and reducing bureaucracy. I heard stories of him automatically firing the bottom 10% of his managers every year, regardless of overall corporate performance, while lavishly rewarding the top 20%. He once said, "If you pick the right people and give them the opportunity to spread their wings and put compensation as a carrier behind it you almost don't have to manage them."[42] That sounds like a man who is encouraging innovation and minimizing overhead, not a man implementing a process-driven culture.

Upon doing some research, I did find the speech that I believe our PMO department was paraphrasing. It was a speech on Six Sigma given at a university,[43] and the context was a discussion of factory floors. GE, among other things, manufactured space shuttle parts. They did extensive time-and-motion studies of the factory floor assembly process, and had a very rigorous process that must be followed every time,

---

[42] http://bit.ly/2E4P9O5.

[43] I apologize, but I never wrote down the reference for this when I found it more than 15 years ago. I have never been able to find the reference again.

widget after widget, hour after hour, day after day to ensure the highest product quality. They didn't want some factory floor worker deciding that screw 143-B didn't really need to be tightened more than hand-tight.

That makes some sense, but it applies only in an environment where the work is *exactly* the same, day after day, year after year. Work like our security provisioning or regression testing. And I think you'll agree that there *should* be consequences if a front line employee takes shortcuts with the security provisioning process, even if it worked faster this one time. But I suggest that on the other side of town from the factory floor, GE had research and innovation labs where GE employees were designing new products, facing new challenges every day. Those workers couldn't be tied to a rigid process, but needed to be allowed the flexibility to quickly adapt to changing conditions and to decide what processes were and were not needed.

In our software development company, there were jobs that more closely resembled the factory floor: our call center, our HR department, our mailroom. However, there were other jobs that more closely resembled the research lab, including software development. In fact, you can think of the factory floor as operations, where the results of design and development are supported in production.

In my mind, treating software development like a factory floor job results in a process flowchart that would (and did) cover an entire wall. Each time a project failed, another step was added to the process to make sure that the same failure never happened again. Every single project had to follow the entire process, whether it made sense or not. I remember ordering a writing tablet (basically a big mouse pad) and having to wait more than two months while our technology team followed all the processes necessary to ensure that no sensitive data was being stored on the hardware. It was a mouse pad!

I'm not suggesting process is unnecessary in the development environment. Process is good, a necessary tool for giving management insight on project progress, but the process needs to provide more business value than it consumes in productivity loss.

This company where I worked had several software development managers that seemed to fail at every project they were given. They just weren't capable of overseeing new development, recognizing obstacles quickly and adapting the project to changing conditions. Yet often enough, it was the developers underneath the manager who received all the blame, while the manager was given yet another project to lead over the cliff. In my opinion, this was very nearly fatal to the company, adding an order of magnitude to the overhead of every project – projects which were our bread-and-butter. Our company was actually acquired by another company who wanted our product line. That acquisition resulted in extreme changes to our development methodology, most of which were *sorely* needed.

I see less extreme examples of this same *death-by-flowchart,* process-centric culture happening at other companies and consider it primarily a failure of middle management. In every case I've been involved in, this incremental growth of the development process flowchart of requirements was due to development managers who weren't capable of managing their projects under changing conditions without an explicit process to follow. When their projects failed after rigidly following the current process, a post-mortem analysis was held, and a new step added to the process which every project would have to include from that point on.

In my opinion, these managers were simply in the wrong position. The problems were being caused by a lack of creativity, foresight, and innovation, but they were being fixed by creating more complex, more rigid processes. No flowchart is going to give a solution to every possible software development obstacle. Software development managers must be capable of seeing what's going on and taking whatever steps are necessary to steer around the issues. A software development manager is supposed to be doing more than making sure their staff is entering their time. They are supposed to be managing the development projects, not just the developers.

The manager doesn't necessarily need to be fired, but may be much better suited to a position where there are more rigorous processes which must be followed every day – those factory floor jobs. These jobs aren't second-string positions for people who don't measure up. These critical IT functions demand hardworking, responsible, integrity-driven workers who will protect the company from risk.

I've also seen senior management try to "fix" this extreme process overhead by throwing away the entire process and implementing an agile replacement. Agile is an extremely powerful methodology ideally suited to many projects. There are many very good reasons to switch some kinds of work to Agile (see details on page 195), but "manager incompetence" isn't one of those reasons. If they need a process to follow, agile development is going to be terrifying. If your managers are failing because they aren't flexible enough to manage projects under rapidly changing conditions, then you need to do the right thing and remove them from those positions, hopefully finding them a place better suited to their skills and temperament.

Agile for the wrong reasons: eliminating project overhead

This leads to another poor reason for moving to an Agile development methodology: to strip out administrative overhead. I mentioned earlier (page 199) having worked at a software development company that had such a complex SDLC that we would take our estimates for coding and unit testing, and multiple them by a factor of fourteen in order to estimate the full cost of the project. A company whose lifeblood was software development kept its developers in meetings almost thirty hours each week.

The complexity of the project management flowchart had grown steadily over a very long period. A project would fail miserably, usually due to failure on the leaders to detect and adapt to changing conditions, and, in order to prevent that from ever happening again, the PMO office would add a new step to the flowchart: a new test, a new review, or a new signoff. Instead of dealing with managers who were not able to adapt to each day's challenges, they made the SDLC process more and more complex, making every future manager pay the price of that one manager's poor performance.

I've seen this pattern repeated at many development shops. A manager insists on following the exact same process that he followed on the last project, despite the new project being completely different. Letting people go isn't an easy task, especially when that person has friends and tenure. However, refusing to recognize that the person isn't suited for managing R&D-type projects (and instead adding yet another step to an already overwhelming project management process) isn't the answer either.

This practice is, unfortunately, quite common. In my experience, *many* companies move to agile development simply because they know that they can't live with their current administrative overhead, and they've heard that agile processes will eliminate it. Again, your organization may indeed benefit from moving to Agile, but *not* for this reason. If you don't have the courage to deal with the ineffective managers, retooling them for agile projects isn't going to help. Agile development calls for far more flexibility and foresight than the waterfall SDLC processes you're leaving behind. You will eliminate the overhead, but if you don't take care of the staffing problem, your projects will just fail faster and more efficiently.

I'm not suggesting that these managers need to be fired. Again, different people have different skill sets. A manager who is detail oriented, who has high integrity and a great work ethic, but who is really more comfortable following a well-defined process is *ideal* for managing your productions support and operations, your security, and your change management. Putting a creative cowboy in those roles leads to disaster. However, putting a process-follower in charge of architecture or software development leads to failed projects and a heavy burden of administrative overhead.

Adopt an agile process if the work you do would benefit from that approach, but don't retool your organization to Agile simply to solve communications issues or reduce process overhead.

Requirements gathering

You may recall from the discussion of the NIST framework that a hierarchy of requirements was recommended, with regulatory requirements at the top, followed by a handful of annual corporate goals set by the senior executives. Departmental VPs will set their own goals in support of the corporate goals, generally in the form of high-level projects, and so forth.

The bottom two layers, architectural review and technical details, are often labeled as the "design" phase of the development process, rather than the "requirements" phase.

Level	Type Of Requirement	Author	Typical Form
IR	Industry requirements	Regulatory and certification bodies	Large volumes of ambiguously worded mandates
CR	Annual corporate requirements	Corporate executives	3-5 goals the company needs to focus on, announced annually, usually just after annual budgets are set
DR	Departmental requirements	Department heads	Strategic projects supporting the corporate goals
BR	Business requirements	Business analysts	Lists of feature/function requirements for "what" the functionality should do
FR	Functional requirements	All four domains of architecture	Architectural requirements saying "how" the functionality should be implemented
TR	Technical requirements	Lead technical resources: Developers, data modelers, hardware and software admins	Detailed coding requirements

Table 6 – NIST requirements hierarchy

The NIST requirements hierarchy looks like a very waterfall approach to requirements gathering, where each level of requirements must be completed before the next can begin. How valid is this approach to requirements gathering today, almost three decades later? It turns out that it is still very valid.

You aren't going to have any influence on the industry, corporate, or even departmental levels of the hierarchy. What happens at those levels happens regardless of your development methodology and is beyond your control. Most of the different development methodologies still start with business project requests. The main differences in the various approaches are when and to what degree of formality the bottom three layers of the requirements hierarchy are implemented.

Even if you're implementing a very loose, agile process, there are still business functionality requirements, architectural approach requirements, and technical requirements. They can be passed in formal documents, or they can be shared verbally as the business analyst and the developer sit in a cube iteratively testing changes, but at some level, all of these NIST hierarchy requirements still exist.

For our goal of managing IT complexity at the enterprise level, the most important area to examine is the functional (architectural) requirements. The business requirements and technical requirements are certainly important, but all the development methodologies have strong, though different, solutions in those areas. Regardless of development methodology, your architectural review and guidance is what will determine whether the project will integrate smoothly and efficiently into the corporate infrastructure. You need some kind of architectural review.

Implementing architectural review isn't easy. There are many hurdles to overcome, including:

- There aren't enough architects to go around. Moreover, there are four domains; therefore you really need to get at least four of the most scarce resources in your IT infrastructure involved in every review.

- Even if you can find the resources, in the real world, projects have almost unachievable deadlines, with little time to spare for architectural review.

- Architectural review usually results in changes that make the project harder, meaning it will be more expensive and take longer.

That combination doesn't paint a compelling case for architectural review. Yet, this is the single most critical failure point in the requirements process in most companies, driving millions of dollars in expenses and lost revenue due to short-sighted implementation decisions that result in inefficiencies and integration issues that are compounded with each passing year.

How you implement architectural review will depend on your development methodology, but there are a few key features you need to make sure your requirements governance includes, which are discussed below.

Make sure everyone understands the evolving long-term strategy
Most developers aren't going to intentionally hijack your project and sabotage your strategic vision. The developers aren't stupid, they're just uninformed. They spend their days focused on project-level horizons that are weeks or months in length, not a strategic horizon that's years away. Help them understand the strategic vision, and *why* that vision is a better place than where you are today – not just for the company, but also for them in particular. The antagonism between architect and developer is usually simply a matter of communication. Rather than hand down seemingly arbitrary mandates from on high, schedule regular meetings where you discuss the vision and solicit feedback. You have to be

careful not to distract them too much from their day job, but these men and women need to be convinced you're on the same team.

They're also your pool of future architects, and keeping the architectural conversation flowing allows you to keep an eye out for those who really have the mindset necessary for the architecture role.

This natural tendency toward antagonism is one reason why I think it is always better to use matrixed architectural resources that are embedded in real development areas, not full-time architects sitting in an isolated ivory tower somewhere, working on a strategic plan while living in a vacuum unconnected to the reality of the business.

Provide well-documented and communicated standards

These take time to write, but not as long as it would take for an architect to review every single project for compliance with architectural concepts you haven't bothered to write down. Every time you do review a project and find something wrong about the approach, you should consider adding that to your body of standards to help prevent you from having to document it again in the next project.

This may sound as if it contradicts my earlier advice against adding process steps to your SDLC every time you find a new problem. The difference here is that everyone is required to follow every step in the SDLC, where standards are only followed where they apply. Standards don't create unnecessary overhead for projects; they just give guidelines for things you were going to do anyway.

Documenting standards is always a good idea and worth the time, but it must be combined with good communication skills and a plan for continuous review. Most standards reflect a best practice captured at a point in time, under a particular environment and technological capability. As the environment and technology continue to change, you can't let your standards be what holds you back. Architecture and governance frameworks like TOGAF and ITIL that provide the most detailed standards suffer the most risk of becoming outdated. Standards are a living, breathing part of your governance. Make sure to invest in keeping them alive and relevant.

Pick your battles

As with architectural review of software purchases, you're going to have to pick your battles. Look at the project pipeline. Which projects are the most critical to the business, both for immediate operations and as a foundation for the future? Which of these projects have the most potential for architectural review to make a difference? Some very strategic projects may actually not have much architectural risk. Some projects that are less critical in the near term are actually laying down very critical infrastructure groundwork for the long term. Remember that you need to pick your battles based on providing the most value to the business, not based on architectural purity. This is one reason why the business architect is so critical on the EAG team. They are the one with the best understanding of the short and long-term business needs.

Prepare critical architectural approaches well before they are actually needed

Architects usually have some idea what key projects will be ramping up in the next six months, and whether any of these projects will hinge on new strategic infrastructure (information, applications, or hardware). This is an ideal time for the architects from all four domains to work together, without the pressure of project deadlines, to discuss the long-term strategy internally, get training and attend trade shows, and talk to peers, consultants, and vendors. Then use this information to thoughtfully prepare a strategic approach document well before the project begins. These documents will be directed at the most critical new infrastructure components, and may be the single best value that an architect can provide the company.

If an architect doesn't begin working on the approach until a project is launched and technical resources are ready to begin, the project isn't going to get the best the architect has to offer. Using the functional framework is a great way to identify these gaps in strategy, prioritize them, and assign them out to architects to work on. When you have this kind of time, you can assign a small group of architects the task of leading the approach development, and bringing it back to the architecture team for review and feedback. Ideally, once you decide on a framework and get the bulk of your governance in place, fifty percent of the EAG team meeting time is spent reviewing these fast-approaching strategic business initiatives. A good bit of the remaining time should be spent discussing how to handle the potential infrastructure challenges of emerging breakthrough technology.

If most of your architectural meetings are spent taking minutes of who is working on what back in their real jobs, you have a failure in leadership. Rather than providing valuable strategic guidance, you're doing little more than distracting the company's top resources from projects where they are sorely needed.

Perform the architectural review without becoming a bottleneck

One of the most common mistakes is to over-specify. Most architects came up the development path. Before they became an architect, they were top-talent project resources: data modelers, developers, and software and hardware admins. They'll find it hard to simply flesh out the high-level architectural approach and move on. They'll want to use their experience and skills to specify what are more properly technical requirements.

Too much detail is almost as bad as no architectural review at all. Trust your technical people to do their job. In truth, the architect may well be able to do a better job creating the detail technical design than the lead developer on the project, but if you keep doing someone's job for them, they're never going to learn, and you'll be stuck with it forever. Mistakes will be made – costly mistakes. However, they are less costly in the long run than having only one person who knows how to do the job. Remember all the costly mistakes that were made to get you where you are today, and show a little patience with the next generation.

A good architectural approach is seldom more than a couple of pages for most projects. For key projects implementing critical strategic infrastructure, the architectural approach may be ten or twenty pages per architectural domain, but those would have been developed far in advance. The goal is to document enough to keep the architecture on track, headed in the right direction. You aren't trying to have the architect do all the technical work.

Consider adopting an industry standard application model

ITIL contains descriptions of a large number of business processes. Just as you can purchase commercially developed industry-specific data models for the information domain, some industries have developed detailed business operations models which can be used by the application domain. The TMForum, for example, has a two-layer model for business processes: a TAM (target application map) for high-level application functionality, and a Business Process Model, also known as TOM (target operational map) at the more detailed process level. The TOM model is like the information domain's data model diagrams, but instead of mapping tables, fields, and relationships, it maps the business logic and business process flow in the application domain.

A model like this can give you a huge leg up on creating a well-tested list of application domain functions for your functional framework. An industry-recognized model such as this will facilitate interactions with vendors, streamline industry regulatory compliance, and ensure that your internal policies are comprehensive and your roles clear. It can also aid in the collection of business process requirements by leveraging time-tested industry process descriptions. Just remember the limitations of these models described in the discussion of the ITIL framework.

Gathering application requirements isn't new. You already have processes in place that are working just fine to ensure the efficiency and success at the *project level*. To lift your management of project requirements to focus on the success of the larger enterprise, make sure you consider adding the EAG controls mentioned above. Here again, a functional framework is a great tool for keeping *all* the IT functionality in mind, preventing you from slipping into a project-focused architecture mindset.

Developing

There are several different approaches to software development, some of which are discussed beginning on page 193. Those various methods are each the subjects of many fine books authored by some of the brightest minds in our industry. Rather than try to summarize the pros and cons of each here, I want to discuss two aspects of software development that you need to focus on to serve your company well:

- How to integrate your existing software development functions with the other IT management functions for a coordinated, efficient, automated, *enterprise-wide IT infrastructure*.

- How to think about applications and how you develop them in an *increasingly distributed world*.

Developing in an integrated functional framework
A functional framework is designed to keep you aware of the larger picture, an integrated series of IT functions working together in well-orchestrated, automated interactions. The framework serves as a reminder to consider all of the different IT functions that must be coordinated.

You don't have a great deal of control over the integration capabilities of your legacy infrastructure. You might have better luck finding software that meets your needs when you are buying it off the shelf. However, when you are developing software solutions from scratch, there's no excuse for not considering how the solution will have to integrate with all the various IT functions in the larger corporate environment.

Most of you are probably pursuing various security certifications for your infrastructure. One of the phrases you'll hear a lot is, "security by design, and by default." This means that security isn't an afterthought, something that's patched on after you build your solution. Security must be part of the design of every project, right from the beginning. As with any compliance audit, you can't just ensure the auditors that you think about security all your waking hours. You need to show them that your software development process includes security considerations in every step of the lifecycle including design, development, testing, and implementation. Every step along the way, security is an integral, inescapable part of the process.

Not only do you have to show that it's part of your process, you also have to show that you are following that process by handing over audit logs that are automatically captured by the security-related steps in your development process.

As an EAG team building the governance artifacts, you need to provide the policies, standards, system utilities, corporate repositories and the process templates to lead the projects into compliance, and the collection and analysis of the collected audit records and metrics to ensure compliance and continually improve your processes. Your SDLC process documents need to spell out those security consideration points. Your project plans need to include tasks for those activities. Design those considerations into your development processes.

Security is certainly on everyone's mind these days, but there are several other cross-functional integration points where you need to provide similar "by design and by default" governance:

- Software development projects that promised certain Return on Investment (ROI) should include, by design, that means of **collecting and analyzing ROI**. Increased sales, reduced fraud, faster response times – whatever was promised must be measured. This is integrating the development of the infrastructure to support a business function with the tactical roadmap layer of your framework, where the function was justified.

- Software that must meet certain Service Level Agreements (SLAs) for performance and availability should **collect SLA metrics** by design. This is integration of the software development function with other functions in your framework such as contract management and customer support.

- By design, software should access data through loosely coupled DaaS services based on the enterprise logical data model, and should access data from the corporate system of record, rather than batch copying data to a locally-accessed copy. Spell out the activities that you want to occur during software development to ensure your developers are **complying with your architectural strategy for the functionality** they are developing. This is integrating the development function in your framework with the architectural strategic vision layer of that same function.

- These are just a few examples. You'll want to take a look across your functional framework and integrate into your software development processes the hooks to insure "by design and by default" integration with framework functions such as data quality (use of master reference data, integration with QA workflows, etc.), data modeling (compliance with ELDM, correct system of record, no data duplication, etc.), and others. The functional framework gives you a simple way to ensure you consider the full spectrum of issues required to build a fully integrated, automated IT infrastructure in support of the business.

If you think about your standards, many of them take the form, "If you do *this*, do it this way." Other standards and all of your policies will take the form, "Always do *this*." Those "always" tasks are the ones you want to consider making "by design and by default."

This has to be balanced against the aforementioned danger of a software development flowchart that contains thousands of steps and creates a drain on the project. Don't just demand that developers add a step to their process; give them the tools, the APIs, the systems infrastructure, and the templates to make compliance easier than non-compliance. Make compliance automated and default, rather than manual. Make sure that any overhead you add to the IT management process is outweighed by the value it brings.

Developing for a distributed future

Software development is about to be *transformed*. Our infrastructure has suddenly fragmented and scattered to the winds. This is happening in all three IT domains.

- Distributed Information (see Consuming , page 128)
- Distributed Applications (see Trend: Disappearance of the network edge, page 214)
- Distributed Technology (see Trend: The virtualization of hardware, page 233)

In one sense, these trends started several years ago and have been gaining more ground each year for some time. In another sense, we're maybe a decade from the day when these trends will represent the majority, rather than the minority of your infrastructure. The 2016 Gartner Hype Cycle for the Internet of Things[44] predicts many of these distributed infrastructure components becoming mature and commercially viable within two to five years.

Yes, all this bears close watching, but how much should it really impact your development decisions today? After all, this is a business, not a science project. This sounds like a really interesting thing to play around with, but is that good stewardship of the business's time and money today?

The viability tipping point is a decision each company will need to make for themselves. It'll depend on many factors, all of which are in constant motion. My suggestion is to be cautious, but not blind. Using the functional framework, you should go ahead and start planning your strategy for how your infrastructure will evolve as these factors mature. On paper only, figure out as much as you can foresee. You'll likely need to educate yourself in order to flesh out that picture. That's fine – you have a little time. But start now.

As pieces of the architectural strategic plan picture start to fall into place, you can start to develop your tactical roadmap. Again, each step in the roadmap must provide value immediately. Are any of your major business applications in the cloud yet? This is a good time to get your feet wet:

- **Distributed information**. Maybe you have a new analytics project that can benefit from one of the powerful hosted machine learning products, like IBM Watson. This is a good way of taking on cloud-based infrastructure without risk to the operational applications.

- **Distributed applications**. Maybe you're upgrading your HR software, and can consider a hosted solution. Nearly every vendor has a cloud-based solution now, with hundreds of active users. When thinking about our IT application infrastructure, we tend to forget about those HR and accounting apps, but they can be a smart way of moving to a mixed local and cloud solution without the risks that accompany early adoption. Since HR software is applicable to all industries, the software vendors have a lot of installs, and are looking for economies of scale. They can afford to invest more research and development in cloud-based development than vendors of industry-specific software.

---

[44] http://gtnr.it/2FY0UaA.

- **Distributed technology**. Maybe you're overhauling your disaster recovery solution and can consider a hosted DR recovery site. There's a terrific use case for letting someone else manage the entire DR infrastructure and, as an added bonus, during your POC and annual DR testing, you get an excellent preview of the power and challenges of moving your current infrastructure to the cloud.

Each of these examples provides immediate business value while giving you a limited-risk sandbox to figure out issues like security, performance, integration, and support that accompany a cloud-based architecture.

Once you conquer a couple of projects like these, then you might begin to think about turning your development staff loose on a home-grown, cloud-based business application that provides immediate business value. The lessons you learned in the previous examples will stand you well as you try to build out products of your own.

A friend of mine working at a utility company told me that one of their first real forays into cloud-based development was implemented in lower environments (development and test) only. The nature of their core applications resulted in the need for up to six different test environments, used at various times for various purposes. Most of the time they needed only one or two. During a major system upgrade, they decided that it made sense to purchase cloud-based virtual infrastructure for these environments. They could be spun up when needed, and decommissioned just as quickly. The utility company didn't pay for environments when they weren't being used, and the hardware/software infrastructure updates and security patches were the headache of the cloud host, not my friend.

It's still difficult to justify the monthly cost of some cloud-hosted infrastructure solutions for permanent production solutions, but it's *much* easier to make the business case for solutions whose resource requirements fluctuate dramatically over time. The solution worked *so* well that they're now exploring moving their DR solution to the cloud host as well.

I spoke with a peer at a conference recently who stressed the importance of a loosely coupled architecture that communicates via service calls over a standard IP network. When they moved one application's environment to a cloud host, the tightly coupled, proprietary communications points were the main failure point. The business logic that had been implemented using a **Business Process Management (BPM)** engine orchestrating business services over an IP network worked flawlessly and performed so well that the testers of the system often forgot it wasn't local anymore.

Among the tightly coupled components that caused problems was all the batch file data movement to instantiate local copies of data each night. The system still worked, but the advantage of a local copy of data on the cloud solution was more than offset by the degraded performance of all the large file movement. He found that in a cloud solution, it made far more sense to switch to data services against a single system of record. *An infrastructure built for distributed applications worked best with an infrastructure built for distributed information.*

Your development team can handle the mechanics of developing, or you've hired the wrong team. As an architect, your job is to tell them *what* to develop, not *how*. If you want to serve your company well architecturally, you need to be creating a vision for a distributed future.

Change management

There are many fine change management tools available to help you automate the migration of software development projects from environment to environment with the appropriate approvals and back-out controls. These tools are also called software configuration management tools (SCM). They often include features like source version control, workflow management tools, and test harnesses.

I won't attempt to describe all the functionality of these tools. From an enterprise IT management perspective, what's important is the integration of those tools with your other IT functions (such as security and testing) and your ability to leverage a single solution across multiple product lines.

In addition to all the requirements you would need to consider when building a departmental change management solution, you'll need to make sure someone is asking the following enterprise-level questions:

1. Can you use a **single corporate change management tool for multiple application teams**? Even if they work on different platforms? At the very least, all your mainframe development across all application development teams would use the same change management tool; though perhaps your Java developers might all use another. There are several change management toolsets out there that claim to support all these environments. Using a single toolset will reduce administration costs, training costs, and infrastructure costs. You may be able to justify a site license and save dramatically on licensing costs. Many audits these days require a review of your change management processes, i.e. to make sure that no changes can be moved to production without approval. Having a single solution can reduce audit costs, and reduce the risk of failure to comply. If you do need to implement new steps in your processes, they can be made in one location and affect multiple applications. A change management tool can be part of your enterprise regulatory/security compliance.

2. In an increasingly integrated world, your change management tool not only needs to work on multiple development platforms, but it may actually need to **coordinate projects that span multiple platforms**. You may have a mainframe application functionality change that includes Java services to expose the functionality to your ESB, and includes accompanying changes to reports in your enterprise business intelligence tool – all of which need to move up together. Can your change management solution handle this?

3. **Integrating application and information changes.** A single project often involves both changes to code and changes to the data model. When you migrate from development to test, both types of changes need to migrate at the same time. If a problem is found in test, both need to be backed out and taken back to development. Does your change management solution force you to manually coordinate different propagation paths for different parts of the same project? How much time is wasted on this duplicate work, and how many errors are caused by the need for manual coordination?

4. Likewise, a project may **include changes to internal and external documentation**. You need a change management system that can move these artifacts along with the code changes. This includes project documentation, testing documentation, data dictionary and data lineage

information, end user installation and user manuals, marketing literature and more. Can your change management tool integrate with your various documentation repositories?

5. What about **test cases**? Can your change management tool move the test data from environment to environment along with the code?

6. Can your change management tooling be **integrated with your project management system** so that approval of a project in the project tracking system for one environment automates the migration to the next? Change management involves many signoffs by different roles at different points, and may involve a workflow management tool to route tasks and track responses. Ideally, this would be the enterprise-standard workflow management tool used across all IT functions.

7. Can it be **integrated with your defect reporting/tracking system** so that each software release can automatically be tied to the defects it addresses, and the defect log updated with the status of the fix as it moves toward production?

8. Does your change management **automate the build of each environment**, including both code and database changes? It is good practice to have separation of duties. Developers should not be able to change code in the test environment, because the migration to test is itself a test of the process that will be used to migrate to prod. You aren't just testing a code change; you are testing the propagation of a code change. But separation of duties doesn't require human intervention. Automation is, in fact, preferred, as it's more predictable, less prone to error, and ensures an auditor that a process was always followed. A DBA, for example, shouldn't have to be involved to make manual changes to the database during code propagation. These changes should be implemented automatically by software. The DBAs should review the automated change, and perhaps reject the way it was done, forcing the cycle to be repeated, but the change itself should be automated.

9. Can your change management solution be **integrated with your testing solution** so that when a project is moved from development to test, an automated test cycle is run?

10. Is your change management solution **part of your disaster recovery planning**, or will all development grind to a halt in the event of an emergency? Is your change management repository part of your regular backups?

As you can see, your change management functionality must integrate into the larger enterprise-level plan to manage all the IT functionality. Change management has ties to project requests, bug tracking, information management, testing, disaster recovery, security, and more. Mature enterprise-level change management is difficult to achieve. Many companies find change management and testing the hardest parts of achieving CMMI[45] certification.

Here again, the functional framework is a convenient way to see all the integration points at a glance, to help insure your change management solution is fully integrated into all the other IT supported functions.

---

[45] Capability Maturity Model Integration – a measure of the maturity of your infrastructure and processes.

Testing

Software testing is difficult to do well. I've seen many cases where the software testing area might as well have been sent home. You can easily work very hard at testing and still be wasting everyone's time and money. Most of the time this occurs because everyone believes they know how to test, but very few people really do.

Most of the other software development processes at your organization are being done quite well, though perhaps not consistently across the enterprise. Software testing is the one function of the software development lifecycle where most of us are fooling ourselves into believing we know what we're doing.

If you want to step up to more efficient, more productive testing across your enterprise, I would recommend you set up a corporate software testing center of excellence, and get them trained and certified. Get an independent audit of your testing processes.

The **ISO 9000** and **ISO 9126** standard (now **ISO 25010:2011**) focuses on testing functionality (including accuracy and security), reliability, usability, efficiency, maintainability, and portability. Think of it as your dimensions of data quality, but for business logic and processes rather than information.

For testing security functions, you should check out the **Open Source Security Testing Methodology Manual (OSSTMM)**. It consists of peer-reviewed methodology for assessing operational security in data networks, telecommunications, wireless, physical security, and human security.

Of course, there are several stages of testing:

- **Unit Testing (UT)**. Performed by the development team in the development environment, focused on whether the code changes themselves function as designed.

- **User Acceptance Testing (UAT)**. Usually performed in a test environment, where the resource who initiated the project request will determine if the solution met expectations.

- **System Integration Testing (SIT)**. Usually a simulation of the production environment, where all processes are run, and regression testing performed to ensure the change didn't have any unexpected impact on other functionality. Often referred to as the "model office."

- You may also have performance testing, penetration testing, and any number of other specialized test environments.

This short bullet list is actually quite complex and, contrary to most development organization's beliefs, is something you're probably not doing very well today, even within the scope of a single project.

That's something I seriously urge you to look into, but it's not in the scope of this book. Instead, we want to discuss what differences there are between testing done well on a project-by-project, or even information system by information system level, and testing that is coordinated across the enterprise. The challenge here is that *our IT systems are, at the same time, becoming both more tightly integrated and more distributed.*

In your production environments, the different information systems don't function in isolation the way they did thirty years ago. Information and processing requests constantly flow between them in a complex web of activity. Even when performing testing within a single system, you have to test these interfaces, both outbound and inbound.

In the increasingly integrated world, you have to figure out how to coordinate this testing across your enterprise. For example, any decisions about masking data in lower environments must be made at the enterprise level, so that the masked values in one information system synch with the masked values in the systems that talk to it.

Likewise, any decisions about making the lower environments a subset of production in order to speed the test performance must be coordinated across all the system testing environments at the corporate level through the EAG team. You need to come up with a long-term strategy and work to achieve it over time. This isn't going to happen overnight.

To complicate matters further, in the future, many of the services you call may be hosted in the cloud by other companies who are unlikely to share your strategies for masking and for making subsets.

How are you going to coordinate upgrades? When one application changes, the impact can cascade throughout the enterprise. This is another good reason to design an architecture consisting of information systems that are loosely coupled to each other via services. If one application accesses another application's database directly, then the two are tightly coupled, and very prone to failure if the data mode changes. But if a services interface is used, then each application is insulated from internal changes in the other (as long as the API is preserved).

How are you going to coordinate maintenance windows across multiple integrated SIT environments? Actually, probably the same way you do in production. Unfortunately, production systems often have failover and redundancy that make them higher availability than lower environments.

As systems continue to grow in volume and velocity, how are we going to provide realistic lower environments in the first place? Does Google have a pre-production SIT environment? Does Amazon? Does eBay? Do they rebuild their entire infrastructure every night? If they don't have a static image of the system, how do they know if a change worked or not? How do you regression test in a non-deterministic, distributed system where each test run happens over dynamically fluid information, application and technology?

As software architecture changes, becoming increasingly distributed and outsourced, and the individual infrastructure components continue to grow in scale, we are going to have to re-think the way we test. That thinking is the responsibility of the EAG team, and should be part of your architectural strategy for the testing function on your functional framework.

Trend: Disappearance of the network edge

If you consider the implications of the increasingly distributed architecture described earlier, you may be struck by how this will affect application design in the years to come. In years past, we designed applications with three different levels of scope:

1. By far, most applications were designed to serve the needs of the **internal business**. The application sat inside the firewall and was accessed only by some of the company's employees. The applications were designed to support that volume of workload, and, while there was certainly user authentication, the internal network was considered pretty safe.

2. A far smaller subset of applications exposed very modest functionality to **external customers** outside the firewall. The company likely has a much larger number of customers than employees, so these applications had to scale higher, a goal made possible mainly by the limited processing required to support the minimal feature/function exposed through these customer portals. Authentication in this domain is much more strict, and the risk of breaches much higher.

3. A very small set of generic, no-risk information might be supported on a **public** interface such as a corporate website. This site may have to support a user base even larger than the customer base, but in most cases, the information is basically static, the risk low, and the processing demand minimal.

In this scenario, there was a very real *edge* to our network, and most of our applications, both built and bought, operated strictly inside the firewall, in a relatively secure, relative low volume zone. The applications were designed for that environment.

Today this network edge that our applications have hidden behind is blurring and disappearing. Increasingly, our applications are moving across the firewall into the cloud, and the demand for more robust, interactive customer solutions is driving our customer base deeper into the territory once reserved for our internal apps. Our applications are increasingly integrated across the web, calling and being called by partner companies outside our firewall.

You can no longer afford to design applications the way we did twenty years ago. Applications must be loosely coupled via services, and they must be designed to support the much heavier demands of an increasingly integrated, yet geographically distributed world. From a scalability and authentication standpoint, can you really afford to develop under the pretense that your application will remain forever tucked away behind a protective firewall, accessed only by a few trusted users?

Two kinds of people – conflict embracers versus conflict avoiders

There are two kinds of people in this world: those that embrace conflict, and those that avoid it.

I don't know of anyone who particularly enjoys conflict. I'm sure those people exist, but fortunately, I haven't run across them. There are, however, people who thrive on conflict. They realize how uncomfortable people are with it, and have learned to use that to their own advantage.

During the cold war, the United States found negotiating with the Soviets to be very challenging,[46] primarily because the two nations approached the table with such different mindsets. Because of the way our political system and four-year election cycles worked, American negotiators felt a lot of pressure to come home with some kind of result. The Soviets, on the other hand, were perfectly willing to walk

---

[46] http://nyti.ms/2FWZFs2.

away with nothing rather than give up anything important. While the American political system was built on democratic compromises, the Soviets viewed compromise as a weakness. Their attitude seemed to be, "What's mine is mine, and what's yours is negotiable." Due to the differences in political planning horizons, national objectives, and the relative value placed on keeping secrets versus transparency, negotiations were tense, often baffling affairs. One reason many political historians believe the Soviets did so well in these negotiations was that the Soviets understood how to use the stress of the negotiating table to their advantage. An American negotiator would feel more and more stress building throughout the meeting to come home with something to show. The Soviets knew this, and would patiently stonewall; the Americans would put more and more on the table to make their offer more tempting. The Soviets knew that the longer they waited, the sweeter the deal would be.

This is how I see the people who thrive on conflict. They'll stir things up, causing a great deal of stress in those who just want to avoid conflict, knowing that they'll be offered increasingly desperate solutions. The more stress they cause and the longer they can keep it up, the better their position will become. All they have to do is generate conflict, and their opponent will be willing to agree to almost anything in order to end it. I've worked with several people like this over the years: abrasive and deliberately belligerent, professionally unpleasant people who love to stir things up. This kind of conflict is poisonous. I don't care how good these people are at their job, if they don't share your corporate values, they have to go.

On the other hand, avoiding conflict is also bad. Conflict happens even when neither side is intentionally provocative. We all need to be able to remain professional, but supervisors and managers have a special responsibility to act as a point of escalation and resolution. In my experience, the hardest working person on the team is the department administrative assistant, who probably has a lower salary than anyone else on the floor. Most of the time a supervisor or mid-level manager gets paid pretty good money for how hard they actually have to work. Part of the reason they get paid that salary is that there are times they have to step up and make the difficult decisions, or take care of things that are getting ugly, or enforce unpleasant corporate policies. They may not love conflict, but they are literally being paid to deal with it.

Companies that promote staff into supervisor and manager positions based purely on tenure often face the problem of having turned a very good front line employee into a very poor supervisor. Skills as a developer have little to do with skills as a supervisor. If someone really doesn't want to deal with conflict, that's fine, but in that case they shouldn't take the supervisor job. If you cash the paycheck, the company has a right to expect that you will do the job. Saying "no" to a supervisor position because you know you will not be able to handle the conflict resolution is quite *brave*. Saying "yes" and then avoiding every possible conflict even when the result damages the company is *cowardly*. If you have a coward in a management or supervisor position, you need to cut them loose immediately and replace them with someone who will do the right thing for the company, even when the process is unpleasant. There is no place for cowards in an enterprise architecture and governance program.

Problems don't just go away because you avoid them. They get worse. While not enjoyable, conflict brings opportunity. If you keep your head, remain professional, and don't compromise your decisions solely to make the problem go away, conflict can actually be a means of making progress much more quickly than would otherwise have been the case. Things that might have lain festering in the dark for years will be brought out into the light where they can be dealt with. You'll probably never enjoy the process, but you will learn to use conflict to move things forward.

Software services functions

In the application domain of the functional framework, we have discussed two functional areas: the software infrastructure lifecycle, and the software development lifecycle. Occasionally, you will find a need for a third application functional area, software services.

As with information services, there's no need to call out each software service, as long as they fall under the architecture and governance in the application infrastructure lifecycle. Most of your applications can be considered services in the ITIL sense, regardless of whether or not they were developed with a service-oriented architecture. That doesn't mean you need to call each out as a separate function in the framework. The goal of the functional framework is to simplify the complexity of managing IT functionality on behalf of the business, not to make it more and more complicated.

If the release management, security, and operational support for a software application or service fall under the policies, standards, processes, and roles built into the software infrastructure lifecycle, then it's counterproductive to call an application out as its own service function, with its own requirements for separate architectural strategy and roadmap, and separate application governance policies and processes.

If the application does have separate policies and processes than your other software, you have to ask yourself the question, "Should it?" In most cases, the answer should be, "No."

The few applications that I've seen really justified as separate services have always fallen under the heading of "systems functions." These are services written to centralize the functionality that exists in many applications.

In the early days of corporate computing, applications were created as monolithic infrastructures, containing all the software services that were needed, because, frankly, they didn't exist anywhere else. Every application would have its own database management software (DBMS), its own report writer, its own customer management system, and its own print management system, and they were all unique and different. Since all their internal components were dedicated, these business applications could be managed as completely isolated units of functionality, with no components shared with other applications.

Over time, as technology improved, we developed the capability to take some functionality out of the individual solutions, and manage it an enterprise level across all solutions. In the information domain, customer data was removed from individual applications and managed in a cross enterprise CDI/MDM (Customer Data Integration/Master Data Management) system. In the application domain, enterprise print management solutions replaced application-specific solutions. Technology domain storage Area Networks allowed the creation of virtual dedicated disk storage out of an enterprise pool of disk resources.

It would be an unusual application today that included an internal, custom **database management system (DBMS)**. That's really the point. In the old days, the DBMS was considered part of the business software. Your account management software would have its own embedded, proprietary code to read and write its data to disk. Today, the DBMS is considered a software support system and managed separately from the primary business application software. These are almost always third party infrastructure products, and in fact are often managed by the technology domain.

Even in this day and age, though, you may still find yourself occasionally creating cross-application system service applications. Internally developed systems-infrastructure applications are a different breed of application than your core business application functionality, and are one of the few good cases to call out as application functions of their own. Enterprise-level system applications often have different policies, standards, processes and roles than business applications.

As enterprise assets, you may wish to call these services out separately, so that the unique architecture and governance of these cross-functional services don't get buried within the functions that make use of them. Another way of thinking about this is to consider them "systems" functions. Most large companies have many "software" developers, and a small handful of "systems" programmers whose job it is not to write software for the business, but to write software utilities and APIs for use by the other developers. These "systems" applications are not business-facing, but are used internally by IT to help make the business facing application development more consistent and efficient. If the development and support of these systems applications is *significantly* different from the development and support of normal applications, you may want to have them operate under different policies, standards, processes, and roles. In that case, you would want to consider them a separate function in your functional framework. If the policies and standards aren't significantly different from the rest, then there's no need to needlessly complicate the framework by calling these out as separate functions. The idea is to keep the high-level framework as simple as possible.

Contact management

One example of this internally developed, enterprise-level systems-application I've worked with was a system to integrate contact information. In one sense, this was an extension of MDM (see page 168), but at the business logic level.

Many applications contain customer contact information, including things like:

Preferred contact information:

- Channel information – email address, phone number, and physical address
- Preferred channel – email, text, phone, postal
- Preferred contact language
- Time of day (for phone and text)
- Opt in/out information

Offer management:

- Actions
  - Campaigns and offers (generated by campaign management)
  - Real-time offers (generated at time of call)
  - Event-driven actions (i.e. welcome letters for new customers)
  - Other actions (i.e. a note to ask customer to confirm email address)
- Responses
  - Rejections (may terminate offer, or may simple suspend it for a time)

o   Acceptance

o   Other responses (customer provided email address)

Contact notes

- Call center notes
- Emails from customer
- Social media posts

Customers get very frustrated when they call in and get transferred around. It's even worse when the customer is told over and over by each successive transfer that they have been "specially selected for an exciting new limited-time offer." Or when a customer calls in about an offer they received in the mail, and the call center has no idea what they are talking about.

We had this problem at a company where I worked. Our business architect asked us to design an integrated solution that could (like the DBMS of old) completely replace the application-by-application logic that had grown over the years. Yet the solution had to be integrated. We didn't want the call center staff to open yet another application window; the contact management functionality needed to be embedded in the existing call center application interface.

The architectural vision for this system function was much different from for our core business applications. The governance policies, processes, and roles were also much different. Instead of supporting business users, we were supporting business applications. Licensing and security were quite different from that of a customer facing application. Service level agreements for supporting applications were materially different than for supporting customers. The development and support roles were not embedded in an any one information system, but were instead a pool of matrixed developers working outside of the core information systems. Upgrading a systems function is much more complicated than upgrading an application embedded in a single information system.

This is a case where it might make sense to call out the application as a separate software function rather than simply one more business application subject to the software infrastructure lifecycle functions.

CHAPTER 6

The Technology Domain

Technology is the foundation upon which all of the rest of your infrastructure depends. The business depends on information, information depends on applications, and applications depend on technology. Poorly managed information domain functions will kill a company within a few years. Poorly managed application domain functions will kill a company within a few months. Poorly managed technology functions can kill a company within hours.

I've mentioned several times in this book the precedence of the architectural domains: Business, Information, Application, and then Technology. That makes it sound as if the architectural process should be managed as a traditional "waterfall" workflow, where each domain completes their work in isolation, then throws their work product over the fence to the next domain. That's clearly unwise. Architecture is an agile process. Yes, there are some decisions that come before others, but those decisions are often made in a group effort.

For example, the business may decide there's a regulatory requirement that is going to require encrypted data. Before the information and application architects spend a bunch of time and effort designing encryption solutions, the technology architect needs to be able to point out that the storage solution you're already using automatically encrypts data at rest. Architecture is a *team* effort.

Two kinds of people – deep focus versus broad focus

There are two kinds of people in this world, those that have demonstrated deep mastery of one particular subject area, and those that demonstrate a broad understanding of the bigger picture.

Most of us have worked at companies where tenure plays a larger part than performance when determining promotions and raises and, assuming we were the ones with lack of tenure, we complained bitterly about this. It seems obvious to all that the person who gets promoted to the level four job description should be the one who's doing level-four work, not necessarily the one who's been there 15 years. If you're trying to attract and retain the best people, not just the oldest, then promotions should be based on ability, not tenure.

The problem is that there are lots of different abilities. When you hire a developer fresh out of school, pretty much all they can really do is code subroutines to specifications you give them. As their coding skills grow stronger, they start to develop extended skills. You can give them specifications at a higher level, and they can figure out the subroutines they need to orchestrate. Given even more time, most developers will take on other challenges, such as the ability to work with the business to get their own requirements, or developing written communication skills, or bettering their understanding of the business model or their understanding of emerging software development tools and techniques.

Becoming a better software developer isn't increasing mastery of one "software development" skill; it's mastery of more and more related skills. There's always another skill to master, another mountain to climb. No one climbs them all, and no one climbs them in the same order or to the same height. Some people can't manage the public speaking mountain. Some hit the wall on project management.

Fortunately, there's a lot of room in software development for people with different strengths, as long as their weaknesses aren't critical to their job role.

Unfortunately, I often see cases where a developer, based on exceptional skills in one area, is promoted to a position that requires other strengths. There seems to be an assumption that the natural progression of any developer's career is to eventually graduate into management of a team of developers, or a position in strategic architecture.

A manager needs to understand the job that they are managing, and an architect needs to understand the process they are architecting, but having come up through the ranks isn't enough, by itself, to justify a promotion to those positions. Architecture and manager roles require the candidate to master additional skills. There comes a point in the career of a developer when they ask, "Do I want to climb higher on these skills I use today, or do I want to start climbing new skill-slopes?" They have to make the decision of whether to developer deeper development skills or widen their skillset to include those skills necessary to another role. In ten years' time, would they rather be a ninja level coder or a mid-level manager or an architect?

Different developers are going to make different choices. Your best programmer may really rather continue to sit in their cube getting better and better at what they do, and have no interest in giving that up to jump to another career track. This is why your best developers may actually make incredibly poor managers of developers, and really struggle if pushed into an architect position. You have to make all of those options available as viable career tracks. Don't top out your developer pay classes so that great developers have to give up development if they want a raise. Don't promote purely because of tenure, but if a developer continues to improve, providing increasing value to the company as a developer, that should be a reasonable career option.

Both manager and architect positions require strategic thinking, communications skills, and leadership ability to degrees that are not really all that necessary to a developer. In order to *jump tracks* into management or architecture, you need to demonstrate some mastery of skills that weren't really all that important to you as a developer.

I think most companies have figured out that jumping tracks into management requires new skills, although I've certainly seen some questionable internal promotions there, too. I think it's far more common for a company to think of an architect as simply the next level of programmer (or data modeler, or technician), a continued mastery of the same skills that have gotten you where you are today. The architect role isn't yet common enough for companies to see the patterns of their promotion decisions emerging. Most times, when these architects fail, they bring down the EAG program with them, and companies believe that the EAG program itself, not the staffing, was the problem.

When I'm looking for an EAG architect, I look for people who have developed a specific set of skills:

- They are already demonstrating experience and skill at managing processes in one or more domains. Don't make an EAG architect responsible for setting up architecture and governance over IT processes they have never mastered in the real world.

- They are constantly saying "if they had only asked me, what we should have done was…" Not in a derogatory way, but in a way that demonstrates insight into the larger picture and an understanding of long-term strategy.

- They always have a well-reasoned opinion, but are willing to listen to opposing viewpoints and be persuaded. They have strong personalities, but they never get caught up in dominance games, wanting to be the one who won the argument, rather than wanting the company to win.

- They are always thinking big-picture, always trying to put things in the larger context. They are the ones with the reputation for addressing a problem by saying, "The way I see it, we have three options…," listing the pros and cons of each, and ending by naming their preferred option. They don't jump on one solution; they see the larger context, thinking through all possible approaches before picking the best.

- They are always taking every opportunity to explain things clearly, with easy to understand pictures. They are always drawing on the whiteboard. The have a knack for making complex ideas easier to understand.

- They clearly understand the business model, not just IT, and understand that IT exists to support the business, not the other way around.

Perhaps the worst mistake I've ever made personally in recommending a person for an architecture role was hiring a person we'll call Andy. Andy was an outside hire who had been a consultant for more than a decade, and had a fantastic resume that checked all the boxes. Not only did he have years of experience with the necessary IT skills, he had that experience in our industry, working at companies just like ours on projects just like the ones we were staffing up for. He only worked a couple of years at each location, but he was a consultant, and people don't stick with one job their whole careers as they used to, so we didn't count that against him. We confirmed his work history, and offered him a job.

Big mistake! The question we didn't ask was what part of the project lifecycle he worked on at all those positions. It turned out that his whole career was based on coming in during the planning phase, setting up "the way things ought to be," and handing it over to someone else to implement. Despite twelve years of experience in the position we were hiring for, he had never had to implement his conceptual architecture and governance, and deal with them in the *real world*.

You don't want to hire EAG architects who's only experience is being an architect. Make sure you hire architects who have actually been there and done that in the real world, and understand what works and what doesn't. They need to understand that we aren't building a perfect architecture to hand in to a professor as an assignment in a college class. We are building an EAG program to support a business in the real world, where things are *not* perfect, and we don't have all the time and all the money to make them perfect. We have to create architecture and governance that can work in that environment.

Hardware lifecycle functions

As I've said before, your hardware lifecycle functions are undoubtedly the most mature architecture and governance in your company. The other domains have *much* more work to do before they reach that same level of maturity. The problem with the hardware domain is that it has become the victim of its own success.

The hardware domain has existed in a silo for decades, making decisions on their own, without consulting other domains. Why? Because at the enterprise level, there *were* no other domains to consult with. The main thing you're going to have to do with your hardware IT functions is to work on integrating them with the emerging enterprise-level architecture and governance of the other domains.

The goal of the hardware domain *isn't* to fill the computer room with the latest, shiniest, fastest devices on the market. The goal of the hardware domain is to support the needs of the business as efficiently as possible. This shouldn't be a Field of Dreams, "build it, and they will come" approach. The purpose of the hardware is to support the applications that support the data that supports the business.

Think again about that Charles Dickens bookkeeper sitting on a high stool all day, entering and totaling numbers in a ledger book with a quill pen. This is how people ran business for centuries before the advent of computers. Computers were adopted by businesses solely to automate the retention and manipulation of business information. They aren't an end to themselves. Computers exist in the data center only to automate those quill-pen business processes and let Bob Cratchit go home for Christmas.

New IT skills had to be brought into the business to support all the new hardware and software that was purchased to automate the business processes, but, over time, it seems we IT people have gotten so focused on the hardware and software that we've forgotten about Bob. While we sit in the warm computer room admiring the shiny new hardware, Bob Cratchit is back at his cold desk trying to get his job done, and Tiny Tim is home waiting.

Old Ebenezer Scrooge was very good at his job, but he had forgotten the true meaning of Christmas. If you want to integrate your technology management into a larger EAG program, you're going to have to remember the true meaning of Information Technology.

Hardware acquisition

The first function in the technology lifecycle, the first ghost to visit old Hardware Scrooge, is hardware acquisition. Hardware acquisition is much the same as application acquisition (page 175). It's a complicated subject, with intricate vendor pricing discounts and bundling, complex integration requirements, and a deep, specialized understanding of rapidly changing technology. The main message from the ghost of IT past is that you re-examine the way you collect requirements. The main modification you're going to need to make to a functioning hardware acquisition process is to integrate the business, information, and application domains into the mix. Those are your customers. They don't exist so that you can buy hardware. You buy hardware to support them! If you think you don't have to involve those groups in your planning and purchasing decisions, then you are definitely *not* treating them as your customer.

It's going to be difficult, politically, to stop the technology tail from wagging the EAG dog. They key is for everyone to understand that the technology team is *not* being *put in their place*. You have to approach this from the standpoint of opening up the doors to one of the most mature processes in your infrastructure, so that, rather than pushing the technology domain down, you are pulling the other domains up, and integrating them into something even broader in scope, leveraging the technology team's process maturity as a platform on which to model and integrate the other EAG domains.

Hardware licensing

Hardware licensing is a form of asset inventory. It needs to integrate with the inventory of your information and application assets. There are relationships between these different domain assets, and capturing those relationships is just as important as capturing the assets themselves. You need to know which information assets and which application assets are associated with which technology assets.

Asset inventory is usually accomplished these days through applications: network scanners and software agents running on the hardware. Those applications generate triggers and alerts, and have business logic that must be configured. The application domain will have a great deal to say about the architecture of these applications.

All the asset inventory information will be collected in some central repository, integrating information, application, and technology assets and their relationships in one data store, exposed through data services, with an audit trail, information security, quality control, analytics, and information delivery. Contract information from the contract management system will also need to be integrated into this enterprise asset inventory repository, so that contractual license compliance can be measured. This centralized enterprise asset inventory repository will be architected and governed by the information domain.

No one domain exists in isolation. Decisions that affect the enterprise have to be made at the enterprise level. Enterprise architecture and governance must have equal involvement from all domains.

Hardware security

Hardware security is a bit of a misnomer. There is no need to secure hardware. What you secure is the information that resides on, flows through, or is gained access through the hardware. Hardware security exists to protect information.

The main thing that needs to happen in the hardware security function to make it part of an integrated EAG program is to coordinate with the other domain security initiatives to understand what information sits on and flows through the hardware, and what applications on the hardware provide access to or alter that information. You cannot implement a security program over technology components without understanding the relationships between each piece of technology and the specific information it protects.

Hardware security is critically important. Just make sure you understand what you're securing, and why.

Hardware standup, configuration, and maintenance

There are quite a few other technology domain functions, all of which are quite mature in most organizations. The main areas to examine when integrating these functions into an EAG program are the ones that have information and application components.

Hardware maintenance, for example, can be due to security issues in the microcode on the hardware. You need to make sure the relevant microcode release levels are accurately and automatically collected in your asset inventory information by the asset inventory applications, so that the extent of risk across the enterprise can be measured. Again, you are not measuring the number of hardware platforms that are at risk, you are measuring the extent of business information residing on or flowing through those platforms that is at risk.

Older hardware release levels will eventually no longer be supported by the manufacturer. As with security, this release level and expiration date needs to be tracked in the asset inventory system, so that the hardware supporting the business is always supported in turn by the manufacturer, assuming always that the risk to the business is outweighed by the cost of support. Whether to keep hardware under vendor support or not is a business decision, not an IT decision.

Many aspects of hardware configuration are actually a configuration of application code embedded in the technology. It's quite common for the technology domain to own this embedded software, but when that is the case, they need to carefully consider how much of the application domain software ownership lifecycle architecture and governance needs to apply, and the lines between software owned by the application domain and software owned by the technology domain need to be clearly defined and agreed upon. For many appliance solutions, this line is going to be quite fuzzy. It is the job of an EAG program to clarify that line. The functional framework offers a good platform for that clarification.

Hardware tuning

Hardware tuning is a vast, extremely complicated subject that changes rapidly as new technologies are constantly introduced. No one person can master all aspects of this subject. I wouldn't even consider myself to know enough to qualify as a summer intern. I have great respect for the men and women who do this well. My hat's off to them.

From the standpoint of an integrated, cross-functional enterprise-level program to manage IT complexity, the important thing to remember is that hardware tuning can't be done in isolation. No matter how much money you have to throw at the solution, there's no one hardware solution that's going to be a silver-bullet for every possible workload. *Hardware selection and tuning must be performed with the information and application requirements in mind.* You can't just tune hardware; you have to tune it for some purpose. That understanding seems to be missing within many organizations today. Different business purposes will require different tuning even if they use the same hardware components.

Still without claiming to be an expert, I want to call out a few hardware selection/tuning areas that seem to consistently come up as challenges. In every case, the issues arise when hardware selection and tuning is performed in isolation, without waiting for or taking the time to understand the nature of the workload the hardware will be asked to serve.

Tune the entire stack, not just CPU and memory

Proper selection, configuration, and monitoring of the hardware stack are crucial to the success of an organization. Many organizations stand up all new equipment using the factory recommended infrastructure including CPU, memory, and network cards. When business function performance degrades, they mainly look at CPU and memory. Rarely is anything else considered until those two are first maxed out. Every three years or so, they will budget for a hardware refresh that basically buys the latest version of the equipment you already have, with no real analysis of how well that stack is working. With even a little bit of thought, it's clear that this isn't the right approach. Nevertheless, in my experience this is the way most organizations work. There are two problems with this approach.

The first problem is that there's a lot more to the stack than memory and CPU. Typically, the application software and the application database will be implemented on separate, dedicated hardware servers. In this case, your stack will include things like:

- Application Server

    o CPU
    o Memory
    o Ram Disk
    o Application Software configuration
    o Security/encryption software
    o Number and throughput of network cards

- IP Network

    o Cabling
    o Routers
    o Firewalls

- DB Server

    o Number and throughput of network cards
    o CPU
    o Memory
    o Configuration of database software
    o Number and throughput of Host Bus Adapter (HBA) cards (to connect to SAN network)

- SAN Network

    o Fiber channels
    o Switches

- Disk

    o Disk controller cards
    o Caching
    o Number and size of disks
    o Read and seek time of disk

The throughput of the business processes you are serving depends on all of these factors and more. A bottleneck with any component limits the throughput of the entire stack. You need to be able to proactively monitor the *entire* stack, so that you know ahead of time where you're approaching capacity, and so that, in the event of a problem, you have the tools in place to immediately identify the bottleneck. How many times have you experienced degraded performance, only to be told that the CPU and memory utilization did not show them maxed out? Why don't we have the tools in place to proactively monitor the rest of the stack?

In many cases, software licensing is based on CPU specifications. If you keep throwing CPU at a problem, it can have significant impact on your software license costs, when the CPU may, in fact, not even be the problem.

Know whether you are tuning for TPS or MBPS
Say you purchase a new database server. Odds are that you'll configure it with the RAM, CPU, network cards, and HBA cards that come recommended by the factory, or perhaps by the database software. However, that isn't always appropriate.

By far, most database installs are intended for operational applications. These applications have an activity *footprint* that consists of a very high volume of very small transactions. This is practically the definition of Online Transaction Processing (OLTP). Since most databases will be set up to support this type of activity, the configuration recommendations for the hardware and software will be designed to maximize the transactions per second (TPS) throughput. You would look at each layer of your hardware stack, above, and determine the TPS it will support, making sure there are no bottlenecks.

However, sometimes the database will need to support Online Analytical Processing (OLAP), with a small number of very large transactions. Optimizing the stack for TPS is *not* appropriate in this case. Rather than look at the TPS specification for a component, you need to look at the megabytes per second (MBPS) each component in the stack supports, and make sure that the appropriate capacity is supported throughout the stack.

One advantage of purchasing an analytical appliance solution such as Teradata or Netezza is that it is a stack-in-a-box, pre-tuned for analytical of access. If you're going to build the stack yourself from components, you *must* understand how to configure and monitor it for the type of activity you want to support. You can't just tune hardware; you have to tune hardware for a particular application activity footprint.

SMP versus MPP storage
Databases can also be purchased in SMP or MPP configurations. Some, such as DB2, can be configured using either technology, depending on your need. What need is better served by each technology?

SMP, or **Symmetrical Multi Processing**, takes the approach of giving every CPU access to all of the data in the repository. This is also known as a *shared-all* configuration, because access to all of the information is shared by all of the processors. Technically, it's the underlying hardware that is SMP, but the software that runs on that hardware must be written in such a way as to take advantage of it. Oracle, Sybase, SQL Server, and other databases are examples of database applications written to take advantage of SMP hardware, distributing workload into threads that can run on different processors, all accessing the entire data store.

MPP, or **Massively Parallel Processing**, takes the approach of distributing large workloads to many different processors as well, but in this case the processors (or groups of processors) are truly independent, each working on a separate slice of the data in what is known as a *shared-none* configuration. In a MPP enabled database application, the data is hashed into as many slices as there are independent hardware nodes. Each node works only on the slice of data it can see. The results are passed up to an administration node, which integrates the data and returns it to the requestor.

Both SMP and MPP are powerful solutions, each of which is more appropriate for certain kinds of activity.

When speaking of database solutions, MPP is most powerful when the data can be sliced and distributed in such a way that the query will find all the information that must be joined together all on the same node. Back in 2005, I worked on a call-detail data mart for a large telecommunications company that loaded 4.5 terabytes of data daily, maintained a full 60 days of history, and required a response time of less than 5 seconds to *any* query. This database was used to monitor call activity for fraud, and to alter the switching paths between cell towers to minimize cost of routing calls from tower to tower. Because the call detail data was basically one large table, it could be hashed in such a way that the queries would run very, very efficiently. The queries never needed to join detail data that was on one node with data from another node. This data mart was credited with saving the company more than $8 million in expenses each month. When the queries and the data allow the workload to be split in such a way as to be run in isolation on each node, MPP is extremely scalable, with very little loss of efficiency. If you want the solution to run twice as fast, you can simply double the number of nodes.

However, there are times when the workload can't be split this way. The example above worked well because it was one large table. If you have several large tables, but they all have some field that ties them together, you can still hash them on that unifying variable so that all the rows in each table that belong together to be co-located on the same node, and still run efficiently. Order header and order line could both be hashed on the order number. A claim header, claim line, adjustments to the line, and the diagnosis and procedure codes that go with each line, can all be hashed on the claim key so that all the information for a single claim, across all of these tables, is always located on the same node.

But if you need to join those claim tables to enrollment tables and provider tables, it becomes impossible to hash everything on one common hash key across all the tables so that the provider and the enrollment and the claim information that go together are always guaranteed to be located on the same node. In this case, the MPP use-case falls apart rapidly. The MPP engine has to analyze the query, and pick one or more tables and collect all the detail information for those tables together in one place, either on the administration node, or, worse, place a complete copy of the table on each node. Suddenly, you are spending a great deal of time shuffling data around, then running almost the full workload on each of the smaller nodes.

MPP is a powerful solution, but only when you can guarantee co-location. If you can't, then SMP is probably going to work better. Guaranteeing co-location involves either a very simplistic data model, or being able to guarantee ahead of time the exact nature of the queries. If you have ad-hoc queries running over a complex data model composed of many large tables that cannot all be collocated, MPP is not going to work well for you. Unfortunately, one of the main applications people use MPP solutions for these days is data warehousing. MPP can be an excellent choice for analytical reporting data marts, but is usually a poor choice for ad-hoc reporting in the operationally modeled layer of a warehouse.

Big data platforms are, in many ways, very similar to MPP architecture, because they distribute data across an array of independent commodity servers. They work best when the workload can be split into many different units of work that can run in isolation using the data on each node of the big data array. However, if the workload involves joining data that isn't co-located on a single node, big data suffers the same challenges as MPP architecture. Some NoSQL implementations, such as MongoDB, also use an array of commodity servers and share the same limitations.

You can't select the most appropriate hardware (technology domain) without a good understanding of the data itself (information domain) and the kinds of queries that will be used to access it (application domain). Appropriate hardware selection requires involvement of all three IT domains.

Row-based versus column-based storage

Another area where inappropriate decisions are often made because the workload isn't well understood is row versus columnar database engines.

Traditionally, database engines have used a row-based storage approach. If you were to examine the data on the database disk, you would see each database row stored all together in one place. If you examined each block of data (the unit of I/O used for database disk reads and writes) you would see a number of rows from a database table, stored back to back, with a unused free area at the end of the block typically sized to allow the insertion of several additional complete records in that block before requiring the block to be split in two. If the table has a large number of fields, then the block may actually only have a handful of records. I can recall one instance where the most used table in an application was so wide that only seventeen records were stored in each block.

A columnar database, on the other hand, stores data by column, not by row. While not precisely accurate, you can think of this as taking the data in a traditional table and splitting it into a number of tables, each with the primary key and one non-key field.

Now imagine a query that is summing the contents of one field across all the rows in a very large, very wide table. In a row-based table, each block you read will give you only a handful of records, of which only a very small fraction of the data is relevant to your query. Unfortunately all of that data has to be read from the disk, sent to the database application server, loaded into memory, and processed by the CPU just to extract the one field you want. In the one example above where each block contained only 17 rows, you would be reading 16K (the block sized that tablespace used, which is pretty typical), for each 17 rows.

In a columnar solution, that same block would contain an array of very small chunks of data, each containing only the information you are looking for. Instead of processing 17 rows per block, you'll probably process closer to 1000 rows per block. If you're joining data from multiple tables, this advantage is multiplied. Columnar solutions often run an average of 600 times faster than row-based solutions. Not 600 *percent* faster, but 600 *times* faster.

However, here again, columnar isn't a perfect solution for every kind of workload. Imagine now a query that selected all the fields from that same table, a "SELECT *". In a row based table, a single read pulls together all the fields, where, in a columnar solution, each of the non-key columns are instantiated separately, and must be joined together to produce the desired output. In this case, the columnar solution would take far longer than the row-based solution to retrieve the same data.

Columnar solutions work best when the query returns a small number of columns from a very wide table. If there are only a few rows, columnar won't make much of a difference. If the table only has a few columns, then columnar won't make much difference. When queries return most of the fields in the table, columnar is going to hurt, not help the performance. But given the right conditions, columnar-organized databases can produce amazing results, performing several orders of magnitude faster than row-based databases.

I went to an industry conference once where I sat in a breakout session that was a case study of a company that replaced the hardware infrastructure of the database for a major application with columnar technology. In their presentation, they showed sample query results both before and after the migration. They concluded their presentation saying they were disappointed to have only gotten a fourteen percent average increase in performance rather than the significant lift they had expected. Some queries actually ran much slower. However, the slides that showed the before and after performance were showing queries that selected a very large number of fields. I was very embarrassed for the presenters, who clearly chose a technology without understanding their application workload or the types of workload for which the technology was suited.

On the other hand, I worked on a project that produced a dimensional model for reporting through a high-end business intelligence tool. The fact and dimension tables in our star schema were quite large, but any one query would only return a small number of fields to be displayed on the screen. Because of pre-existing infrastructure, the platform where all of this was built was a row-based database with no failover or redundancy, with large batch windows where the data was unavailable. The dimensional data was created on this platform, and then copied to a smaller columnar database that had much higher availability. Our business analysts could point their BI tool to the row based solution to verify the data before it was moved to the columnar solution where our end users accessed it. The difference in performance between the row based solution (running on beefier hardware) and the columnar solution was almost exactly 600 times performance improvement. Because the access was all through a BI reporting tool that typically only brought a small number of columns to the screen, the query footprint for this database was ideally suited to a columnar database's sweet spot.

Here again, this is a good example of why the hardware (technology domain) can't be selected and tuned until the data (information domain) and query (application domain) requirements are understood. In an enterprise-wide, holistic IT management solution, the technology domain must be developed subject to the requirements of the workload it will serve. Technology decisions can no longer be made in a vacuum.

Analytical disk solutions

Disk performance and flexibility increases every year. We are getting to the point where you really don't have to worry too much about disks at all, as they're all a virtualized commodity.

Back in the day, for an analytical database disk array, we would purchase lots of small disks, and only use about half the tracks on each. This had the effect of minimizing seek time, the time it takes to move the read head from one track to another. We would dedicate the disk to the analytical database, because if another app was using the disk, then the read heads kept getting pulled off "our" data. We would deliberately locate data table spaces and index table spaces on different spindles, so that the disk did not have to seek back and forth between index and data. We would configure this stack for MBPS, optimized with caching for reads, because we do a lot more reading than writing, and seldom in mixed workloads. And so forth.

Our technology teams don't do this much anymore. Nearly every part of that setup goes against the principles of SAN management. The modern trend is to have fewer, larger disks, to use 100% of the disk, and to share that disk virtually with many applications, not allowing them to control what data is on what disk.

I understand the advantages of SAN management, but I wonder if we are truly to the point where all the stuff we used to do back in the day is really irrelevant. Are our SAN management principles optimizing SAN cost at the expense of business analytics performance? I don't know. Not my field. Moreover, I seem to create a lot of ill will whenever I ask those kinds of questions. It seems to me that if the technology truly had surpassed the need for all those things we used to do, as it someday must, then we could talk about it openly, and not treat the subject as the elephant in the middle of the room.

OK, maybe I'm a little bitter about that one...

Hardware end of life

A recent study[47] by Forrester Research among IT leaders at more than 3,700 companies estimated that an average of 72% of a company's total IT budget is spent on sustaining existing infrastructure, while just 28% is applied to new investments.

With our goal of efficiently managing IT complexity in support of the business, we need to consider whether or not we're being good stewards of the company's financial resources by upgrading every hardware device as soon as the vendor tells us to. Hardware vendors and grocery stores have a vested interest in keeping us terrified of expiration dates.

There are several things to keep in mind when discussing hardware end-of-life:

- **Performance**. If the hardware platform is not meeting the business service level needs, it may need to be replaced. In this case, the hardware may not be at the end of life – just the end of usefulness for its original purpose. The hardware may be repurposed for other solutions with lower demands, perhaps a lower environment (DEV, TEST) for the same application. Note that the decision of whether the hardware is fast enough or not is a business decision, not an IT

---

[47] http://bit.ly/2Dtm7eM.

decision. Hardware should not be replaced simply because there is a new, faster version if there is no business need.

- **Support**. You define end-of-life, not the vendor. Most vendors actually have two dates for end-of-life, one date for when they stop marketing and selling the product, and another date for when they stop supporting it. The difference between those dates is often as much as five years, and can sometimes be negotiated for longer at a rate far below the cost of upgrading hardware that is meeting your needs just fine. Even when the product has no vendor support, you still need to consider whether the risk of extended outage while a replacement is found is worth the cost of replacement. The information system the technology supports may be non-critical, or may be about to be replaced. This is a business decision.

- **Security**. In many cases, hardware needs to be replaced even if the performance is fine, because a security flaw has been uncovered that cannot be addressed with maintenance. These security flaws may relate to increased risk for information breach, or they may simply expose a risk for non-compliance with some regulatory standard. Depending on the data that the hardware exposes, this may need to be a priority replacement. However, if the hardware does not expose any sensitive data, there may be cases where the minimal risk exposure is outweighed by the cost of upgrading the hardware. This is a business decision, not an IT decision. Even if the security flaw is significant and disruptive, you may still be able to use the technology for a lower environment, if those environments use deidentified or test data.

We also need to consider the option of replacing an on-site solution with a hosted solution. Most cloud-based technology is managed by the third-party vendor, including the task and cost of keeping the solution current. If 72% of your non-payroll IT budget is spent on keeping the solution current, isn't it worth at least exploring whether that function can be delegated to the external vendor?

Trend: The virtualization of hardware

The final spirit to visit old Ebenezer was the Ghost of Christmas Yet-to-Come. I think the spirit of hardware yet-to-come would show our Scrooge a vision of an empty data center, quiet and cold; a vision of a time when most of the hardware and network we support today is in the cloud; a vision of a day where the corporate firewall has fallen, and our corporate infrastructure spilled out into the web.

Hardware is increasingly a virtual commodity. Hardware virtualization *within* the corporate network (i.e. SAN arrays and virtual servers) is commonplace today. It's so pervasive that it would be a very unusual datacenter that does *not* support a significant volume of virtual disk and virtual servers. You also find more and more hardware implemented as a third-party virtualized service. To the average user sitting at their desk, even a server in the corporate data center is, for all intents and purposes, a virtual implementation. The actual server is hidden away somewhere in a remote location where dedicated experts manage its existence. To the average user, there's no real difference between a server in a local data center and a server in a cloud solution somewhere, as long as the performance, availability, and security meet the business need.

In 1950, Alan Turing developed a test to determine if a machine could exhibit intelligent human behavior. If a human used only a keyboard and monitor to conduct a conversation with a computer in another room, would the human be able to tell that the other side of the conversation wasn't human? I'm suggesting that the increasingly connected world we live in has extended the Turing test in many interesting ways. If the business user is unable to distinguish whether the service they're using is local or remote, can it be said that the remote service is exhibiting the character of a local service to the extent that it can be replaced? Are cloud-based hardware solutions one day going to completely replace the corporate data center?

It's not just the data center hardware that's moving farther away from the corporate network. The traditional network and workstation is leaving as well. Remote access through web portals and mobile devices is eating away at the need to stand up and support large farms of desktop workstations in cubicles. Telecommuting is on the rise. I once did some work for a company where about half the cubicles were shared. Five different employees would share each desktop, each coming in to the office one day a week and working from home the rest. There are some service industry jobs (e.g. firefighter, police) that aren't going to be working remote any time soon, but many service roles (e.g. doctors) are increasingly able to work remotely. Thirty-four states now have laws in place setting guidelines for telemedicine.[48] In many of those states, there's no requirement for even one physical consultation before a doctor can begin treating the patient remotely. Mobile devices are investing billions of dollars to provide the accessories and protocols necessary to support this transition.

For most of us, the necessary technology to do our work remotely exists today. If we aren't already working remotely, the roadblock is probably a matter of corporate preferences, not a matter of technology. As yesterday's old-school executives are replaced by young men and women who grew up tethered to smart phones, corporate attitudes are going to shift, and shift quickly. Walls are going to fall, and the presentation layer of the corporate hardware infrastructure will quickly spill out into the web. Your organization may only be one retirement away from embracing large scale telecommuting.

Even five years ago, many companies were very reluctant to trust their infrastructure to the cloud. The cloud was viewed as very high risk from a security, scalability, performance, and availability standpoint. Any discussions in that direction were shut down quickly. Comparing that to today, the difference in attitude is nothing short of astounding. If the back-end goes to the cloud, and the front end goes to the web, what will be left in the managed corporate infrastructure in ten years?

In this new world, the amount of corporate hardware maintained on premise by IT to support the business is dwindling. I'm not suggesting you ignore the technology domain. You'll be managing corporate hardware assets for many years to come. In addition, even cloud-based services require management on your part. Rather, my point is that you need to take a close look at your long-term strategic vision for your technology infrastructure, and begin putting the architecture and governance in place within your functional framework to manage this trend at an enterprise level.

---

[48] http://bit.ly/2mTFFhp.

One Kind of People

I'm not sure how this "two kinds of people" thing got started. After two or three, I just couldn't stop myself. However, I'm concerned now that I'm leaving you with a divisive attitude; that I'm encouraging a mentality of *us-versus-them*. That wasn't my intention at all.

I worked for many years at a company which developed software for the banking industry. The company was exciting and innovative, but the building was *not*. The area where we worked consisted of row after row of identical cubicles.

My cubical was on the end of a row, and like every other, shared a back wall with a developer in the next row over. My neighbor, who was older than me, cursed like a sailor. That may be normal where you work, but in the Deep South, that sort of thing just wasn't considered polite behavior. For the good part of a year, I was silently furious about this guy's inappropriate language. I would clench my fists and grind my teeth, and go home and complain to my patient wife. Wait. It gets worse.

After literally months of this stress, I finally decided I needed to go confront the guy and give him a piece of my mind. But, since this guy didn't work on my team, we only knew each other in passing. So I decided that I would go introduce myself first, and say hello. Then, the *next* time he started spewing foul language while I was on the phone with a client, I would have a platform to go tell him off. That's the South for you; we can be rude, but there are forms to be observed first.

So, purely as preparation for calling the guy a jerk, I went over one day and introduced myself. We chatted for a minute, and, lo and behold, the guy actually *was* a sailor. In fact, he had been through Korea at the same time as I lived there (my father was Army Corps of Engineers). We got to talking about Korea and other things, and I somehow never got around to giving him a piece of my mind. My new friend had to pass my cubical on the way to the elevator and coffeepot. He started dropping in for a short chat once or twice a day.

Not long after that, I noticed that the guy's language didn't bother me as much as it used to. If he did get fired up while I was on the phone, I would wad up a piece of paper and toss it over the shared cubical wall at him, and he would stop immediately and apologize later. We actually became fairly close friends, and a couple of years later when he retired, I was the one who threw his retirement party.

That was an eye-opening moment in my life. This guy was, at one time, my hated tormentor who I would gladly consider running over in the parking lot if no one was looking. And a few months later we were close friends. What just happened? He hadn't changed. I had changed.

A few years before that I had the opportunity to spend three months installing software in Siberia. This would have been in the mid 90's, shortly after Boris Yeltsin became the first democratically elected leader in Russia's thousand year history. I grew up during the Cold War subject to constant fearmongering about the *Iron Curtain*, *Communism*, and the *Red Menace*. I had a Hollywood stereotype in my head about the kind of people I would find in Russia and the reception I would receive. Russia was very different from America culturally and historically, but I found it to be full of exactly the same kinds of people you meet here. I had lived my whole life to that point thinking in terms of America versus Russia, two superpowers struggling for dominance; thinking that they were out to crush us. But I was wrong. I met wonderful, interesting people who did the same kind of work I did, had the same hopes and the same fears. The Russian government has changed again under more than 15 years of Vladimir Putin, but I'll never be able to return to the false ideology that the Russian people are our collective enemy. Once you get to know someone, it's hard to hate or fear them,

In her novel *To Kill a Mockingbird*, Harper Lee gives Scout the line "I think that there is just one kind of folks. Folks." It's been interpreted as the naiveté of a child, not yet aware of the realities of the world. But maybe that's backwards, and maybe Scout was right. Maybe we're the ones being childish.

People are different in many ways, and you need to recognize that. But there is no *us* and *them*. Not really. If you start drawing borders like that, you start to dehumanize people, and you can become capable of saying and doing the most hateful things. Don't let that happen to you. If there's someone you have to work with that really rubs you the wrong way, don't talk *about* them; talk *to* them. Get to know them. You'll turn around one day and realize that they aren't near as irritating as they used to be.

Atticus, he was real nice.

Most people are, Scout, when you finally see them.

Harper Lee, To Kill a Mockingbird

Forms and Templates

The following forms and templates are intended as starting points only, illustrating some common best practices. Your organization will have specific style guides. Your legal department and your security office will have specific verbiage that must be included. Your project management office and technical writers will all have requests and requirements that will impact your final version.

Your method of publication may also impact the content and style of these documents. These are presented in their simplest form, as if they were paper documents. But your company may expose these as HTML, or may even store the individual snippets of content in a homegrown or third-party database with a front end that pulls the pieces together on demand, such as the Rational Suite of products acquired by IBM in 2003. These database-driven architecture and requirements systems retain version history and have a built-in publication interface assuring the most current version of the documentation is always available. But for our purposes, old school paper forms will illustrate the basic points.

Architecture template (strategic vision and tactical roadmap)

<FunctionName> Architectural Plan

This is a formal corporate document. It should follow all corporate standards for logos, typesetting, colors, headers and footers, confidentiality notices and disclaimers.

Functional Area	The name of the functional area within the framework, i.e. "Software Development Lifecycle (SLDC)"
Function	The name of the function within the functional area, i.e. "System Integration Testing (SIT)"

1. Purpose

    1.1. The purpose of this architectural plan is to outline <insert organization name, i.e. MyCompany> architectural strategic plan and tactical roadmap for <insert clear, direct description of the function. Keep sentences clear, simple, and direct.>

2. Scope

2.1. This architectural plan applies to <Insert clear, direct description of who/what/where is covered by this architectural plan (e.g., "all third-party, cloud-based applications which directly interface to MyCompany business processes and data"). >

3. Business Need

3.1. This is where you will document the business justification for this function. If you can't clearly articulate how this architectural strategy will benefit the business, then there is no need to go any further. The goal is not just to explain how an investment of budget and time on this strategy will pay for itself, but to create a compelling case why an investment here will provide more return for the business than other projects the business is considering funding. This section is typically only one or two paragraphs.

4. Long-Term Strategy

4.1. This is where you cast the vision for what the function will look like in three to five years, or whatever your planning horizon is. This is not necessarily the ultimate end-state, but rather a best possible realistic scenario for that time frame, given the constraints of your environment (i.e. legacy application limitations and competitive pressures). Diagrams are encouraged, but keep them simple. You are creating a napkin-drawing to explain the concept, not giving all the design details for a technician to implement. This section is the bulk of the document, typically two to ten pages.

5. Tactical Roadmap

This is the cycle-by-cycle plan for moving from current state to the architectural vision above. The planning cycles are typically aligned with your budget cycles, with a documented tactical roadmap plan for each year. For each planning cycle iteration, you should limit the goals to four or fewer projects.

Each of those goals should briefly state where the ROI for that cycle will be coming from, and how soon it is to be expected. Keep in mind that by listing the ROI here, you are committing to incorporate the collection of these metrics into the project.

For example:

5.1. 2017-01 - Implement automated System Integration Testing in Environment X. Will reduce time projects spend in test environment and increase speed to development.

It isn't necessary for the tactical roadmap to spell out the complete path to the final destination, but it should extend at least two years into the future.

In some cases, the maturity of your organization has already achieved the end state. You still need to document the business need (section 3) and strategic vision (section 4) in this document, but the roadmap can simply note that no additional changes are necessary.

The tactical roadmap for the most immediate planning cycle may name specific business-requested projects, but beyond that it will contain primarily IT-requested projects – descriptions of the types of infrastructure change that the architects would like to see. As each planning cycle approaches, though, the architects will use this tactical plan information to help identify the business-requested projects that can be used instead. Ideally, by the time each planning cycle begins, all of the tactical goals will be able to be addressed through business-sponsored projects.

6. Communication Plan

6.1. *How is this vision to be communicated?* The <insert position title, not name> or their designee shall be responsible for determining what job roles, if any, must take specific training.

6.2. *Will there be training available? Is that training mandatory? For what roles? Whose responsibility is it to ensure that all of the correct people are educated? How often should the training be repeated in order to stay current?* "The <insert position title, not name> or designee will develop requirements for any specific security training deemed necessary, to be administered and tracked through <corporate education portal>."

7. Revision Cycle

7.1. *Both the long-term strategic goal and the tactical roadmap will be undergoing constant revision as business priorities, regulatory requirements, competitive pressures, and the latest technology change. How often should the document be reviewed and updated? How are changes made and approved?*

Document Owner	The single person accountable for this document. Best given as a role name rather than a resource name. Include contact information. This will usually be either the Director of Enterprise Architecture or one of their direct reports (EA Project manager, EA Technical writer). Alternatively, the document owner may be the EA domain lead for the function. For example, the strategic plan for the hardware acquisition function may be owned by the EA Technical Architect lead. This is the person to contact regarding questions, concerns, clarifications and suggestions for revision.
Document Approvers	This will include all the people who have to sign off on any modifications to this document. It will typically be the EA group, but may include the executive sponsors, and sometimes specific subject matter experts, such as the legal department.
Document Location	This is the URL of the location of the official version of this document in the document repository.
Document Revision	The revision number and date.

Governance policy templates

A policy should be corporate-wide, and is typically rather brief. Details that are allowed to vary from department to department should be implemented in standards and processes rather than the corporate policy document.

Governance Policy Template

<PolicyName> Policy

This is a formal corporate document. It should follow all corporate standards for logos, typesetting, colors, headers and footers, confidentiality notices and disclaimers.

Functional Area	The name of the functional area within the framework, i.e. "Software Development Lifecycle (SLDC)"
Function	The name of the function within the functional area, i.e. "System Integration Testing (SIT)"

In the policy document, each paragraph should be numbered, to facilitate compliance discussion, including identifying the specific policy section for which a waiver is being requested.

1 Purpose

   1.1 The purpose of this policy is to outline <insert organization name, i.e. MyCompany> policy for <insert clear, direct description of WHAT the policy is intended to do (e.g., outline acceptable use of MyCompany equipment, or outline MyCompany requirements for controlling access to MyCompany resources. Keep sentences clear, simple, and direct.>

   1.2 This policy supports <insert the list of regulatory or certification requirements. The details of the requirement need not be included. Just the name and a link for more information, if possible. If no such governing body applies, omit this paragraph.>

2 Scope

   2.1 This policy applies to < Insert clear, direct description of who/what/where is covered by this policy (e.g., all MyCompany systems, all MyCompany employees).>

3 Policy

   3.1 <Insert clear, direct statements outlining the requirements of the policy using will/shall liberally throughout.>

      3.1.1 <Use ordinal numbered bullets for outline levels when applicable>

      3.1.1 <Use ordinal numbered bullets for outline levels when applicable>

3.2 <Insert clear, direct statements outlining the requirements of the policy using will/shall liberally throughout>.

    3.2.1   <Use ordinal numbered bullets for outline levels when applicable>

    3.2.2   <Use ordinal numbered bullets for outline levels when applicable>

4   Implementation TimeLine and Effective Date

3.2 <insert "who or what", i.e. "All MyCompany Applications," "All MyCompany systems," or "All MyCompany personnel"> shall be compliant with this policy by <Insert Date>.

4   Policy Questions and Risk Acceptance

4.1 Questions, concerns or complaints regarding <information security> policies, procedures or compliance shall be submitted by email to the policy owner listed at the end of this document. Submissions will be documented and tracked to disposition without reprisal.

4.2 Any system or group not able to comply with corporate policy must have an approved Risk Acceptance Form on file in the <insert name of enterprise governance organization> by the policy effective date.

    4.2.1   The Policy Waiver and Risk Acceptance Form, <insert location>, includes a mandatory mitigation plan and instructions for submitting the form.

    4.2.2   For any non-compliance identified after the effective date, notify the <insert name of enterprise governance organization> at <insert contact information> for guidance to document the gap.

5   Compliance Management

5.1 Compliance will be monitored by <insert role responsible for monitoring compliance> *Describe how frequent they are required to monitor it, where the results are stored and how and to whom they will be communicated. Monitoring of compliance is an important requirement of a mature, continually improving governance process. For example, "A weekly automated desktop scanning audit will be run by the LAN Desktop Services department on all workstations to detect the presence of unlicensed software. The results of that scan will be archived on the LAN Desktop Services departmental website, and any unlicensed software reported to the desktop owner, their supervisor and manager."*

6   Non Compliance

6.1 Failure to comply with this policy will result in <insert consequences of non-compliance>. **This is not what will happen to the company (i.e. a regulatory fine), but rather what will happen to the employee who elected not to comply with the corporate policy. For example, "Any employee found to have violated this corporate policy or failed to report any non-compliance shall be subject to disciplinary action, up to and including termination of employment."**

7   Communication Plan

7.1 **How is this vision to be communicated?** The <insert position title, not name> or their designee shall be responsible for determining what job roles, if any, must take specific training.

7.2 *Will there be training available? Is that training mandatory? For what roles? Whose responsibility is it to ensure that all of the correct people are educated? How often should the training be repeated in order to stay current?* "The <insert position title, not name> or designee will develop requirements for any specific security training deemed necessary, to be administered and tracked through <corporate education portal>."

8   Revision Cycle

8.1 **How often should this policy be reviewed and updated? How are changes made and approved?**

Document Owner	The single person accountable for this document. Best given as a role name rather than a resource name. Include contact information. This will usually be either the Director of Enterprise Architecture or one of their direct reports (EA Project manager, EA Technical writer). Alternatively, the document owner may be the EA domain lead for the function. For example, the policy for the software end-of-life function may be owned by the EA Application Architect lead. This is the person to contact regarding questions, concerns, clarifications and suggestions for revision.
Required Approvers	This will include all the people who have to sign off on any modifications to this document. It will typically be the EA group, but may include the executive sponsors, and sometimes specific subject matter experts, such as the legal department or the regulatory compliance area. Policies which have the potential of employee termination should be reviewed by HR.
Document Location	This is the URL of the location of the official version of this document in the document repository.
Document Revision	The revision number and issue date.

Policy Waiver (Risk Acceptance Form)

Policy Risk Acceptance Form	
Functional Area	The name of the functional area within the framework, i.e. "Software Development Lifecycle (SLDC)"
Function	The name of the function within the functional area, i.e. "System Integration Testing (SIT)"
Policy	The name of the policy which is at risk.
Risk Details	
Risk ID	Unique identifier assigned to this risk
Raised By	Name and job title of person raising the risk
Date Raised	Date the risk was raised to the Executive Governance committee
Risk Description	
A brief description of the risk identified and its area of impact such as security risk, regulatory compliance risk, and financial risk	
Risk Likelihood	
☐ Low ☐ Medium ☐ High	
Risk Impact Level	
☐ Low ☐ Medium ☐ High	
Supporting Documentation	
Reference any supporting documentation used to substantiate this risk	
Risk Mitigation	
Recommended Preventative Actions	
A brief description of any actions that should be taken to prevent the risk from realization	
Recommended Contingent Actions	
A brief description of any actions to be take in the event that the risk is realized, to minimize its impact	
Approval Details (to be completed by Executive Governance committee)	
☐ Approved ☐ Not Approved Date: _____ Give any details that were used to justify the decision. If the risk is time limited, specify the expiration date, after which the risk should be resolved, or re-submitted. All job roles on the policy "Required Approvers" list must approve any risk acceptance.	

Standard templates

The following template can be used as a base from which to build your own standards.

\<DepartmentName\> \<FunctionName\> Standards

Standards may be declared at the corporate or at the department level. Regardless, they are formal management artifacts, and should follow all corporate standards for logos, typesetting, colors, headers and footers, confidentiality notices and disclaimers.

Functional Area	The name of the functional area within the framework, i.e. "Software Development Lifecycle (SLDC)"
Function	The name of the function within the functional area, i.e. "System Integration Testing (SIT)"

In the standards document, each paragraph should be numbered, to facilitate discussion of standards, including identifying the specific standard for which a waiver is being requested. Even the paragraphs in the purpose, scope, and communication plan should be numbered so that they can be discussed with clarity.

1 Purpose

    1.1 The purpose of this standard is to outline \<insert department name, if applicable\> \<insert organization name, i.e. MyCompany\> standards for \<insert functional area and function name\>

2 Scope

    2.1 This policy applies to \< Insert clear, direct description of who/what/where is covered by this policy (e.g. "all hardware within the data centers. It does not apply to third party hosted solutions or to Lan desktop hardware.")\>

3 Standards

List standards below using logical groupings. It is perfectly acceptable to refer to external artifacts such as spreadsheets of approved abbreviations to be used in database field names and images of company logos to be used in report headers, but any such artifacts must also be included in the document repository.

    3.1 \<Insert clear, direct statements outlining the standard using will/shall liberally throughout\>.

        3.1.1 \<Use ordinal numbered bullets for outline levels when applicable\>

        3.1.2 \<Use ordinal numbered bullets for outline levels when applicable\>

    3.2 \<Example\> Database Field Naming Conventions.

3.2.1 <Example> Pascal Case - Database table and field names in this environment should use Pascal case, where the first letter of each word is capitalized, with no spaces or underscores, i.e. TranStatus…

3.2.2 <Example>Database Field name Suffix –

3.2.2.1 <Example> All database fields which represent calendar dates should be named with a "Dt" suffix.

3.2.2.2 <Example> All database fields which represent currency amounts should be named with an "Amt" suffix and be declared as DECIMAL(20,2).

4   Implementation TimeLine and Effective Date

4.1 <insert "who or what", i.e. "All MyCompany Applications," "All MyCompany systems," or "All MyCompany personnel"> shall be compliant with these standards by, <Insert Date>.

5   Questions, Feedback, and

5.1 Questions, concerns or complaints regarding these standards shall be submitted by email to the Standard owner listed at the end of this document. Submissions will be documented and tracked to disposition without reprisal.

5.2 Request for new standards or alterations to existing standards shall be submitted by email to the Standard owner listed at the end of this document. *Explain who/how/when submissions will be acknowledged, reviewed, and accepted or rejected.*

6   Waivers and Risk Acceptance

6.1 Any system or group not able to comply with these standards must have an approved Standard Waiver and Risk Acceptance Form on file in the <insert name of standards body> by the policy effective date.

6.1.1   The Standard Waiver and Risk Acceptance Form, <insert location>, includes a mandatory mitigation plan and instructions for submitting the form.

6.1.2   *Explain escalation process if the submitter does not accept the decision of the standards body.*

7   Compliance Management

7.1 Explain how compliance with the standard will be monitored. Explain who is responsible for monitoring compliance to standards, when that monitoring occurs, and where the results are recorded. Monitoring of compliance is an important requirement of a mature, continually improving governance process.

For example, "Before moving code from the development to the test environment, it must pass a code review by the team technical lead. Code review is automatically as part of the change management request process, and the results are discussed in the code review meeting on Tuesdays and Fridays."

8 Non Compliance

8.1 What are the consequences of non-compliance? For example, "Any code which does not pass a code review cannot be moved to the test environment without an approved waiver."

9 Communication Plan

9.1 **How are these standards to be communicated?** The <insert position title, not name> or their designee shall be responsible for determining what job roles, if any, must take specific training.

9.2 *Will there be training available? Is that training mandatory? For what roles? Who is responsibility to ensure that all of the correct people are educated? How often should the training be repeated in order to stay current?* The <insert position title, not name> or designee will develop requirements for any specific standards training deemed necessary, to be administered and tracked through <corporate education portal>.

10 Revision Cycle

10.1 *How often should this standard be reviewed and updated? How are changes made and approved?*

Document Owner	The single person accountable for this document. Best given as a role name rather than a resource name. Include contact information. This will usually be either the Director of Enterprise Architecture or one of their direct reports (EA Project manager, EA Technical writer). Alternatively, the document owner may be the EA domain lead for the function. For example, the standards for the software design and testing functions may be owned by the EA Application Architect lead. This is the person to contact regarding questions, concerns, clarifications and suggestions for revision.
Standard/Waiver Approval Team	This will include all the people who have to sign off on any modifications to this document. It will typically be the relevant EA Domain Architects (not the entire EA team), but may include the executive sponsors, and sometimes specific subject matter experts. For example, external reporting standards may need to be reviewed by corporate branding.
Document Location	This is the URL of the location of the official version of this document in the document repository.
Document Revision	The revision number and issue date.

Process and role templates

Blank Process and Role Template Document

<Information System Name><Functional Area Name><Process Name>

1. Purpose:

The purpose of this procedure is to <insert clear description of WHAT the procedure is intended to describe (e.g., outline specific steps to create accounts for X application)>.

This process and its roles support the <list of names and locations of corporate-wide policy documents that this process implements. This should never be an empty list.>

This process supports the <names and locations of applicable standards. These are often department-specific, which is fine as long as each department standard is documented and complies with the overarching corporate policy>

2. Scope:

This Process applies to <list clear, direct description of who/what/where is addressed by this policy (e.g. all MyCompany employees). >

3. Process:

< Insert the specific steps necessary to execute the purpose listed in section 1.0. This should be sufficiently detailed to enable a new employee to successfully execute the procedure with limited guidance/oversight>

<make sure to note if any sections are optional. When these process and role documents are initially captured, they should be reviewed by the enterprise governance board. You should expect that there are some gaps. These should be identified, and feedback returned to the authors of the document, along with a timeline for remediation.>

3.1. Roles and Responsibilities

<Insert your RACI Matrix here, showing all roles for each step in the process. The Process flow in section 3.3 will only show roles for those responsible for actually performing the work.>

3.2. Process Location

<Describe the location within your organization (not the geographic location) that is subject to this document.>

3.3. Process Flow

<This is the bulk of the document. Begin with a flowchart showing all the process steps, separated into swimlanes representing each responsible role. After that overview, being again describing each process step in detail. Explain how each process step works, how the process is approved or rejected and how the process step transitions to another step of the process.>

3.4. Process Timeline and Service Level Agreements

<Describe any specific timelines or service levels. Remember that service levels are not always related to time. They may be related to quantity, quality, etc. Spell out the nature of the process goals, including how they are measured, where the measurements are stored, who is responsible for taking the measurements, who is responsible for reviewing them. Some measurements are contractual, and should be integrated with the contract management function.>

3.5. Process Controls

3.5.1. Management Oversight

<In addition to the roles responsible for each step of the process, there is usually an executive responsible for the overall process. How is this manager kept abreast of the overall state of the process. This may also include reporting to the project management office.>

3.5.2. Exception/Waiver process

<How does one request a waiver or exception to the process? How is it granted, and by whom? Where are exceptions stored? What is the escalation process if the requester disagrees with the ruling on the request?>

4.0 Procedure Information

Procedure Owner/Point of Contact:	Procedure Manager:
< Insert ABCBS employee who approved this procedure >	< Insert this ABCBS employee's MGR who will approved this procedure >
Issue Date:	Effective Date:
<Insert Date of Issuance (when posted internally) >	<Insert Date when employees are accountable for provisions in procedure>

Index